STOCK TRADER'S ALMANAC 2006

D1368648

Yale Hirsch & Jeffrey A. Hirsch

WILEY

John Wiley & Sons, Inc.

 The Hirsch Organization Inc. ♦ 79 Main Street, Suite 3 ♦ Nyack, NY 10960
www.hirschorg.com

Published by John Wiley & Sons, Inc., Hoboken, New Jersey
Published simultaneously in Canada

HG
4661
H584
2006

Editor in Chief	Jeffrey A. Hirsch
Editor at Large	Yale Hirsch
Vice President	J. Taylor Brown
Data Coordinator	Christopher Mistal
Web Development	Nexgen
Graphic Design	Darlene Dion Design

For general information on our other products and services, or technical support, please contact our Customer Care Department within the United States at 800-762-2974, outside the United States at 317-572-3993 or fax 317-572-4002.

Wiley also publishes its books in a variety of electronic formats. Some content that appears in print may not be available in electronic books.

For more information about Wiley products, visit our Web site at www.wiley.com.

ISBN: 0-471-70956-5

Printed in the United States of America

10 9 8 7 6 5 4 3 2 1

This Thirty-ninth Edition is respectfully dedicated to:

Robert and Sam Stovall

For two generations, Robert and Sam have been providing Wall Street with market research, analysis and commentary nonpareil. Besides being two of our favorite colleagues on the Street, this father and son duo has always responded to our inquiries, and been an inspiration to us as well. Robert is Managing Director at Wood Asset Management and Sam is Chief Investment Strategist at Standard & Poor's.

The *Stock Trader's Almanac*® is an organizer. Its wealth of information is presented on a calendar basis. The Almanac puts investing in a business framework and makes investing easier because it:

- updates investment knowledge and informs you of new techniques and tools.
- is a monthly reminder and refresher course.
- alerts you to both seasonal opportunities and dangers.
- furnishes an historical viewpoint by providing pertinent statistics on past market performance.
- supplies forms necessary for portfolio planning, record keeping and tax preparation.

We are constantly searching for new insights and nuances about the stock market and welcome any suggestions from our readers.

Have a healthy and prosperous 2006!

 Signifies THIRD FRIDAY OF THE MONTH on calendar pages and alerts you to extraordinary volatility due to expiration of equity and index options and index futures contracts. Triple-witching days appear during March, June, September and December.

  The BULL SYMBOL on calendar pages signifies favorable trading days based on the S&P 500 rising 60% or more of the time on a particular trading day during the 21-year period January 1984 to December 2004. A BEAR SYMBOL on calendar pages signifies unfavorable trading days based on the S&P falling 60% or more of the time for the same 21-year period. Market Probability numbers for the same 21-year period for the Dow, S&P and NASDAQ (see pages 120-125) appear every day that the market is open. Other seasonalities near the ends, beginnings and middles of months; options expirations, around holidays and other times are noted for *Almanac* investors' convenience on the weekly planner pages.

INTRODUCTION TO THE THIRTY–NINTH EDITION

We are pleased and proud to introduce the Thirty-ninth Edition of the *Stock Trader's Almanac*. The Almanac provides you with the necessary tools to invest successfully in the twenty-first century.

J.P. Morgan's classic retort "Stocks will fluctuate" is often quoted with a wink-of-the-eye implication that the only prediction one can make about the stock market is that it will go up, down, or sideways. Many investors agree that no one ever really knows which way the market will move. Nothing could be further from the truth. We discovered that while stocks do indeed fluctuate, they do so in well-defined, often predictable patterns. These patterns recur too frequently to be the result of chance or coincidence. How else do we explain that since 1950 practically all the gains in the market were made during November through April compared to almost nothing May through October? (See page 50.)

The Almanac is a practical investment tool. Its wealth of information is organized on a calendar basis. It alerts you to those little-known market patterns and tendencies on which shrewd professionals enhance profit potential.

You will be able to forecast market trends with accuracy and confidence when you use the Almanac to help you understand:

- How our presidential elections affect the economy and the stock market — just as the moon affects the tides. Many investors have made fortunes following the political cycle. You can be sure that money managers who control billions of dollars are also political cycle watchers. Astute people do not ignore a pattern that has been working effectively throughout most of our economic history.
- How the passage of the Twentieth Amendment to the Constitution fathered the January Barometer. This barometer has an outstanding record for predicting the general course of the stock market each year with only five major errors since 1950 for a 90.9% accuracy ratio.
- Why there is a significant market bias at certain times of the day, week, month and year.

Even if you are an investor who pays scant attention to cycles, indicators and patterns, your investment survival could hinge on your interpretation of one of the recurring patterns found within these pages. One of the most intriguing and important patterns is the symbiotic relationship between Washington and Wall Street. Aside from the potential profitability in seasonal patterns, there's the pure joy of seeing the market very often do just what you expected.

"Sixth" years since 1886 have a mixed record (page 126) but most years ending in six have provided excellent buying opportunities (page 26). 2006 is also a Midterm Election Year "where bottom pickers find paradise" (page 34). Nine Midterm bottoms have occurred in the last 10 four-year cycles over the past 44 years. Five came in October.

Last edition in this space, we noted that a Three Peaks and Domed House pattern was forming. It is currently in the process of tracing out a correction that should bring the market back to the October 2004 lows over the next few months. Our likely protracted involvement in the Persian Gulf is bound to keep a lid on stock prices (both patterns are detailed on page 42).

This first bull market of the 21st century is tiring under the weight of high energy prices and a tightening Fed among other factors. After a late 2005/early 2006 rally, the market will likely stall — short of new all-time highs — in the face of the four-year Presidential Election cycle, global market pressures and geopolitical entanglements. 2006 promises to provide the next great buying opportunity of the new millennium. We expect the next major bottom, perhaps the low for the millenium, to occur in summer or autumn of 2006.

— Jeffrey A. Hirsch, August 5, 2005

THE 2006 STOCK TRADER'S ALMANAC

CONTENTS

DIRECTORY OF TRADING PATTERNS & DATABANK

STRATEGY PLANNING AND RECORD SECTION

2006 STRATEGY CALENDAR
(Option expiration dates encircled)

MONDAY	TUESDAY	WEDNESDAY	THURSDAY	FRIDAY	SATURDAY	SUNDAY
26 Chanukah	27	28	29	30	31	1 JANUARY New Year's Day
2	3	4	5	6	7	8
9	10	11	12	13	14	15
16 Martin Luther King Day	17	18	19	(20)	21	22
23	24	25	26	27	28	29
30	31	1 FEBRUARY	2	3	4	5
6	7	8	9	10	11	12
13	14 ♥	15	16	(17)	18	19
20 Presidents' Day	21	22	23	24	25	26
27	28	1 MARCH Ash Wednesday	2	3	4	5
6	7	8	9	10	11	12
13	14	15	16	(17) ♣ St. Patrick's Day	18	19
20	21	22	23	24	25	26
27	28	29	30	31	1 APRIL	2 Daylight Saving Time Begins
3	4	5	6	7	8	9
10	11	12	13 Passover	14 Good Friday	15	16 Easter
17	18	19	20	(21)	22	23
24	25	26	27	28	29	30
1 MAY	2	3	4	5	6	7
8	9	10	11	12	13	14 Mother's Day
15	16	17	18	(19)	20	21
22	23	24	25	26	27	28
29 Memorial Day	30	31	1 JUNE	2	3	4
5	6	7	8	9	10	11
12	13	14	15	(16)	17	18 Father's Day
19	20	21	22	23	24	25
26	27	28	29	30	1 JULY	2

Market closed on shaded weekdays; closes early when half-shaded.

2006 STRATEGY CALENDAR

(Option expiration dates encircled)

MONDAY	TUESDAY	WEDNESDAY	THURSDAY	FRIDAY	SATURDAY	SUNDAY	
3	4 Independence Day	5	6	7	8	9	JULY
10	11	12	13	14	15	16	
17	18	19	20	(21)	22	23	
24	25	26	27	28	29	30	
31	1 AUGUST	2	3	4	5	6	
7	8	9	10	11	12	13	AUGUST
14	15	16	17	(18)	19	20	
21	22	23	24	25	26	27	
28	29	30	31	1 SEPTEMBER	2	3	
4 Labor Day	5	6	7	8	9	10	SEPTEMBER
11	12	13	14	(15)	16	17	
18	19	20	21	22	23 Rosh Hashanah	24	
25	26	27	28	29	30	1 OCTOBER	
2 Yom Kippur	3	4	5	6	7	8	OCTOBER
9 Columbus Day	10	11	12	13	14	15	
16	17	18	19	(20)	21	22	
23	24	25	26	27	28	29 Daylight Saving Time Ends	
30	31	1 NOVEMBER	2	3	4	5	
6	7 Election Day	8	9	10	11 Veterans' Day	12	NOVEMBER
13	14	15	16	(17)	18	19	
20	21	22	23 Thanksgiving	24	25	26	
27	28	29	30	1 DECEMBER	2	3	
4	5	6	7	8	9	10	DECEMBER
11	12	13	14	(15)	16	17	
18	19	20	21	22	23	24	
25 Christmas	26 Chanukah	27	28	29	30	31	

PROGNOSTICATING TOOLS AND PATTERNS FOR 2006

For 39 years, Almanac readers have profited from being able to predict the timing of the Political Market Cycle, plus various seasonal and other recurring patterns. To help you gain perspective in 2006, a Midterm Election year, a valuable array of tables, charts and pertinent information can be found on the pages noted.

THE SIXTH YEAR OF DECADES

The last two losses were Midterm Years and both bottomed in October. Most "sixth" years delivered genuine buying opportunities. The last three produced solid gains. Midterm 2006 promises a super buying opportunity. *Page 26*.

MARKET CHARTS OF MIDTERM ELECTION YEARS

Individual charts for each of the last 21 Midterm Election years, including President in office. *Page 28*.

MIDTERM ELECTION YEARS: WHERE BOTTOM PICKERS FIND PARADISE

Nine of the last ten quadrennial cycles experienced bottoms in the Midterm Year. Five of those low points came in October. *Page 34*.

PROSPERITY MORE THAN PEACE DETERMINES OUTCOME OF MIDTERM CONGRESSIONAL RACES

The President's party tends to hold on to more Congressional seats when the economy and stock market are on solid footing. Prosperity is of greater importance to the electorate than peace. *Page 36*.

500+% MOVES FOLLOW WARTIME INFLATION AND 3 PEAKS & DOMED HOUSE — 2 AMAZING PATTERNS

These two classic recurring patterns may help you divine the market's future course. Markets tend to catch up to inflation after protracted military involvements have ended. Most major market tops have traced a pattern that resembles Three Peaks and a Domed House. *Page 42*.

WHY A 50% GAIN IN THE DOW IS POSSIBLE FROM ITS 2006 LOW TO ITS 2007 HIGH

Since 1914 the Dow Jones Industrials has averaged a 50% gain from the Midterm low to the Pre-Election Year high. This follows an average 22.2% drop from the Post-Election Year high to the Midterm low. *Page 78*.

MIDTERM ELECTION TIME UNUSUALLY BULLISH

Perhaps it is a bullish feeling that accompanies the opportunity to make a change in Washington. The Dow Jones Industrials average a 3.4% gain during the eight days surrounding the Midterm elections when the percentage of seats lost by the President's party is double digit. *Page 102*.

POLITICS AND STOCK MARKETS, THE 172-YEAR SAGA CONTINUES

Stock prices have been impacted by presidential elections for 172 years, gaining 745.9% in second halves of terms vs. 227.6% in first halves. *Page 127*.

Week After Triple Witching Dow Up 11 of Last 14

MONDAY

D 47.6
S 52.4
N 52.4

19

I never buy at the bottom and I always sell too soon. — Baron Nathan Rothchild's success formula (London financier, 1777-1836)

TUESDAY

D 47.6
S **38.1**
N 52.4

20

Governments last as long as the under-taxed can defend themselves against the over-taxed.
— Bernard Berenson (American art critic, 1865-1959)

WEDNESDAY

D 57.1
S **61.9**
N 52.4

21

If you bet on a horse, that's gambling. If you bet you can make three spades, that's entertainment.
If you bet cotton will go up three points, that's business. See the difference? — Blackie Sherrod

Watch for the Santa Claus Rally (Page 114)

THURSDAY

D **61.9**
S **66.7**
N **76.2**

22

First-rate people hire first-rate people; second-rate people hire third-rate people. — Leo Rosten (American author, 1908-1997)

Last Trading Day Before Christmas Has Been Weak 4 in a Row

FRIDAY

D 57.1
S 52.4
N **61.9**

23

Every age has a blind eye and sees nothing wrong in practices and institutions, which its successors view with just horror.
— Sir Richard Livingston (On Education)

SATURDAY

24

Christmas Day

SUNDAY

25

JANUARY ALMANAC

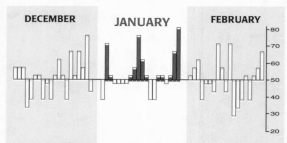

JANUARY								FEBRUARY						
S	M	T	W	T	F	S		S	M	T	W	T	F	S
													1	2	3	4
1	2	3	4	5	6	7		5	6	7	8	9	10	11
8	9	10	11	12	13	14		12	13	14	15	16	17	18
15	16	17	18	19	20	21		19	20	21	22	23	24	25
22	23	24	25	26	27	28		26	27	28				
29	30	31												

Market Probability Chart above is a graphic representation of the S&P 500 Recent Market Probability Calendar on page 121.

◆ January Barometer predicts year's course with .800 batting average ◆ Every down January on the S&P since 1950, *without exception*, preceded a new or extended bear market, or a flat market (page 44) ◆ S&P gains January's first five days preceded full-year gains 85.7% of the time, but in midterm year it is almost a contrary indicator (page 14) ◆ November, December and January constitute the year's best three-month span, a 4.8% S&P gain, 21% annualized (pages 46 & 138) ◆ At this rate, $1000 since 1950 grew to over $40 million ◆ January NASDAQ powerful 3.7% since 1971 (pages 54 & 139) ◆ "January Effect" now starts in mid-December and favors small-cap stocks (pages 104 & 110) ◆ Midterm Januarys since 1950 net loser, down half the time and strongly up *only* in major bull trends.

JANUARY DAILY POINT CHANGES DOW JONES INDUSTRIALS

Previous Month	1996	1997	1998	1999	2000	2001	2002	2003	2004	2005
Close	5117.12	6448.27	7908.25	9181.43	11497.12	10786.85	10021.50	8341.63	10453.92	10783.01
1	H	H	H	H	S	H	H	H	H	S
2	60.33	− 5.78	56.79	S	S	− 140.70	51.90	265.89	− 44.07	S
3	16.62	101.60	S	S	− 139.61	299.60	98.74	− 5.83	S	− 53.58
4	− 20.23	S	S	2.84	− 359.58	− 33.34	87.60	S	S	− 98.65
5	7.59	S	13.95	126.92	124.72	− 250.40	S	S	134.22	− 32.95
6	S	23.09	− 72.74	233.78	130.61	S	S	171.88	− 5.41	25.05
7	S	33.48	− 3.98	− 7.21	269.30	S	− 62.69	− 32.98	− 9.63	− 18.92
8	16.25	− 51.18	− 99.65	105.56	S	− 40.66	− 46.50	− 145.28	63.41	S
9	− 67.55	76.19	− 222.20	S	S	− 48.80	− 56.46	180.87	− 133.55	S
10	− 97.19	78.12	S	S	49.64	31.72	− 26.23	8.71	S	17.07
11	32.16	S	S	− 23.43	− 61.12	5.28	− 80.33	S	S	− 64.81
12	− 3.98	S	66.76	− 145.21	40.02	− 84.17	S	S	26.29	61.56
13	S	5.39	84.95	− 125.12	31.33	S	S	1.09	− 58.00	− 111.95
14	S	53.11	52.56	− 228.63	140.55	S	− 96.11	56.64	111.19	52.17
15	− 17.34	− 35.41	− 92.92	219.62	S	H	32.73	− 119.44	15.48	S
16	44.44	38.49	61.78	S	S	127.28	− 211.88	− 25.31	46.66	S
17	− 21.32	67.73	S	S	H	− 68.32	137.77	− 111.13	S	H
18	57.45	S	S	H	− 162.26	93.94	− 78.19	S	S	70.79
19	60.33	S	H	14.67	− 71.36	− 90.69	S	S	H	− 88.82
20	S	10.77	119.57	− 19.31	− 138.06	S	S	H	− 71.85	− 68.50
21	S	40.03	− 78.72	− 71.83	− 99.59	H	S	H	94.96	− 78.48
22	34.68	− 33.87	− 63.52	− 143.41	S	− 9.35	− 58.05	− 124.17	0.44	S
23	− 27.09	− 94.28	30.14	S	S	71.57	17.16	50.74	− 54.89	S
24	50.57	− 59.27	S	S	− 243.54	− 2.84	65.11	− 238.46	S	− 24.38
25	− 26.01	S	S	82.65	21.72	82.55	44.01	S	S	92.95
26	54.92	S	12.20	121.26	3.10	− 69.54	S	S	134.22	37.03
27	S	− 35.79	102.14	− 124.35	− 4.97	S	S	− 141.45	− 92.59	− 31.19
28	S	− 4.61	100.39	81.10	− 289.15	S	25.67	99.28	− 141.55	− 40.20
29	33.23	84.66	57.55	77.50	S	42.21	− 247.51	21.87	41.92	S
30	76.23	83.12	− 66.52	S	S	179.01	144.62	− 165.58	− 22.22	S
31	14.09	− 10.77	S	S	201.66	6.16	157.14	108.68	S	62.74
Close	5395.30	6813.09	7906.50	9358.83	10940.53	10887.36	9920.00	8053.81	10488.07	10489.94
Change	278.18	364.82	− 1.75	177.40	− 556.59	100.51	− 101.50	− 287.82	34.15	− 293.07

Dow & S&P 1950-June 2005, NASDAQ 1971-June 2005, Russell 1K & 2K 1979-June 2005. Options data 1980-June 2005

20th Amendment made "Lame Ducks" disappear
Now, "As January goes, so goes the odd-numbered year"

DECEMBER 2005/JANUARY 2006

Chanukah (Market Closed)

MONDAY

26

The way a young man spends his evenings is a part of that thin area between success and failure. — Robert R. Young

First Trading Day After Christmas Dow Up 9 in a Row 1990-1998 - Down 3 of Last 6

TUESDAY

D 76.2
S 66.7
N 66.7

27

---

*It is the growth of total government spending as a percentage of gross national product—
not the way it is financed—that crowds out the private sector.* — Paul Craig Roberts (*Business Week*, 1984)

FREE LUNCH Menu of New Lows E-mailed to Almanac Investor *Subscribers*

WEDNESDAY

D 57.1
S 57.1
N 57.1

28

Get to the Point! Blurt it out! Tell me plainly what's in it for me! — Roy H. Williams
(The Wizard of Ads, A reader's mental response to a poorly constructed advertisement. Quoted in *Your Company*, December 1998)

THURSDAY

D 57.1
S 76.2
N 71.4

29

---

*If you destroy a free market, you create a black market. If you have ten thousand regulations,
you destroy all respect for the law.* — Winston Churchill (British statesman, 1874-1965)

Last Day of the Year Dow Down 6 of Last 9 — NASDAQ Down 5 Straight After Being Up 29 in a Row!

FRIDAY

D 42.9
S 42.9
N 76.2

30

People with a sense of fulfillment think the world is good, while the frustrated blame the world for their failure.
— Eric Hoffer (*The True Believer*, 1951)

SATURDAY

31

New Year's Day
January Bullish Seasonalities: see pages 80 and 116.

SUNDAY

1

JANUARY'S FIRST FIVE DAYS AN "EARLY WARNING" SYSTEM

The last 35 up First Five Days were followed by full-year gains 30 times for an 85.7% accuracy ratio and a 13.7% average gain in all 35 years. The five exceptions include flat 1994 and four related to war. Vietnam military spending delayed start of 1966 bear market. Ceasefire imminence early in 1973 raised stocks temporarily. Saddam Hussein turned 1990 into a bear. The war on terrorism, instability in the Mideast and corporate malfeasance shaped 2002 into one of the worst years on record. The 20 down First Five Days were followed by 10 up years and 10 down (50% accurate).

In Midterm Election Years this indicator has had a spotty record — almost a contrary indicator. In the last 14 Midterm Years only six full years followed the direction of the First Five Days and none did in the last seven. The full-month January Barometer (page 16) has a better Midterm record of 64.3% accurate.

THE FIRST-FIVE-DAYS-IN-JANUARY INDICATOR

	Chronological Data				Ranked By Performance		
	Previous Year's Close	January 5th Day	5-Day Change	Year Change	Rank		5-Day Change	Year Change
1950	16.76	17.09	2.0%	21.8%	1	1987	6.2%	2.0%
1951	20.41	20.88	2.3	16.5	2	1976	4.9	19.1
1952	23.77	23.91	0.6	11.8	3	1999	3.7	19.5
1953	26.57	26.33	−0.9	− 6.6	4	2003	3.4	26.4
1954	24.81	24.93	0.5	45.0	5	1983	3.3	17.3
1955	35.98	35.33	−1.8	26.4	6	1967	3.1	20.1
1956	45.48	44.51	−2.1	2.6	7	1979	2.8	12.3
1957	46.67	46.25	−0.9	−14.3	8	1963	2.6	18.9
1958	39.99	40.99	2.5	38.1	9	1958	2.5	38.1
1959	55.21	55.40	0.3	8.5	10	1984	2.4	1.4
1960	59.89	59.50	−0.7	− 3.0	11	1951	2.3	16.5
1961	58.11	58.81	1.2	23.1	12	1975	2.2	31.5
1962	71.55	69.12	−3.4	−11.8	13	1950	2.0	21.8
1963	63.10	64.74	2.6	18.9	14	2004	1.8	9.0
1964	75.02	76.00	1.3	13.0	15	1973	1.5	−17.4
1965	84.75	85.37	0.7	9.1	16	1972	1.4	15.6
1966	92.43	93.14	0.8	−13.1	17	1964	1.3	13.0
1967	80.33	82.81	3.1	20.1	18	1961	1.2	23.1
1968	96.47	96.62	0.2	7.7	19	1989	1.2	27.3
1969	103.86	100.80	−2.9	−11.4	20	2002	1.1	−23.4
1970	92.06	92.68	0.7	0.1	21	1997	1.0	31.0
1971	92.15	92.19	0.04	10.8	22	1980	0.9	25.8
1972	102.09	103.47	1.4	15.6	23	1966	0.8	−13.1
1973	118.05	119.85	1.5	−17.4	24	1994	0.7	− 1.5
1974	97.55	96.12	−1.5	−29.7	25	1965	0.7	9.1
1975	68.56	70.04	2.2	31.5	26	1970	0.7	0.1
1976	90.19	94.58	4.9	19.1	27	1952	0.6	11.8
1977	107.46	105.01	−2.3	−11.5	28	1954	0.5	45.0
1978	95.10	90.64	−4.7	1.1	29	1996	0.4	20.3
1979	96.11	98.80	2.8	12.3	30	1959	0.3	8.5
1980	107.94	108.95	0.9	25.8	31	1995	0.3	34.1
1981	135.76	133.06	−2.0	− 9.7	32	1992	0.2	4.5
1982	122.55	119.55	−2.4	14.8	33	1968	0.2	7.7
1983	140.64	145.23	3.3	17.3	34	1990	0.1	− 6.6
1984	164.93	168.90	2.4	1.4	35	1971	0.04	10.8
1985	167.24	163.99	−1.9	26.3	36	1960	−0.7	− 3.0
1986	211.28	207.97	−1.6	14.6	37	1957	−0.9	−14.3
1987	242.17	257.28	6.2	2.0	38	1953	−0.9	− 6.6
1988	247.08	243.40	−1.5	12.4	39	1974	−1.5	−29.7
1989	277.72	280.98	1.2	27.3	40	1998	−1.5	26.7
1990	353.40	353.79	0.1	− 6.6	41	1988	−1.5	12.4
1991	330.22	314.90	−4.6	26.3	42	1993	−1.5	7.1
1992	417.09	418.10	0.2	4.5	43	1986	−1.6	14.6
1993	435.71	429.05	−1.5	7.1	44	2001	−1.8	−13.0
1994	466.45	469.90	0.7	− 1.5	45	1955	−1.8	26.4
1995	459.27	460.83	0.3	34.1	46	2000	−1.9	−10.1
1996	615.93	618.46	0.4	20.3	47	1985	−1.9	26.3
1997	740.74	748.41	1.0	31.0	48	1981	−2.0	− 9.7
1998	970.43	956.04	−1.5	26.7	49	1956	−2.1	2.6
1999	1229.23	1275.09	3.7	19.5	50	2005	−2.1	??
2000	1469.25	1441.46	−1.9	−10.1	51	1977	−2.3	−11.5
2001	1320.28	1295.86	−1.8	−13.0	52	1982	−2.4	14.8
2002	1148.08	1160.71	1.1	−23.4	53	1969	−2.9	−11.4
2003	879.82	909.93	3.4	26.4	54	1962	−3.4	−11.8
2004	1111.92	1131.91	1.8	9.0	55	1991	−4.6	26.3
2005	1211.92	1186.19	−2.1	??	56	1978	−4.7	1.1

Based on S&P 500

JANUARY

(Market Closed)

MONDAY
2

The bigger a man's head gets, the easier it is to fill his shoes. — Anonymous

First Trading Day of the Year Dow Up 9 of Last 14, Down 4 of Last 6,
Huge Winner in 2003, Up 266 Dow Points

TUESDAY
D 57.1
S 38.1
N 57.1
3

The only title in our democracy superior to that of President is the title of citizen.
— Louis D. Brandeis (U.S. Supreme Court Justice 1916-1939, 1856-1941)

Second Trading Day of the Year Dow Up 9 of Last 12,
Big Loser in 2000, Off 360 Dow Points; Huge Winner in 2001, Up 300 Dow Points

WEDNESDAY
D 71.4
S 71.4
N 85.7
4

Victory goes to the player who makes the next-to-last mistake.
— Savielly Grigorievitch Tartakower (Chess master, 1887-1956)

THURSDAY
D 47.6
S 52.4
N 61.9
5

A man isn't a man until he has to meet a payroll. — Ivan Shaffer (*The Stock Promotion Game*)

FRIDAY
D 57.1
S 47.6
N 61.9
6

A cynic is a man who knows the price of everything and the value of nothing. — Oscar Wilde

SATURDAY
7

SUNDAY
8

THE INCREDIBLE JANUARY BAROMETER (DEVISED 1972) ONLY FIVE SIGNIFICANT ERRORS IN 55 YEARS

Devised by Yale Hirsch in 1972, our January Barometer states that as the S&P goes in January, so goes the year. The indicator has registered **only five major errors since 1950 for a 90.9% accuracy ratio**. Vietnam affected 1966 and 1968; 1982 saw the start of a major bull market in August; two January rate cuts and 9/11 affected 2001; and the anticipation of military action in Iraq held down the market in January 2003. (*Almanac Investor* newsletter subscribers were warned at the time not to heed the January Barometer's negative reading as it was being influenced by Iraqi concerns.)

Including the six flat years yields an 80.0% accuracy ratio. A full comparison of all monthly barometers for the Dow, S&P and NASDAQ at *http://www.hirschorg.com/jb* details January's market forecasting prowess. Bear markets began or continued when Januarys suffered a loss *(see page 44)*. Full years followed January's direction in the nine of the last fourteen Midterm years. Three of the five errors (1970, 1978 & 1994) were flat; the other two were 1966 (Vietnam) and 1982 (new bull). *See pages 18, 22 and 24 for more January Barometer items.*

AS JANUARY GOES, SO GOES THE YEAR

Market Performance In January

	Previous Year's Close	January Close	January Change	Year Change
1950	16.76	17.05	1.7%	21.8%
1951	20.41	21.66	6.1	16.5
1952	23.77	24.14	1.6	11.8
1953	26.57	26.38	−0.7	− 6.6
1954	24.81	26.08	5.1	45.0
1955	35.98	36.63	1.8	26.4
1956	45.48	43.82	−3.6	2.6
1957	46.67	44.72	−4.2	−14.3
1958	39.99	41.70	4.3	38.1
1959	55.21	55.42	0.4	8.5
1960	59.89	55.61	−7.1	− 3.0
1961	58.11	61.78	6.3	23.1
1962	71.55	68.84	−3.8	−11.8
1963	63.10	66.20	4.9	18.9
1964	75.02	77.04	2.7	13.0
1965	84.75	87.56	3.3	9.1
1966	92.43	92.88	0.5	−13.1 X
1967	80.33	86.61	7.8	20.1
1968	96.47	92.24	−4.4	7.7 X
1969	103.86	103.01	−0.8	−11.4
1970	92.06	85.02	−7.6	0.1
1971	92.15	95.88	4.0	10.8
1972	102.09	103.94	1.8	15.6
1973	118.05	116.03	−1.7	−17.4
1974	97.55	96.57	−1.0	−29.7
1975	68.56	76.98	12.3	31.5
1976	90.19	100.86	11.8	19.1
1977	107.46	102.03	−5.1	−11.5
1978	95.10	89.25	−6.2	1.1
1979	96.11	99.93	4.0	12.3
1980	107.94	114.16	5.8	25.8
1981	135.76	129.55	−4.6	− 9.7
1982	122.55	120.40	−1.8	14.8 X
1983	140.64	145.30	3.3	17.3
1984	164.93	163.41	−0.9	1.4
1985	167.24	179.63	7.4	26.3
1986	211.28	211.78	0.2	14.6
1987	242.17	274.08	13.2	2.0
1988	247.08	257.07	4.0	12.4
1989	277.72	297.47	7.1	27.3
1990	353.40	329.08	−6.9	− 6.6
1991	330.22	343.93	4.2	26.3
1992	417.09	408.79	−2.0	4.5
1993	435.71	438.78	0.7	7.1
1994	466.45	481.61	3.3	− 1.5
1995	459.27	470.42	2.4	34.1
1996	615.93	636.02	3.3	20.3
1997	740.74	786.16	6.1	31.0
1998	970.43	980.28	1.0	26.7
1999	1229.23	1279.64	4.1	19.5
2000	1469.25	1394.46	−5.1	−10.1
2001	1320.28	1366.01	3.5	−13.0 X
2002	1148.08	1130.20	−1.6	−23.4
2003	879.82	855.70	−2.7	26.4 X
2004	1111.92	1131.13	1.7	9.0
2005	1211.92	1181.27	−2.5	??

Ranked By Performance

Rank		January Change	Year Change
1	1987	13.2%	2.0%
2	1975	12.3	31.5
3	1976	11.8	19.1
4	1967	7.8	20.1
5	1985	7.4	26.3
6	1989	7.1	27.3
7	1961	6.3	23.1
8	1997	6.1	31.0
9	1951	6.1	16.5
10	1980	5.8	25.8
11	1954	5.1	45.0
12	1963	4.9	18.9
13	1958	4.3	38.1
14	1991	4.2	26.3
15	1999	4.1	19.5
16	1971	4.0	10.8
17	1988	4.0	12.4
18	1979	4.0	12.3
19	2001	3.5	−13.0 X
20	1965	3.3	9.1
21	1983	3.3	17.3
22	1996	3.3	20.3
23	1994	3.3	− 1.5 flat
24	1964	2.7	13.0
25	1995	2.4	34.1
26	1972	1.8	15.6
27	1955	1.8	26.4
28	1950	1.7	21.8
29	2004	1.7	9.0
30	1952	1.6	11.8
31	1998	1.0	26.7
32	1993	0.7	7.1
33	1966	0.5	−13.1 X
34	1959	0.4	8.5
35	1986	0.2	14.6
36	1953	−0.7	− 6.6
37	1969	−0.8	−11.4
38	1984	−0.9	1.4 flat
39	1974	−1.0	−29.7
40	2002	−1.6	−23.4
41	1973	−1.7	−17.4
42	1982	−1.8	14.8 X
43	1992	−2.0	4.5 flat
44	2005	−2.5	??
45	2003	−2.7	26.4 X
46	1956	−3.6	2.6 flat
47	1962	−3.8	−11.8
48	1957	−4.2	−14.3
49	1968	−4.4	7.7 X
50	1981	−4.6	− 9.7
51	1977	−5.1	−11.5
52	2000	−5.1	−10.1
53	1978	−6.2	− 1.1 flat
54	1990	−6.9	− 6.6
55	1960	−7.1	− 3.0
56	1970	−7.6	0.1 flat

X = 5 major errors   *Based on S&P 500*

JANUARY

January's First Five Days Act as an "Early Warning" (Page 14)

MONDAY
D 42.9
S 47.6
N 47.6
9

In politics as in chess, or in the military or in business, when you have the advantage you must press it quickly — or lose it. For the first time in history, we are in a position to checkmate tyranny. Momentum is largely on the side of democracy.
— Garry Kasparov (World Chess Champion, 1985-2000)

TUESDAY
D 47.6
S 47.6
N 57.1
10

"Be yourself!" is about the worst advice you can give to some people. — Tom Masson

WEDNESDAY
D 47.6
S 47.6
N 57.1
11

Companies already dominant in a field rarely produce the breakthroughs that transform it. — George Gilder

THURSDAY
D 57.1
S 52.4
N 57.1
12

In the stock market those who expect history to repeat itself exactly are doomed to failure. — Yale Hirsch

FRIDAY
D 52.4
S 57.1
N **66.7**
13

Age is a question of mind over matter. If you don't mind, it doesn't matter.
— Leroy Robert "Satchel" Paige (Negro League and Hall of Fame Pitcher, 1906-1982)

SATURDAY
14

SUNDAY
15

JANUARY BAROMETER IN GRAPHIC FORM SINCE 1950

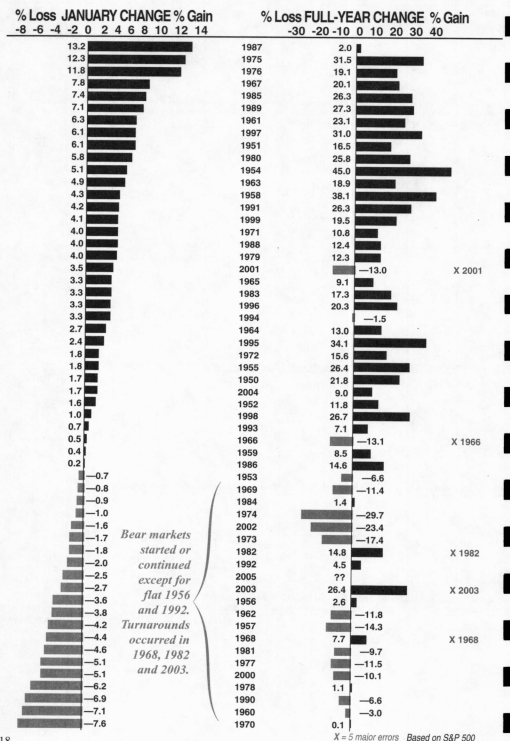

% Loss — JANUARY CHANGE — % Gain	Year	% Loss — FULL-YEAR CHANGE — % Gain	
13.2	1987	2.0	
12.3	1975	31.5	
11.8	1976	19.1	
7.8	1967	20.1	
7.4	1985	26.3	
7.1	1989	27.3	
6.3	1961	23.1	
6.1	1997	31.0	
6.1	1951	16.5	
5.8	1980	25.8	
5.1	1954	45.0	
4.9	1963	18.9	
4.3	1958	38.1	
4.2	1991	26.3	
4.1	1999	19.5	
4.0	1971	10.8	
4.0	1988	12.4	
4.0	1979	12.3	
3.5	2001	—13.0	X 2001
3.3	1965	9.1	
3.3	1983	17.3	
3.3	1996	20.3	
3.3	1994	—1.5	
2.7	1964	13.0	
2.4	1995	34.1	
1.8	1972	15.6	
1.8	1955	26.4	
1.7	1950	21.8	
1.7	2004	9.0	
1.6	1952	11.8	
1.0	1998	26.7	
0.7	1993	7.1	
0.5	1966	—13.1	X 1966
0.4	1959	8.5	
0.2	1986	14.6	
—0.7	1953	—6.6	
—0.8	1969	—11.4	
—0.9	1984	1.4	
—1.0	1974	—29.7	
—1.6	2002	—23.4	
—1.7	1973	—17.4	
—1.8	1982	14.8	X 1982
—2.0	1992	4.5	
—2.5	2005	??	
—2.7	2003	26.4	X 2003
—3.6	1956	2.6	
—3.8	1962	—11.8	
—4.2	1957	—14.3	
—4.4	1968	7.7	X 1968
—4.6	1981	—9.7	
—5.1	1977	—11.5	
—5.1	2000	—10.1	
—6.2	1978	1.1	
—6.9	1990	—6.6	
—7.1	1960	—3.0	
—7.6	1970	0.1	

Bear markets started or continued except for flat 1956 and 1992. Turnarounds occurred in 1968, 1982 and 2003.

X = 5 major errors   Based on S&P 500

JANUARY

Martin Luther King Jr. Day (Market Closed)

MONDAY
16

People's spending habits depend more on how wealthy they feel than with the actual amount of their current income.
— A.C. Pigou (English economist, *The Theory of Unemployment*, 1877-1959)

First Trading Day of January Expiration Week Dow Up 10 of Last 13

TUESDAY
17
D 61.9
S 76.2
N 61.9

Every time everyone's talking about something, that's the time to sell. — George Lindemann (Billionaire, *Forbes*)

WEDNESDAY
18
D 61.9
S 61.9
N 71.4

The advice of the elders to young men is very apt to be as unreal as a list of the best books.
— Oliver Wendell Holmes Jr. (*The Mind and Faith of Justice Holmes*, edited by Max Lerner)

THURSDAY
19
D 38.1
S 52.4
N 76.2

While one person hesitates because he feels inferior, the other is busy making mistakes and becoming superior. — Henry C. Link

January Expiration Day Dow Down 6 of Last 7, 2004 Broke a 5-Year Dog Run

FRIDAY
20
D 38.1
S 38.1
N 38.1

I really do inhabit a system in which words are capable of shaking the entire structure of government, where words can prove mightier than ten military divisions. — Vaclav Havel (Czech dramatist, essayist, political leader and president b.1936)

SATURDAY
21

SUNDAY
22

HOT JANUARY INDUSTRIES BEAT S&P NEXT 11 MONTHS

The S&P 500 in January tends to predict the market's direction for the year. In turn, Standard & Poor's top ten industries in January outperform the index over the next eleven months.

Our friend Sam Stovall, Chief Investment Strategist at S&P, has crunched the numbers over the years. He calls it the "January Barometer Portfolio" or JBP. Since 1970 a portfolio of the top ten S&P industries during January has beaten the S&P 500 itself — and performed even better in years when January was up.

The JBP went on to outperform the S&P 500 during the remaining 11 months of the year 74% of the time, 16.1% to 6.9%, on average. When the S&P 500 is up in January, a top-10 industries portfolio increases the average portfolio gain to 21.4% for the last 11 months of the year vs. 12.7% for the S&P.

For more check Sam's Sector Watch at *businessweek.com* or our March 2005 *Almanac Investor* newsletter in the archives at *stocktradersalmanac.com*. Also highlighted are Sam's selected stocks from within the top ten sectors.

AS JANUARY GOES, SO GOES THE YEAR
FOR TOP PERFORMING INDUSTRIES
January's Top 10 Industries vs. S&P 500 Next 11 Months

	11 Month % Change		S&P Jan	After S&P Up in January		After S&P Down in January	
	Portfolio	S&P	%	Portfolio	S&P	Portfolio	S&P
1970	− 4.7	− 0.3	− 7.6			− 4.7	− 0.3
1971	23.5	6.1	4.0	23.5	6.1		
1972	19.7	13.7	1.8	19.7	13.7		
1973	5.2	− 20.0	− 1.7			5.2	− 20.0
1974	− 29.2	− 30.2	− 1.0			− 29.2	− 30.2
1975	57.3	22.2	12.3	57.3	22.2		
1976	16.3	8.1	11.8	16.3	8.1		
1977	− 9.1	− 9.6	− 5.1			− 9.1	− 9.6
1978	7.3	6.5	− 6.2			7.3	6.5
1979	21.7	8.1	4.0	21.7	8.1		
1980	38.3	20.4	5.8	38.3	20.4		
1981	5.0	− 6.9	− 4.6			5.0	− 6.9
1982	37.2	18.8	− 1.8			37.2	18.8
1983	17.2	13.9	3.3	17.2	13.9		
1984	− 5.0	− 1.1	− 0.9			− 5.0	− 1.1
1985	28.2	20.8	7.4	28.2	20.8		
1986	18.1	19.4	0.2	18.1	19.4		
1987	− 1.5	− 8.9	13.2	− 1.5	− 8.9		
1988	18.4	10.4	4.0	18.4	10.4		
1989	16.1	22.1	7.1	16.1	22.1		
1990	− 4.4	− 3.3	− 6.9			− 4.4	− 3.3
1991	35.7	19.4	4.2	35.7	19.4		
1992	14.6	4.7	− 2.0			14.6	4.7
1993	23.7	7.2	0.7	23.7	7.2		
1994	− 7.1	− 4.6	3.3	− 7.1	− 4.6		
1995	25.6	30.9	2.4	25.6	30.9		
1996	5.4	16.5	3.3	5.4	16.5		
1997	4.7	23.4	6.1	4.7	23.4		
1998	45.2	25.4	1.0	45.2	25.4		
1999	67.9	14.8	4.1	67.9	14.8		
2000	23.6	− 5.3	− 5.1			23.6	− 5.3
2001	− 13.1	− 16.0	3.5	− 13.1	− 16.0		
2002	− 16.2	− 22.2	− 1.6			− 16.2	− 22.2
2003	69.3	29.9	− 2.7			69.3	29.9
2004	9.9	7.1	1.7	9.9	7.1		
2005			− 2.5				
Averages	16.1%	6.9%		21.4%	12.7%	7.2%	− 3.0%

JANUARY

MONDAY
D 33.3
S 38.1
N 47.6
23

Press on. Nothing in the world can take the place of persistence. Talent will not: nothing is more common than unrewarded talent. Education alone will not: the world is full of educated failures. Persistence alone is omnipotent. — Calvin Coolidge

TUESDAY
D 38.1
S 52.4
N 57.1
24

Three passions, simple but overwhelmingly strong, have governed my life: the longing for love, the search for knowledge, and unbearable pity for the suffering of mankind. — Bertrand Russell (British mathematician and philosopher, 1872-1970)

"January Barometer" 90.9% accurate (Page 16)
Almanac Investor *Subscribers E-mailed Official Reading Alert*

WEDNESDAY
D 71.4
S 52.4
N 42.9
25

While markets often make double bottoms, three pushes to a high is the most common topping pattern.
— John Bollinger (Bollinger Capital Management, created Bollinger Bands, *Capital Growth Letter, Bollinger on Bollinger Bands*)

THURSDAY
D 61.9
S 47.6
N 71.4
26

The trend is your friend...until it ends. — Anonymous

FRIDAY
D 57.1
S 52.4
N 61.9
27

Those heroes of finance are like beads on a string, when one slips off, the rest follow. — Henrik Ibsen

SATURDAY
28

February Bullish Seasonalities: see pages 80 and 116.

SUNDAY
29

FEBRUARY ALMANAC

FEBRUARY						
S	M	T	W	T	F	S
				1	2	3	4
5	6	7	8	9	10	11
12	13	14	15	16	17	18
19	20	21	22	23	24	25
26	27	28				

MARCH						
S	M	T	W	T	F	S
				1	2	3	4
5	6	7	8	9	10	11
12	13	14	15	16	17	18
19	20	21	22	23	24	25
26	27	28	29	30	31	

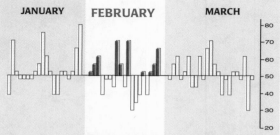

Market Probability Chart above is a graphic representation of the S&P 500 Recent Market Probability Calendar on page 121.

◆ February is the weak link in "Best Six Months" (pages 46, 50 & 138) ◆ RECENT RECORD improving: S&P 14 up, 8 down, average change 0.6% for 22 years ◆ Fourth ranking NASDAQ month in Midterm Election Years (page 150) average –0.3% loss, up 4, down 4 ◆ Day before Presidents' Day weekend S&P down 12 of 14, 11 straight 1992-2002, day after improving lately, up 8 of 14 (see below and page 86) ◆ Many technicians modify market predictions based on January's market.

FEBRUARY DAILY POINT CHANGES DOW JONES INDUSTRIALS

Previous Month Close	1996 5395.30	1997 6813.09	1998 7906.50	1999 9358.83	2000 10940.53	2001 10887.36	2002 9920.00	2003 8053.81	2004 10488.07	2005 10489.94
1	9.76	S	S	– 13.13	100.52	96.27	– 12.74	S	S	62.00
2	– 31.07	S	201.28	– 71.58	– 37.85	– 119.53	S	S	11.11	44.85
3	S	– 6.93	52.57	92.69	10.24	S	S	56.01	6.00	– 3.69
4	S	27.32	– 30.64	– 62.31	– 49.64	S	– 220.17	– 96.53	– 34.44	123.03
5	33.60	– 86.58	– 12.46	– 0.26	S	101.75	– 1.66	– 28.11	24.81	S
6	52.02	26.16	72.24	S	S	– 8.43	– 32.04	– 55.88	97.48	S
7	32.51	82.74	S	S	– 58.01	– 10.70	– 27.95	– 65.07	S	– 0.37
8	47.33	S	S	– 13.13	51.81	– 66.17	118.80	S	S	8.87
9	2.17	S	– 8.97	– 158.08	– 258.44	– 99.10	S	S	– 14.00	– 60.52
10	S	– 49.26	115.09	44.28	– 55.53	S	S	55.88	34.82	85.50
11	S	51.57	18.94	186.15	– 218.42	S	140.54	– 77.00	123.85	46.40
12	58.53	103.52	55.05	– 88.57	S	165.32	– 21.04	– 84.94	– 43.63	S
13	1.08	60.81	0.50	S	S	– 43.45	125.93	– 8.30	– 66.22	S
14	– 21.68	– 33.48	S	S	94.63	– 107.91	12.32	158.93	S	– 4.88
15	– 28.18	S	S	H	198.25	95.61	– 98.95	S	S	46.19
16	– 48.05	S	H	22.14	– 156.68	– 91.20	S	S	H	– 2.44
17	S	H	28.40	– 101.56	– 46.84	S	S	H	87.03	– 80.62
18	S	78.50	52.56	103.16	– 295.05	S	H	132.35	– 42.89	30.96
19	H	– 47.33	– 75.48	41.32	S	H	– 157.90	– 40.55	– 7.26	S
20	– 44.79	– 92.75	38.36	S	S	– 68.94	196.03	– 85.64	– 45.70	S
21	57.44	4.24	S	S	H	– 204.30	– 106.49	103.15	S	H
22	92.49	S	S	212.73	85.32	0.23	133.47	S	S	–174.02
23	22.03	S	– 3.74	– 8.26	– 79.11	– 84.91	S	S	– 9.41	62.59
24	S	76.58	– 40.10	– 144.75	– 133.10	S	S	– 159.87	– 43.25	75.00
25	S	30.01	87.68	– 33.33	– 230.51	S	177.56	51.26	35.25	92.81
26	– 65.39	– 55.03	32.89	– 59.76	S	200.63	– 30.45	– 102.52	– 21.48	S
27	– 15.89	– 58.11	55.05	S	S	– 5.65	12.32	78.01	3.78	S
28	– 43.00	– 47.33	S	S	176.53	– 141.60	– 21.45	6.09	S	– 75.37
29	– 20.59				89.66				S	
Close	5485.62	6877.74	8545.72	9306.58	10128.31	10495.28	10106.13	7891.08	10583.92	10766.23
Change	90.32	64.65	639.22	– 52.25	– 812.22	– 392.08	186.13	– 162.73	95.85	276.29

Either go short, or stay away
The day before Presidents' Day

JANUARY/FEBRUARY

January Ends "Best Three-Month Span" (Pages 46, 54, 138 and 139)

MONDAY
D61.9
S66.7
N57.1
30

Regulatory agencies within five years become controlled by industries they were set up to regulate. — Gabriel Kolko

FOMC Meeting (2 Days)
Historically One of Three Best Trading Days of the Year (Page 121)

TUESDAY
D66.7
S81.0
N71.4
31

If you are not willing to study, if you are not sufficiently interested to investigate and analyze the stock market yourself,
then I beg of you to become an outright long-pull investor, to buy good stocks, and hold on to them;
for otherwise your chances of success as a trader will be nil. — Humphrey B. Neill (Tape Reading and Market Tactics, 1931)

First Trading Day in February Dow Up 5 of Last 6

WEDNESDAY
D52.4
S52.4
N71.4
1

Industrial capitalism has generated the greatest productive power in human history. To date, no other socioeconomic system has
been able to generate comparable productive power. — Peter L. Berger (The Capitalist Revolution)

THURSDAY
D52.4
S57.1
N71.4
2

Wall Street's graveyards are filled with men who were right too soon. — William Hamilton

FRIDAY
D42.9
S61.9
N61.9
3

Those who cast the votes decide nothing. Those who count the votes decide everything. — Joseph Stalin

SATURDAY
4

SUNDAY
5

1933 "LAME DUCK" AMENDMENT
REASON JANUARY BAROMETER WORKS

There would be no January Barometer without the passage in 1933 of the Twentieth "Lame Duck" Amendment to the Constitution. Since then it has essentially been "As January goes, so goes the year." January's direction has correctly forecasted the major trend for the market in most of the subsequent years.

Prior to 1934, newly elected Senators and Representatives did not take office until December of the following year, 13 months later (except when new Presidents were inaugurated). Defeated Congressmen stayed in Congress for all of the following session. They were known as "lame ducks."

Since 1934, Congress convenes in the first week of January and includes those members newly elected the previous November. Inauguration Day was also moved up from March 4 to January 20. As a result several events have been squeezed into January, which affect our economy and our stock market and quite possibly those of many nations of the world.

The basis for January's predictive capacity comes from the fact that so many important events occur in the month: new Congresses convene; the President gives the State of the Union message, presents the annual budget and sets national goals and priorities. Switch these events to any other month and chances are the January Barometer would become a memory.

The table shows the January Barometer in odd years. In 1935 and 1937, the Democrats already had the most lop-sided Congressional margins in history, so when these two Congresses convened it was anticlimactic.

The January Barometer in subsequent odd-numbered years had compiled a perfect record until two January interest rate cuts and 9/11 affected 2001 and the anticipation of military action in Iraq held the market down in January 2003.

See the January Barometer compared to prior "New Congress Barometers" at *http://www.hirschorg.com/lameduck*.

JANUARY BAROMETER (ODD YEARS)

January % Change	12 Month % Change	Same	Opposite
− 4.2%	41.2%		1935
3.8	− 38.6		1937
− 6.9	− 5.4	1939	
− 4.8	− 17.9	1941	
7.2	19.4	1943	
1.4	30.7	1945	
2.4	N/C	1947	
0.1	10.3	1949	
6.1	16.5	1951	
− 0.7	− 6.6	1953	
1.8	26.4	1955	
− 4.2	− 14.3	1957	
0.4	8.5	1959	
6.3	23.1	1961	
4.9	18.9	1963	
3.3	9.1	1965	
7.8	20.1	1967	
− 0.8	− 11.4	1969	
4.0	10.8	1971	
− 1.7	− 17.4	1973	
12.3	31.5	1975	
− 5.1	− 11.5	1977	
4.0	12.3	1979	
− 4.6	− 9.7	1981	
3.3	17.3	1983	
7.4	26.3	1985	
13.2	2.0	1987	
7.1	27.3	1989	
4.1	26.3	1991	
0.7	7.1	1993	
2.4	34.1	1995	
6.1	31.0	1997	
4.1	19.5	1999	
3.5	− 13.0		2001
− 2.7	26.4		2003
− 2.5	??	2005?	2005?

12 months' % change includes January's % change
Based on S&P 500

FEBRUARY

MONDAY
D38.1
S38.1
N61.9
6

*I write an e-mail about every week to 10 days…and within about 24 hours everyone will have read it.
The amazing thing is how I can change the direction of the entire company within 24 hours. Ten years ago I couldn't do that.*
— Michael Marks (CEO Flextronics, *Forbes*, July 7, 2003)

TUESDAY
D52.4
S47.6
N57.1
7

Beware of inside information…all inside information. — Jesse Livermore (*How to Trade in Stocks*)

NASDAQ Flattened in 2001 Down 22.4% in February

WEDNESDAY
D38.1
S47.6
N52.4
8

The greatest discovery of my generation is that human beings can alter their lives by altering their attitudes.
— William James (Philosopher, psychologist, 1842-1910)

THURSDAY
D47.6
S42.9
N47.6
9

*Charts not only tell what was, they tell what is; and a trend from was to is (projected linearly into the will be)
contains better percentages than clumsy guessing.* — R. A. Levy

FRIDAY
D61.9
S71.4
N57.1
10

*Intellect and Emotion are partners who do not speak the same language. The intellect finds logic to justify what the emotions have
decided. WIN THE HEARTS OF PEOPLE, THEIR MINDS WILL FOLLOW.* — Roy H. Williams (*The Wizard of Ads*)

SATURDAY
11

SUNDAY
12

THE SIXTH YEAR OF DECADES

The three losses below were all war-related: 1916 (during WWI), 1946 (post-WWII top and sell-off) and 1966 (Vietnam bear market). The last two losses were Midterm Years and both bottomed in October. Most "sixth" years delivered genuine buying opportunities. The last three produced solid gains. Midterm 2006 promises a super buying opportunity.

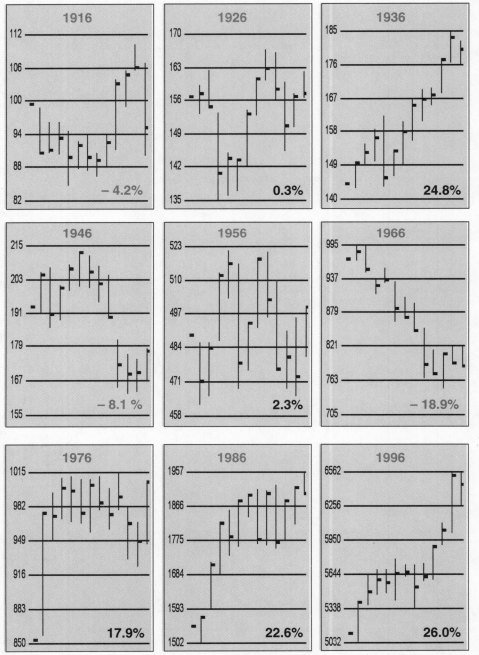

Based on Dow Jones Industrial Average monthly ranges and closing prices

FEBRUARY

Monday Before February Expiration Dow Up 11 of Last 12, 2005 Ended Streak

MONDAY
D 52.4
S 57.1
N 47.6
13

What the superior man seeks, is in himself. What the inferior man seeks, is in others. — Confucius

Valentine's Day ♥

TUESDAY
D 52.4
S 42.9
N 61.9
14

It is a funny thing about life; if you refuse to accept anything but the best, you very often get it. — W. Somerset Maugham

WEDNESDAY
D 71.4
S 71.4
N 66.7
15

The most valuable executive is one who is training somebody to be a better man than he is.
— Robert G. Ingersoll (American lawyer and orator, "the Great Agnostic," 1833-1899)

THURSDAY
D 33.3
S 28.6
N 33.3
16

Ignorance is not knowing something; stupidity is not admitting your ignorance. — Daniel Turov (Turov on Timing)

February Expiration Day Dow Down 4 of Last 6
Day Before Presidents' Day S&P Down 12 of Last 14 — 11 Straight 1992-2002

FRIDAY
D 33.3
S 33.3
N 47.6
17

No profession requires more hard work, intelligence, patience, and mental discipline than successful speculation. — Robert Rhea

SATURDAY
18

SUNDAY
19

MARKET CHARTS OF MIDTERM ELECTION YEARS

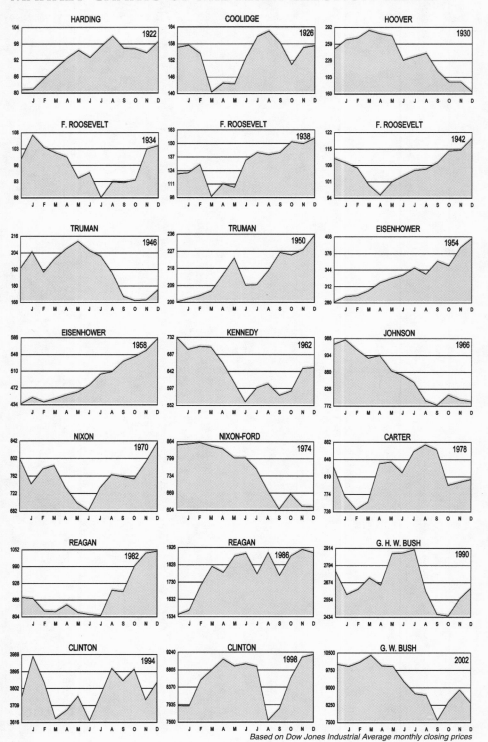

Based on Dow Jones Industrial Average monthly closing prices

FEBRUARY

Presidents' Day (Market Closed)

MONDAY
20

Whenever a well-known bearish analyst is interviewed {Cover story} in the financial press, it usually coincides with an important near-term market bottom. — Clif Droke (Clifdroke.com, November 15, 2004)

Day After Presidents' Day S&P Up 8 of 14 — Major Losses When Down

D 47.6
S 38.1
N 42.9

TUESDAY
21

The greatest good you can do for another is not just to share your riches, but to reveal to him his own. — Benjamin Disraeli (British prime minister, 1804-1881)

WEDNESDAY

D 52.4
S 52.4
N 52.4

22

A statistician is someone who can draw a straight line from an unwarranted assumption to a foregone conclusion. — Anonymous

THURSDAY

D 42.9
S 38.1
N 57.1

23

For want of a nail, the shoe was lost. For want of a shoe, the horse was lost. For want of a horse, the rider was lost. For want of a rider, the battle was lost. For want of a battle, the kingdom was lost. And all for the want of a nail! — English proverb

FRIDAY

D 52.4
S 52.4
N 52.4

24

I don't believe in intuition. When you get sudden flashes of perception, it is just the brain working faster than usual. — Katherine Anne Porter (American author, 1890-1980)

SATURDAY
25

March Bullish Seasonalities: see pages 80 and 116.

SUNDAY
26

MARCH ALMANAC

MARCH						
S	M	T	W	T	F	S
				1	2	3	4
5	6	7	8	9	10	11
12	13	14	15	16	17	18
19	20	21	22	23	24	25
26	27	28	29	30	31	

APRIL						
S	M	T	W	T	F	S
						1
2	3	4	5	6	7	8
9	10	11	12	13	14	15
16	17	18	19	20	21	22
23	24	25	26	27	28	29
30						

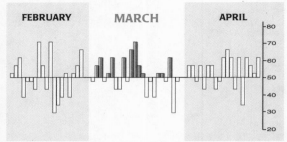

Market Probability Chart above is a graphic representation of the S&P 500 Recent Market Probability Calendar on page 121.

◆ Early and mid-month strength and late-month weakness are most evident above ◆ RECENT RECORD: S&P 14 up, 8 down, average gain 0.9%, sixth best ◆ Rather stormy in recent years with wild fluctuations and large gains and losses ◆ March has been taking some mean end-of-quarter hits — revealed below, down 1469 Dow points March 9-22, 2001 ◆ Last three or four days a net loser eleven out of last fourteen years ◆ NASDAQ hard hit in 2001, down 14.5% after 22.4% drop in February ◆ Market much luckier the day before St. Patrick's Day ◆ Strong in Midterm Election Years up better than 60% of the time with 1+% average gains, ranks third on NASDAQ and fourth on Dow and S&P.

MARCH DAILY POINT CHANGES DOW JONES INDUSTRIALS

Previous Month	1996	1997	1998	1999	2000	2001	2002	2003	2004	2005
Close	5485.62	6877.74	8545.72	9306.58	10128.31	10495.28	10106.13	7891.08	10583.92	10766.23
1	50.94	S	S	18.20	9.62	− 45.14	262.73	S	94.22	63.77
2	S	S	4.73	− 27.17	26.99	16.17	S	S	− 86.66	− 18.03
3	S	41.18	34.38	− 21.73	202.28	S	S	− 53.22	1.63	21.06
4	63.59	− 66.20	− 45.59	191.52	S	S	217.96	− 132.99	− 5.11	107.52
5	42.27	93.13	− 94.91	268.68	S	95.99	− 153.41	70.73	7.55	S
6	− 12.65	− 1.15	125.06	S	− 196.70	28.92	140.88	− 101.61	S	S
7	11.92	56.19	S	S	− 374.47	138.38	− 48.92	66.04	S	− 3.69
8	− 171.24	S	S	− 8.47	60.50	128.65	47.12	S	− 66.07	− 24.24
9	S	S	− 2.25	− 33.85	154.20	− 213.63	S	S	− 72.52	− 107.00
10	S	78.50	75.98	79.08	− 81.91	S	S	− 171.85	− 160.07	45.89
11	110.55	5.77	32.63	124.60	S	S	38.75	− 44.12	− 168.51	− 77.15
12	2.89	− 45.79	− 16.19	− 21.09	S	− 436.37	21.11	28.01	111.70	S
13	− 15.17	− 160.48	− 57.04	S	18.31	82.55	− 130.50	269.68	S	S
14	17.34	56.57	S	S	− 135.89	− 317.34	15.29	37.96	S	30.15
15	− 1.09	S	S	82.42	320.17	57.82	90.09	S	− 137.19	− 59.41
16	S	S	116.33	− 28.30	499.19	− 207.87	S	S	81.78	− 112.03
17	S	20.02	31.14	− 51.06	− 35.37	S	S	282.21	115.63	− 6.72
18	98.63	− 58.92	25.41	118.21	S	S	− 29.48	52.31	− 4.52	3.32
19	− 14.09	− 18.88	27.65	− 94.07	S	135.70	57.50	71.22	− 109.18	S
20	− 14.09	− 57.40	103.38	S	85.01	− 238.35	− 133.68	21.15	S	S
21	− 28.54	− 15.49	S	S	227.10	− 233.76	− 21.73	235.37	S	− 64.28
22	9.76	S	S	− 13.04	− 40.64	− 97.52	− 52.17	S	− 121.85	− 94.88
23	S	100.46	− 90.18	− 218.68	253.16	115.30	S	S	− 1.11	− 14.49
24	7.22	− 29.08	88.19	− 4.99	− 7.14	S	S	− 307.29	− 15.41	− 13.15
25	7.22	− 29.08	− 31.64	169.55	S	S	− 146.00	65.55	170.59	H
26	26.74	4.53	− 25.91	− 14.15	S	182.75	71.69	− 50.35	− 5.85	S
27	− 43.72	− 140.11	− 50.81	S	− 86.87	260.01	73.55	− 28.43	S	S
28	3.97	H	S	S	− 89.74	− 162.19	− 22.97	− 55.68	S	42.78
29	− 43.71	S	S	184.54	82.61	13.71	H	S	116.66	− 79.95
30	S	S	− 13.96	− 93.52	− 38.47	79.72	S	S	52.07	135.23
31	S	− 157.11	17.69	− 127.10	− 58.33	S	S	− 153.64	− 24.00	−37.17
Close	5587.14	6583.48	8799.81	9786.16	10921.92	9878.78	10403.94	7992.13	10357.70	10503.76
Change	101.52	− 294.26	254.09	479.58	793.61	− 616.50	297.81	101.05	− 226.22	− 262.47

March has Ides and St. Patrick's Day
Begins bullishly, then fades away

MONDAY
D 47.6
S 57.1
N 52.4
27

You are your own Promised Land, your own new frontier. — Julia Margaret Cameron (19th century English photographer)

TUESDAY
D 52.4
S 66.7
N 61.9
28

[The Fed] is very smart, but [it] doesn't run the markets. In the end, the markets will run [the Fed]. The markets are bigger than any man or any group of men. The markets can even break a president... — Richard Russell (*Dow Theory Letters*, August 4, 2004)

Ash Wednesday
First Trading Day in March Dow Up 8 of Last 10

WEDNESDAY
D 57.1
S 47.6
N 66.7
1

The time to buy is when blood is running in the streets. — Baron Nathan Rothschild (London financier, 1777-1836)

THURSDAY
D 66.7
S 57.1
N 47.6
2

How a minority Reaching majority Seizing authority Hates a minority. — Leonard H. Robbins

March Historically Strong Early in the Month

FRIDAY
D 61.9
S 61.9
N 76.2
3

Edison has done more toward abolishing poverty than all the reformers and statesmen. — Henry Ford

SATURDAY
4

SUNDAY
5

PROFIT ON DAY BEFORE ST. PATRICK'S DAY

We first published Saint Patrick's Day bullishness in the 1977 Almanac. Dan Turov, editor of *Turov On Timing*, notes gains the day before Saint Patrick's Day have proved best, outperforming the days before many legal holidays for an average gain of 0.31% on the S&P. Irish luck, or coincidence?

During the past 53 years, Saint Patrick's Day itself has posted just a wee gain of 0.14%. Saint Pat's 2005 landed on Thursday before Triple-Witching. Both days before got walloped by bad GM news, soaring oil prices and record trade deficits, while Saint Pat's gained a little ground. The entire week was off, as the market began to show signs of deterioration.

Saint Patrick's Day 2006 falls on Triple-Witching Friday, creating a potential up day on Thursday, March 16th. But with the first Triple-Witching Week of the year tending towards weakness of late, we would exercise caution and perhaps jump in only for a quick trade on a selloff Wednesday, March 15th — depending on market conditions.

Perhaps it's the anticipation of the patron saint's holiday that boosts the market and the distraction of the parade down Fifth Avenue that holds the market back — or is it the absent, and then hungover, traders? Or maybe it's the fact that Saint Pat's usually falls in Triple-Witching Week.

ST. PATRICK'S DAY TRADING RECORD (DAYS BEFORE AND AFTER)

Year	St. Pat's Day	% Change 2 Days Prior	% Change 1 Day Prior	S&P 500 St. Pat's Day or Next *	% Change St. Pat's Day *	% Change Day After
1953	Tue	0.19%	0.15%	26.33	0.42%	− 0.34%
1954	Wed	− 0.45	− 0.04	26.62	0.23	0.41
1955	Thu	2.15	0.76	36.12	0.39	0.17
1956	Sat	0.97	0.31	48.59	0.93	0.58
1957	Sun	0.07	− 0.05	43.85	− 0.45	0.43
1958	Mon	0.12	− 0.31	42.04	− 0.69	− 0.36
1959	Tue	0.12	− 1.08	56.52	0.82	− 0.23
1960	Thu	0.77	0.55	54.96	− 0.15	0.09
1961	Fri	0.30	1.01	64.60	0.61	0.40
1962	Sat	0.21	− 0.17	70.85	− 0.13	− 0.27
1963	Sun	− 0.47	0.50	65.61	− 0.49	− 0.21
1964	Tue	0.08	0.00	79.32	0.23	0.08
1965	Wed	0.03	− 0.13	87.02	− 0.13	− 0.24
1966	Thu	− 0.57	0.58	88.17	0.35	0.41
1967	Fri	0.95	1.01	90.25	0.18	− 0.06
1968	Sun	− 1.90	0.88	89.59	0.55	− 0.67
1969	Mon	− 0.67	− 0.40	98.25	0.26	0.24
1970	Tue	− 0.53	− 1.08	87.29	0.44	0.29
1971	Wed	1.14	0.50	101.12	− 0.09	0.07
1972	Fri	0.13	− 0.23	107.92	0.39	− 0.31
1973	Sat	− 0.75	− 0.51	112.17	− 1.21	− 0.20
1974	Sun	− 0.09	− 0.37	98.05	− 1.24	− 0.84
1975	Mon	0.18	1.22	86.01	1.47	− 1.02
1976	Wed	− 1.05	1.12	100.86	− 0.06	− 0.41
1977	Thu	0.55	0.19	102.08	− 0.09	− 0.22
1978	Fri	− 0.26	0.44	90.20	0.77	0.69
1979	Sat	0.15	0.83	101.06	0.37	− 0.55
1980	Mon	− 1.17	− 0.18	102.26	− 3.01	1.80
1981	Tue	− 0.06	1.18	133.92	− 0.56	0.22
1982	Wed	0.77	− 0.16	109.08	− 0.18	1.12
1983	Thu	0.35	− 1.03	149.59	− 0.14	0.21
1984	Sat	0.41	1.18	157.78	− 0.94	0.68
1985	Sun	− 0.20	− 0.74	176.88	0.20	1.50
1986	Mon	0.28	1.44	234.67	− 0.79	0.47
1987	Tue	− 0.46	− 0.57	292.47	1.47	0.11
1988	Thu	− 0.09	0.95	271.22	0.96	− 0.04
1989	Fri	0.52	0.93	292.69	− 2.25	− 0.95
1990	Sat	0.36	1.14	343.53	0.47	− 0.57
1991	Sun	− 0.29	0.02	372.11	− 0.40	− 1.48
1992	Tue	0.48	0.14	409.58	0.78	− 0.10
1993	Wed	0.36	− 0.01	448.31	− 0.68	0.80
1994	Thu	− 0.08	0.52	470.90	0.32	0.04
1995	Fri	− 0.20	0.72	495.52	0.02	0.13
1996	Sun	0.36	0.09	652.65	1.75	− 0.15
1997	Mon	− 1.83	0.46	795.71	0.32	− 0.76
1998	Tue	− 0.12	1.00	1080.45	0.11	0.47
1999	Wed	0.98	− 0.07	1297.82	− 0.66	1.44
2000	Fri	2.43	4.76	1464.47	0.41	− 0.54
2001	Sat	0.59	− 1.96	1170.81	1.76	− 2.41
2002	Sun	− 0.09	1.14	1165.55	− 0.05	0.41
2003	Mon	3.45	0.16	862.79	3.54	0.42
2004	Wed	− 1.43	0.56	1123.75	1.17	− 0.13
2005	Thu	− 0.75	− 0.81	1190.21	0.18	− 0.05
Average		**0.11%**	**0.31%**		**0.14%**	**0.01%**

When St. Patrick's Day falls on Saturday or Sunday, the following trading day is used. Based on S&P 500.

MARCH

NASDAQ Crushed in 2001 Down 14.5% in March After a 22.4% Drop in February

MONDAY

D 47.6
S 47.6
N 52.4

6

Every truth passes through three stages before it is recognized. In the first it is ridiculed; in the second it is opposed; in the third it is regarded as self evident. — Arthur Schopenhauer (German philosopher, 1788-1860)

TUESDAY

D 52.4
S 52.4
N 57.1

7

English stocks…are springing up like mushrooms this year…forced up to a quite unreasonable level and then, for most part, collapse. In this way, I have made over 400 pounds…[Speculating] makes small demands on one's time, and it's worth while running some risk in order to relieve the enemy of his money. — Karl Marx (German social philosopher and revolutionary, in an 1864 letter to his uncle, 1818-1883)

WEDNESDAY

D 52.4
S 61.9
N 52.4

8

If the models are telling you to sell, sell, sell, but only buyers are out there, don't be a jerk. Buy!
— William Silber, Ph.D. (N.Y.U., *Newsweek*, 1986)

Dow Down 1469 Points March 9-22 in 2001

THURSDAY

D 52.4
S 42.9
N 52.4

9

Don't fritter away your time. Create, act, take a place wherever you are and be somebody.
— Theodore Roosevelt (26th U.S. President, 1858-1919)

FRIDAY

D 47.6
S 42.9
N 52.4

10

The men who can manage men manage the men who manage only things, and the men who can manage money manage all.
— Will Durant

SATURDAY

11

SUNDAY

12

MIDTERM ELECTION YEARS: WHERE BOTTOM PICKERS FIND PARADISE

American presidents have danced the Quadrennial Quadrille over the past two centuries. After the midterm congressional election and the invariable seat loss by his party, the president during the next two years jiggles fiscal policies to get federal spending, disposable income and Social Security benefits up and interest rates and inflation down. By Election Day, he will have danced his way into the wallets and hearts of the electorate and, hopefully, will have choreographed four more years in the White House for his party.

After the Inaugural Ball is over, however, we pay the piper. Practically all bear markets began and ended in the two years after presidential elections. Bottoms often occurred in an air of crisis: the Cuban Missile Crisis in 1962, tight money in 1966, Cambodia in 1970, Watergate and Nixon's resignation in 1974, and threat of international monetary collapse in 1982. But remember, the word for "crisis" in Chinese is composed of two characters: the first, the symbol for danger; the second, opportunity. Of the 10 quadrennial cycles in the past 44 years, only one bottom was reached in the post-presidential year. All others came in midterm years.

THE RECORD SINCE 1914

1914	Wilson (D)	Bottom in July. War closed markets.
1918	Wilson (D)	**Bottom 12 days prior to start of year.**
1922	Harding (R)	**Bottom 4-1/2 months prior to start of year.**
1926	Coolidge (R)	Only drop (7 wks, −17%) ends Mar. 30.
1930	Hoover (R)	**Crash of '29 continues through 1930. No bottom.**
1934	Roosevelt (D)	First Roosevelt bear, February to July 26 bottom (−23%).
1938	Roosevelt (D)	Big 1937 break ends in March, DJI off 49%.
1942	Roosevelt (D)	World War II bottom in April.
1946	Truman (D)	Market tops in May, bottoms in October.
1950	Truman (D)	June 1949 bottom, June 1950 Korean War outbreak causes 14% drop.
1954	Eisenhower (R)	*September 1953 bottom, then straight up.*
1958	Eisenhower (R)	*October 1957 bottom, then straight up.*
1962	Kennedy (D)	Bottoms in June and October.
1966	Johnson (D)	Bottom in October.
1970	Nixon (R)	Bottom in May.
1974	Nixon, Ford (R)	December Dow bottom, S&P bottom in October.
1978	Carter (D)	March bottom, despite October massacre later.
1982	Reagan (R)	Bottom in August.
1986	Reagan (R)	**No bottom in 1985 or 1986.**
1990	Bush (R)	Bottom October 11 (Kuwaiti invasion).
1994	Clinton (D)	Bottom April 4 after 10% drop.
1998	Clinton (D)	October 8 bottom (Asian currency crisis, hedge fund debacle).
2002	Bush, GW (R)	October 9 bottom (Corp. malfeasance, terrorism, Iraq).

Bold = No bottom in midterm election year

Graph shows Midterm Election years screened
Based on Dow Jones industrial average monthly ranges

34

Monday Before March Triple Witching Dow Up 14 of Last 18,
but Walloped 4.1% in 2001 and 1.3% in 2004

MONDAY
D 47.6
S 61.9
N 61.9
13

Some people say we can't compete with Intel. I say, like hell you can't... Dominant companies usually don't change unless they're forced to do so. — David Patterson (Chip designing force behind R.I.S.C. and R.A.I.D., *WSJ*, August 28, 1998)

TUESDAY
D 57.1
S 47.6
N 42.9
14

One machine can do the work of fifty ordinary men. No machine can do the work of one extraordinary man.
— Elbert Hubbard (American author, *A Message To Garcia*, 1856-1915)

WEDNESDAY
D 57.1
S 66.7
N 52.4
15

Foolish consistency is the hobgoblin of little minds.
— Ralph Waldo Emerson (American author, poet and philosopher, *Self-Reliance*, 1803-1882)

Market Much Luckier Day Before St. Patrick's Day (Page 32)

THURSDAY
D 71.4
S 71.4
N 76.2
16

Little minds are tamed and subdued by misfortune; but great minds rise above them. — Washington Irving (American essayist, historian, novelist, *The Legend of Sleepy Hollow*, U.S. ambassador to Spain 1842-46, 1783-1859)

St. Patrick's Day ☘
March Triple Witching Dow Down 6 of Last 10, 3 Straight 1999-2001, Up 3 of Last 4

FRIDAY
D 52.4
S 57.1
N 57.1
17

It is tact that is golden, not silence. — Samuel Butler (English writer, 1600-1680)

SATURDAY
18

SUNDAY
19

PROSPERITY MORE THAN PEACE DETERMINES OUTCOME OF MIDTERM CONGRESSIONAL RACES

Though the stock market in presidential election years very often is able to predict if the party in power will retain or lose the White House, the outcome of congressional races in midterm years is another matter entirely. Typically, the President's party will lose a number of House seats in these elections (1934, 1998 and 2002 were exceptions). It is considered a victory for the President when his party loses a small number of seats, and a repudiation of sorts when a large percentage of seats is lost.

The table below would seem to indicate that there is no relationship between the stock market's behavior in the ten months prior to the midterm election and the magnitude of seats lost in the House. Roaring bull markets preceded the elections of 1954 and 1958, yet Republicans lost few seats during one, and a huge number in the other.

If the market does not offer a clue to the outcome of House races, does anything besides the popularity and performance of the Administration? Yes! In the two years prior to the elections in the first ten midterm years listed, no war or major recession began. As a result, the percentage of House seats lost was minimal. A further observation is that the market gained ground in the last seven weeks of the year, except 2002.

Our four major wars last century began under the four Democrats in the shaded area. The percentage of seats lost was greater during these midterm elections. But the seven worst repudiations of the President are at the bottom of the list. These were preceded by: the sick economy in 1930, the botched health proposals in 1994, the severe recession in 1937, the post-war contraction in 1946, the recession in 1957, Watergate in 1974, and rumors of corruption (Teapot Dome) in 1922. **Obviously, prosperity is of greater importance to the electorate than peace!**

LAST 21 MIDTERM ELECTIONS RANKED BY % LOSS OF SEATS BY PRESIDENT'S PARTY

	% Seats Gained or Lost	Year	President	Dow Jones Industrials Jan 1 to Elec Day	Elec Day to Dec 31	Year's CPI % Change
1.	3.6%	2002	R: G.W. Bush	− 14.5%	− 2.7%	1.6%
2.	2.9	1934	D: Roosevelt	− 3.8	8.3	1.5
3.	1.9	1998	D: Clinton	10.1	5.5	1.6
4.	− 1.5	1962	D: Kennedy	− 16.5	6.8	1.3
5.	− 2.7	1986	R: Reagan	22.5	0.1	1.1
6.	− 4.0	1926	R: Coolidge	− 3.9	4.4	− 1.1
7.	− 4.6	1990	R: G.H.W. Bush	− 9.1	5.3	6.1
8.	− 5.1	1978	D: Carter	− 3.7	0.6	9.0
9.	− 6.3	1970	R: Nixon	− 5.3	10.7	5.6
10.	− 8.1	1954	R: Eisenhower	26.0	14.2	− 0.7
11.	− 9.0	1918	D: Wilson (WWI)	15.2	− 4.1	20.4
12.	− 11.0	1950	D: Truman (Korea)	11.2	− 5.8	5.9
13.	− 13.5	1982	R: Reagan	14.9	4.1	3.8
14.	− 15.9	1966	D: Johnson (Vietnam)	− 17.2	− 2.1	3.5
15.	− 16.9	1942	D: Roosevelt (WWII)	3.4	4.1	9.0
16.	− 18.4	1930	R: Hoover	− 25.4	− 11.2	− 6.4
17.	− 20.9	1994	D: Clinton	1.5	0.7	2.7
18.	− 21.3	1938	D: Roosevelt	28.2	− 0.1	− 2.8
19.	− 22.6	1946	D: Truman	− 9.6	1.6	18.1
20.	− 23.9	1958	R: Eisenhower	25.1	7.1	1.8
21.	− 25.0	1974	R: Ford	− 22.8	− 6.2	12.3
22.	− 25.0	1922	R: Harding	21.4	0.3	− 2.3

Week After Triple Witching Dow Down 14 of Last 18

MONDAY
D **61.9**
S 52.4
N **61.9**
20

A loss never bothers me after I take it. I forget it overnight. But being wrong—not taking the loss—that is what does damage to the pocketbook and to the soul. — Jesse Livermore

TUESDAY
D 42.9
S **38.1**
N **38.1**
21

An appeaser is one who feeds a crocodile—hoping it will eat him last. — Winston Churchill (British statesman, 1874-1965)

WEDNESDAY
D **33.3**
S 47.6
N **33.3**
22

A gold mine is a hole in the ground with a liar on top.
— Mark Twain (1835-1910, pen name of Samuel Longhorne Clemens, American novelist and satirist)

THURSDAY
D 42.9
S **38.1**
N 52.4
23

Most people have no idea of the giant capacity we can immediately command when we focus all of our resources on mastering a single area of our lives. — Anthony Robbins (Motivator, advisor, consultant, author, entrepreneur, philanthropist, b. 1960)

March Historically Weak Later in the Month

FRIDAY
D 28.6
S 52.4
N 52.4
24

Behold, my son, with what little wisdom the world is ruled.
— Count Axel Gustafsson Oxenstierna (1648 letter to his son at conclusion of Thirty Years War, 1583-1654)

SATURDAY
25

SUNDAY
26

APRIL ALMANAC

APRIL							MAY					
S	M	T	W	T	F	S	S	M	T	W	T	F	S
						1							1	2	3
2	3	4	5	6	7	8	7	8	9	10	11	12	13
9	10	11	12	13	14	15	14	15	16	17	18	19	20
16	17	18	19	20	21	22	21	22	23	24	25	26	27
23	24	25	26	27	28	29	28	29	30	31			
30													

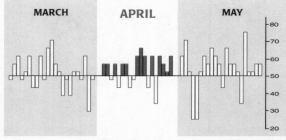

Market Probability Chart above is a graphic representation of the S&P 500 Recent Market Probability Calendar on page 121.

◆ April is still the best Dow month (average 1.8%) since 1950 (page 46) ◆ April 1999 first month ever to gain 1000 Dow points, 856 in 2001, knocked off its high horse in 2002 down 458, 2003 up 489 ◆ Prone to weakness after mid-month tax deadline ◆ Stocks anticipate great first quarter earnings by rising sharply before earnings are reported, rather than after ◆ Rarely a dangerous month except in big bear markets (like 2002), took the brunt of first-half declines in 2004 & 2005 ◆ "Best Six Months" of the year end with April (page 50) ◆ S&P Midterm Election Years up 8, down 6, average –0.01% ◆ End of April NASDAQ strength (pages 124 & 125).

APRIL DAILY POINT CHANGES DOW JONES INDUSTRIALS

	1996	1997	1998	1999	2000	2001	2002	2003	2004	2005
Previous Month Close	5587.14	6583.48	8799.81	9786.16	10921.92	9878.78	10403.94	7992.13	10357.70	10503.76
1	50.58	27.57	68.51	46.35	S	S	– 41.24	77.73	15.63	– 99.46
2	33.96	– 94.04	118.32	H	S	– 100.85	– 48.99	215.20	97.26	S
3	18.06	– 39.66	– 3.23	S	300.01	– 292.22	– 115.42	– 44.68	S	S
4	– 6.86	48.72	S	S	– 57.09	29.71	36.88	36.77	S	16.84
5	H	S	S	174.82	– 130.92	402.63	36.47	S	87.78	37.32
6	S	S	49.82	– 43.84	80.35	– 126.96	S	S	12.44	27.56
7	S	29.84	– 76.73	121.82	– 2.79	S	S	23.26	– 90.66	60.30
8	– 88.51	53.25	– 65.02	112.39	S	S	– 22.56	– 1.49	– 38.12	– 84.98
9	– 33.96	– 45.32	103.38	– 23.86	S	54.06	– 40.41	– 100.98	H	S
10	– 74.43	– 23.79	H	S	75.08	257.59	173.06	23.39	S	S
11	1.09	– 148.36	S	S	100.52	– 89.27	– 205.65	– 17.92	S	– 12.78
12	45.52	S	S	165.67	– 161.95	113.47	14.74	S	73.53	59.41
13	S	S	17.44	55.50	– 201.58	H	S	S	– 134.28	– 104.04
14	S	60.21	97.90	16.65	– 617.78	S	S	147.69	– 3.33	– 125.18
15	60.33	135.26	52.07	51.06	S	S	– 97.15	51.26	19.51	– 191.24
16	27.10	92.71	– 85.70	31.17	S	31.62	207.65	– 144.75	54.51	S
17	– 70.09	– 21.27	90.93	S	276.74	58.17	– 80.54	80.04	S	S
18	1.81	44.95	S	S	184.91	399.10	– 15.50	H	S	– 16.26
19	– 16.26	S	S	– 53.36	– 92.46	77.88	51.83	S	– 14.12	56.16
20	S	S	– 25.66	8.02	169.09	– 113.86	S	S	– 123.35	– 115.05
21	S	– 43.34	43.10	132.87	H	S	S	– 8.75	2.77	206.24
22	29.26	173.38	– 8.22	145.76	S	S	– 120.68	156.09	143.93	– 60.89
23	23.85	– 20.87	– 33.39	– 37.51	S	S	– 47.62	– 47.19	30.67	11.64
24	– 34.69	20.47	– 78.71	S	62.05	– 77.89	– 58.81	– 75.62	S	S
25	13.01	– 53.38	S	S	218.72	170.86	4.63	– 133.69	S	84.76
26	1.08	S	S	28.92	– 179.32	67.15	– 124.34	S	– 28.11	– 91.34
27	S	S	– 146.98	113.12	– 57.40	117.70	S	S	33.43	47.67
28	S	44.15	– 18.68	13.74	– 154.19	S	S	165.26	– 135.56	– 128.43
29	5.42	179.01	52.56	32.93	S	S	– 90.85	31.38	70.33	122.14
30	– 4.33	46.96	111.85	– 89.34	S	– 75.08	126.35	– 22.90	– 46.70	S
Close	5569.08	7008.99	9063.37	10789.04	10733.91	10734.97	9946.22	8480.09	10225.57	10192.51
Change	– 18.06	425.51	263.56	1002.88	– 188.01	856.19	– 457.72	487.96	– 132.13	– 311.25

April "Best Month" for Dow since 1950
Day-before-Good Friday gains are nifty

MONDAY
D 57.1
S 52.4
N 38.1
27

The difference between life and the movies is that a script has to make sense, and life doesn't.
— Joseph L. Mankiewicz (Film director, writer, producer, 1909-1993)

FOMC Meeting

TUESDAY
D 42.9
S 47.6
N 47.6
28

To know values is to know the meaning of the market. — Charles Dow

WEDNESDAY
D **66.7**
S **61.9**
N 52.4
29

You win some, you lose some. And then there's that little-known third category.
— Albert Gore (U.S. Vice President 1993-2000, former 2000 presidential candidate, quoted at the 2004 DNC)

THURSDAY
D 42.9
S **28.6**
N 42.9
30

Women are expected to do twice as much as men in half the time and for no credit. Fortunately, this isn't difficult.
— Charlotte Whitton (Former Ottawa Mayor, feminist, 1896–1975)

Last Trading Day of March Dow Down 12 of Last 16 with Major Losses

FRIDAY
D **38.1**
S 47.6
N **66.7**
31

The words "I am…" are potent words; be careful what you hitch them to. The thing you're claiming has a way of reaching back and claiming you. — A. L. Kitselman (Author, math teacher)

SATURDAY
1

Daylight Saving Time Begins
April Bullish Seasonalities: see pages 80 and 116.

SUNDAY
2

THE DECEMBER LOW INDICATOR: A USEFUL PROGNOSTICATING TOOL

When the Dow closes below its December closing low in the first quarter, it is frequently an excellent warning sign. Jeffrey Saut, managing director of investment strategy at Raymond James, brought this to our attention a few years ago. The December Low Indicator was originated by Lucien Hooper, a *Forbes* columnist and Wall Street analyst back in the 1970s. Hooper dismissed the importance of January and January's first week as reliable indicators. He noted that the trend could be random or even manipulated during a holiday-shortened week. Instead, said Hooper, "Pay much more attention to the December low. If that low is violated during the first quarter of the New Year, watch out!"

Twelve of the 26 occurrences were followed by gains for the rest of the year — and full-year gains — after the low for the year was reached. For perspective we've included the January Barometer readings for the selected years. Hooper's "Watch Out" warning was absolutely correct, though. All but one of the instances since 1952 experienced further declines, as the Dow fell an additional 10.7% on average when December's low was breached in Q1.

Only three significant drops occurred (not shown) when December's low was not breached in Q1 (1974, 1981 and 1987). Both indicators were wrong only three times and three years ended flat. If the December low is not crossed, turn to our January Barometer for guidance. It has been virtually perfect, right nearly 100% of these times (view the complete results at *http://www.hirschorg.com/declow*).

YEARS DOW FELL BELOW DECEMBER LOW IN FIRST QUARTER

Year	Previous Dec Low	Date Crossed	Crossing Price	Subseq. Low	% Change Cross-Low	Rest of Year % Change	Full Year % Change	Jan Bar
1952	262.29	2/19/52	261.37	256.35	− 1.9%	11.7%	8.4%	1.6%[2]
1953	281.63	2/11/53	281.57	255.49	− 9.3	− 0.2	− 3.8	− 0.7
1956	480.72	1/9/56	479.74	462.35	− 3.6	4.1	2.3	− 3.6[2 3]
1957	480.61	1/18/57	477.46	419.79	− 12.1	− 8.7	− 12.8	− 4.2
1960	661.29	1/12/60	660.43	566.05	− 14.3	− 6.7	− 9.3	− 7.1
1962	720.10	1/5/62	714.84	535.76	− 25.1	− 8.8	− 10.8	− 3.8
1966	939.53	3/1/66	938.19	744.32	− 20.7	− 16.3	− 18.9	0.5[1]
1968	879.16	1/22/68	871.71	825.13	− 5.3	8.3	4.3	− 4.4[1 2]
1969	943.75	1/6/69	936.66	769.93	− 17.8	− 14.6	− 15.2	− 0.8
1970	769.93	1/26/70	768.88	631.16	− 17.9	9.1	4.8	− 7.6[2 3]
1973	1000.00	1/29/73	996.46	788.31	− 20.9	− 14.6	− 16.6	− 1.7
1977	946.64	2/7/77	946.31	800.85	− 15.4	− 12.2	− 17.3	− 5.1
1978	806.22	1/5/78	804.92	742.12	− 7.8	0.0	− 3.1	− 6.2
1980	819.62	3/10/80	818.94	759.13	− 7.3	17.7	14.9	5.8[2]
1982	868.25	1/5/82	865.30	776.92	− 10.2	20.9	19.6	− 1.8[1 2]
1984	1236.79	1/25/84	1231.89	1086.57	− 11.8	− 1.6	− 3.7	− 0.9[3]
1990	2687.93	1/15/90	2669.37	2365.10	− 11.4	− 1.3	− 4.3	− 6.9
1991	2565.59	1/7/91	2522.77	2470.30	− 2.1	25.6	20.3	4.2[2]
1993	3255.18	1/8/93	3251.67	3241.95	− 0.3	15.5	13.7	0.7[2]
1994	3697.08	3/30/94	3626.75	3593.35	− 0.9	5.7	2.1	3.3[2 3]
1996	5059.32	1/10/96	5032.94	5032.94	0.0	28.1	26.0	3.3[2]
1998	7660.13	1/9/98	7580.42	7539.07	− 0.5	21.1	16.1	1.0[2]
2000	10998.39	1/4/00	10997.93	9796.03	− 10.9	− 1.9	− 6.2	− 5.1
2001	10318.93	3/12/01	10208.25	8235.81	− 19.3	− 1.8	− 7.1	3.5[1]
2002	9763.96	1/16/02	9712.27	7286.27	− 25.0	− 14.1	− 16.8	− 1.6
2003	8303.78	1/24/03	8131.01	7524.06	− 7.5	28.6	25.3	− 2.7[1 2]
2005	10440.58	1/21/05	10392.59	10071.25	− 3.1	*At Press-time – not in average*		
				Average Drop	− 10.7%			

[1] *January Barometer wrong* [2] *December Low Indicator wrong* [3] *Year flat*

First Trading Day in April Dow Up 8 of Last 11, 6 Straight Winners 1995-2000

MONDAY
D 61.9
S 57.1
N 42.9

3

Don't confuse brains with a bull market. — Humphrey Neill

TUESDAY
D 57.1
S 57.1
N 47.6

4

Pullbacks near the 30-week moving average are often good times to take action. — Michael Burke (*Investors Intelligence*)

Start Looking for the Dow and S&P MACD SELL Signal (Page 52)
Almanac Investor *Subscribers Are E-mailed Alert When It Triggers*

WEDNESDAY
D 42.9
S 47.6
N 61.9

5

Friendship renders prosperity more brilliant, while it lightens adversity by sharing it and making its burden common.
— Marcus Tullius Cicero (Great Roman orator, politician, 106-43 B.C.)

THURSDAY
D 71.4
S 57.1
N 47.6

6

A bull market tends to bail you out of all your mistakes. Conversely, bear markets make you PAY for your mistakes.
— Richard Russell (*Dow Theory Letters*)

FRIDAY
D 38.1
S 42.9
N 38.1

7

When you get into a tight place and everything goes against you, till it seems as though you could not hang on a minute longer, never give up then, for that is just the place and time that the tide will turn.
— Harriet Beecher Stowe (American writer and abolitionist)

SATURDAY

8

SUNDAY

9

500+% MOVES FOLLOW WARTIME INFLATION AND 3 PEAKS & DOMED HOUSE — 2 AMAZING PATTERNS

In the April 1976 issue of *Smart Money* Newsletter (a predecessor of our current *Almanac Investor* Newsletter) Yale Hirsch wrote an article entitled: **Stocks Catch Up With Inflation Eventually — 500% Moves After Both WWI & WWII — Can It Happen Again? Dow 3420?** The piece had an amazing line of rationalization that divined the market.

Little did Yale (or anyone else for that matter) realize at the time that the market would wind up making a 1957% move from the Vietnam low to the bubble high! With the benefit of hindsight we now know that the end of the launching pad — when inflation leveled off— was in August 1982. From its intraday low on August 11, 1982, at 770, the Dow climbed 1447% to its intraday high of 11908.50 on January 14, 2000.

During prolonged military conflicts, the market basically stayed within a defined trading-range. Once peace had set in for several years, the stock market took off to new heights. When the current battle against terror and our involvement in Iraq has passed, then we can expect the Dow to leave 10000 behind for good and put 20000 and beyond in our sights.

Three Peaks and Domed House was discussed in the introduction to the *2005 Almanac*. We have tracked this extraordinary pattern since then. As illustrated below, the current "minor formation" indicates an imminent low in 2005 in the vicinity of the 2004 Dow low of 9750. The longer-term "major formation" (not shown) suggests a 2006 low near the level of the 2002 lows.

The late George Lindsay discovered this pattern studying 150 years of market charts in 1968. In short he observed that, "…the market has followed [the formations] at least 60% of the time…" and that, "The majority of all major advances ended in a pattern which resembled the Three Peaks and a Domed House."

For detailed analyses on both of these important patterns, visit our *Almanac Investor Newsletter* archives at *stocktradersalmanac. com* and see our new book of the same name *Almanac Investor*.

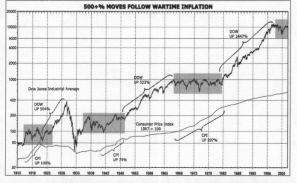

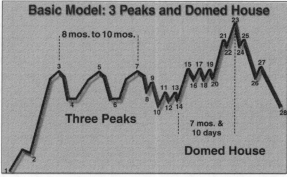

APRIL

April Is the Best Month for the Dow, Average 1.8% Since 1950

MONDAY
D 57.1
S 57.1
N **61.9**
10

Q. What kind of grad students do you take? A. I never take a straight-A student. A real scientist tends to be critical, and somewhere along the line, they had to rebel against their teachers. — Lynn Margulis, (U. Mass science professor, *The Scientist*, June 30, 2003)

TUESDAY
D **61.9**
S 57.1
N **61.9**
11

I have always picked people's brains. That's the only way you can grow. Ninety percent of the information I throw out immediately; five percent I try and discard; and five percent I retain. — Tiger Woods (Top-ranked golfer, on his swing, April 2004)

WEDNESDAY
D 57.1
S 42.9
N 52.4
12

Buy a stock the way you would buy a house. Understand and like it such that you'd be content to own it in the absence of any market. — Warren Buffett

Passover

THURSDAY
D 57.1
S 47.6
N 52.4
13

Sell stocks whenever the market is 30% higher over a year ago. — Eugene D. Brody (Oppenheimer Capital)

Good Friday (Market Closed)

FRIDAY
14

From very early on, I understood that you can touch a piece of paper once...if you touch it twice, you're dead. Therefore, paper only touches my hand once. After that, it's either thrown away, acted on or given to somebody else. — Manuel Fernandez (Businessman, *Investor's Business Daily*)

SATURDAY
15

Easter

SUNDAY
16

DOWN JANUARYS: A REMARKABLE RECORD

In the first third of the 20th century there was no correlation between January markets and the year as a whole (page 24). Then in 1972 we discovered that the 1933 "Lame Duck" Amendment to the Constitution changed the political calendar and the January Barometer was born — its record has been quite accurate (page 16).

Down Januarys are harbingers of trouble ahead, in the economic, political, or military arenas. Eisenhower's heart attack in 1955 cast doubt on whether he could run in 1956 — a flat year. The two other election years with down Januarys were also flat. Eleven bear markets began and four continued into second years with poor Januarys. 1968 started down as we were mired in Vietnam, but Johnson's "bombing halt" changed the climate. January 2003 closed down in the face of imminent military action in Iraq, and the market triple-bottomed in March just before U.S.-led forces began their blitz to Baghdad. The market put three years of the bear behind it as the fall of Baghdad combined with pre-election and recovery forces to fuel 2003 into a banner year.

Unfortunately, bull and bear markets do not start conveniently at the beginnings and ends of months or years. Though some years ended higher, **every down January since 1950 was followed by a new or continuing bear market or a flat year**. Excluding 1956, **down Januarys were followed by substantial declines averaging *minus* 13.0%**, providing excellent buying opportunities later in most years.

FROM DOWN JANUARY S&P CLOSES TO LOW NEXT 11 MONTHS

Year	January Close	% Change	11-Month Low	Date of Low	Jan Close to Low %	% Feb to Dec	Year % Change	
1953	26.38	− 0.7%	22.71	14-Sep	− 13.9%	− 6.0%	− 6.6%	bear
1956	43.82	− 3.6	44.10	28-May	0.9	6.5	2.6	FLAT
1957	44.72	− 4.2	38.98	22-Oct	− 12.8	− 10.6	− 14.3	bear
1960	55.61	− 7.1	52.30	25-Oct	− 6.0	4.5	− 3.0	bear
1962	68.84	− 3.8	52.32	26-Jun	− 24.0	− 8.3	− 11.8	bear
1968	92.24	− 4.4	87.72	5-Mar	− 4.9	12.6	7.7	Cont. bear
1969	103.01	− 0.8	89.20	17-Dec	− 13.4	− 10.6	− 11.4	bear
1970	85.02	− 7.6	69.20	26-May	− 18.6	8.4	0.1	Cont. bear
1973	116.03	− 1.7	92.16	5-Dec	− 20.6	− 15.9	− 17.4	bear
1974	96.57	− 1.0	62.28	3-Oct	− 35.5	− 29.0	− 29.7	bear
1977	102.03	− 5.1	90.71	2-Nov	− 11.1	− 6.8	− 11.5	bear
1978	89.25	− 6.2	86.90	6-Mar	− 2.6	7.7	1.1	Cont. bear
1981	129.55	− 4.6	112.77	25-Sep	− 13.0	− 5.4	− 9.7	bear
1982	120.40	− 1.8	102.42	12-Aug	− 14.9	16.8	14.8	Cont. bear
1984	163.42	− 0.9	147.82	24-Jul	− 9.5	2.3	1.4	FLAT
1990	329.07	− 6.9	295.46	11-Oct	− 10.2	0.4	− 6.6	bear
1992	408.79	− 2.0	394.50	8-Apr	− 3.5	6.6	4.5	FLAT
2000	1394.46	− 5.1	1264.74	20-Dec	− 9.3	− 5.3	− 10.1	bear
2002	1130.20	− 1.6	776.76	9-Oct	− 31.3	− 22.2	− 23.4	Cont. bear
2003	855.70	− 2.7	800.73	11-Mar	− 6.4	29.9	26.4	Cont. bear
2005	1181.27	− 2.5	1137.50	20-Apr	− 3.7	*At Press-time - not in totals or average*		
				Totals	− 260.6%	− 24.4%	− 97.0%	
				Average	− 13.0%	− 1.2%	− 4.9%	

Income Tax Deadline
Monday Before April Expiration Dow Up 13 of Last 17

MONDAY
D 76.2
S 61.9
N 66.7
17

Every great advance in natural knowledge has involved the absolute rejection of authority.
— Thomas H. Huxley (British scientist and humanist, defender of Darwinism, 1825-1895)

TUESDAY
D 76.2
S 66.7
N 47.6
18

If we did all the things we are capable of doing, we would literally astound ourselves.
— Thomas Alva Edison (American inventor, 1093 patents, 1847-1931)

April Prone to Weakness After Tax Deadline

WEDNESDAY
D 57.1
S 61.9
N 61.9
19

Selling a soybean contract short is worth two years at the Harvard Business School.
— Robert Stovall (Managing director, Wood Asset Management)

THURSDAY
D 38.1
S 42.9
N 47.6
20

With enough inside information and a million dollars, you can go broke in a year. — Warren Buffett

April Expiration Day Dow Up 10 of Last 14

FRIDAY
D 57.1
S 61.9
N 52.4
21

He who knows nothing is confident of everything. — Anonymous

SATURDAY
22

SUNDAY
23

TOP PERFORMING MONTHS PAST 55½ YEARS
STANDARD & POOR'S 500 & DOW JONES INDUSTRIALS

Monthly performance of the S&P and the Dow are ranked over the past 55½ years. NASDAQ monthly performance is shown on page 54.

January, April, November and December still hold the top four positions in both the Dow and S&P. This led to our discovery in 1986 of the market's best-kept secret. You can divide the year into two sections and have practically all the gains in one six-month section and very little in the other. September has been the worst month on both lists. (See "Best Six Months" on page 50.)

MONTHLY % CHANGES (JANUARY 1950 – JUNE 2005)

	Standard & Poor's 500					Dow Jones Industrials			
Month	Total % Change	Avg. % Change	# Up	# Down	Month	Total % Change	Avg. % Change	# Up	# Down
Jan	77.5%	1.4%	35	21	Jan	74.8%	1.3%	37	19
Feb	− 1.0	− 0.02	30	26	Feb	11.3	0.2	32	24
Mar	55.3	1.0	36	20	Mar	50.3	0.9	35	21
Apr	71.8	1.3	37	19	Apr	99.1	1.8	34	22
May	17.2	0.3	32	24	May	5.6	0.1	29	27
Jun	13.5	0.2	30	26	Jun	− 5.3	− 0.1	28	28
Jul	45.7	0.8	29	26	Jul	55.9	1.0	33	22
Aug	1.1	0.02	30	25	Aug	− 2.7	− 0.1	31	24
Sep*	− 38.3	− 0.7	22	32	Sep	− 58.4	− 1.1	19	36
Oct	50.8	0.9	33	22	Oct	31.5	0.6	32	23
Nov	95.4	1.7	37	18	Nov	91.7	1.7	37	18
Dec	95.7	1.7	42	13	Dec	98.9	1.8	40	15
% Rank					**% Rank**				
Dec	95.7%	1.7%	42	13	Apr	99.1%	1.8%	34	22
Nov	95.4	1.7	37	18	Dec	98.9	1.8	40	15
Jan	77.5	1.4	35	21	Nov	91.7	1.7	37	18
Apr	71.8	1.3	37	19	Jan	74.8	1.3	37	19
Mar	55.3	1.0	36	20	Jul	55.9	1.0	33	22
Oct	50.8	0.9	33	22	Mar	50.3	0.9	35	21
Jul	45.7	0.8	29	26	Oct	31.5	0.6	32	23
May	17.2	0.3	32	24	Feb	11.3	0.2	32	24
Jun	13.5	0.2	30	26	May	5.6	0.1	29	27
Aug	1.1	0.02	30	25	Aug	− 2.7	− 0.1	31	24
Feb	− 1.0	− 0.02	30	26	Jun	− 5.3	− 0.1	28	28
Sep*	− 38.3	− 0.7	22	32	Sep	− 58.4	− 1.1	19	36
Totals	**484.7%**	**8.6%**			**Totals**	**452.7%**	**8.2%**		
Average		**0.72%**			**Average**		**0.68%**		

*No change 1979

Anticipators, shifts in cultural behavior and faster information flow have altered seasonality in recent years. Here is how the months ranked over the past 15½ years (184 months) using total percentage gains on the S&P 500: October 34.6, November 32.9, December 32.9, May 30.8, April 16.2, March 12.2, January 9.4, February 3.4, June 1.6, July 0.1, September – 16.5, August – 19.6.

During the last 15½ years front-runners of our Best Six Months may have helped push October into the number-one spot. May has also supplanted January, March and April and moved into the number-four spot. January has declined in four of the last six bear-plagued years. October 1987, down 21.8%, is no longer in the most recent 15 years and we've seen some sizeable turnarounds in "bear killing" October the last seven years. Big losses in the period were: August 1990 (Kuwait), off 9.4%; August 1998 (SE Asia crisis), off 14.6%; September 2001 (9/11 attack) off 8.2%; September 2002 (Iraq war drums) off 11.0%.

MONDAY
D 33.3
S 33.3
N 47.6
24

The big guys are the status quo, not the innovators. — Kenneth L. Fisher (*Forbes* columnist)

April 1999 First Month Ever to Gain 1000 Dow Points

TUESDAY
D 61.9
S 61.9
N 52.4
25

Great spirits have always encountered violent opposition from mediocre minds.
— Albert Einstein (German/American physicist, 1921 Nobel Prize, 1879-1955)

WEDNESDAY
D 57.1
S 57.1
N 61.9
26

Companies which do well generally tend to report (their quarterly earnings) earlier than those which do poorly.
— Alan Abelson (*Barron's*)

THURSDAY
D 52.4
S 52.4
N 61.9
27

There is only one corner of the universe you can be certain of improving, and that's yourself.
— Aldous Huxley (English author, *Brave New World*, 1894-1963)

End of "Best Six Months" of the Year (Pages 46, 50 & 138)

FRIDAY
D 52.4
S 61.9
N 76.2
28

All you need to succeed is a yellow pad and a pencil. — Andre Meyer (Top deal maker at Lazard Freres)

SATURDAY
29

May Bullish Seasonalities: see pages 80 and 116.

SUNDAY
30

MAY ALMANAC

MAY						
S	M	T	W	T	F	S
		1	2	3	4	5	6
7	8	9	10	11	12	13
14	15	16	17	18	19	20
21	22	23	24	25	26	27
28	29	30	31			

JUNE						
S	M	T	W	T	F	S
				1	2	3
4	5	6	7	8	9	10
11	12	13	14	15	16	17
18	19	20	21	22	23	24
25	26	27	28	29	30	

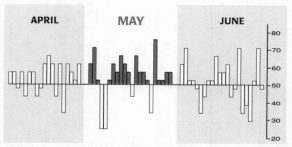

Market Probability Chart above is a graphic representation of the S&P 500 Recent Market Probability Calendar on page 121.

◆ "May/June disaster area" between 1965 and 1984 with 15 out of 20 down Mays ◆ Between 1985 and 1997 May was the best month with 13 straight gains, gaining 3.3% per year on average ◆ RECENT RECORD: S&P 17 up, 5 down, average gain 1.8%, third best ◆ Worst six months of the year begin with May (page 50) ◆ A $10,000 investment compounded to $499,933 for November-April in 55 years compared to $502 loss for May-October ◆ Memorial Day week record: up 12 years in a row (1984-1995), down six of the last ten years ◆ Midterm Election Year Mays down half the time averaging losses.

MAY DAILY POINT CHANGES DOW JONES INDUSTRIALS

Previous Month Close	1996 5569.08	1997 7008.99	1998 9063.37	1999 10789.04	2000 10733.91	2001 10734.97	2002 9946.22	2003 8480.09	2004 10225.57	2005 10192.51
1	6.14	− 32.51	83.70	S	77.87	163.37	113.41	− 25.84	S	S
2	− 76.95	94.72	S	S	− 80.66	− 21.66	32.24	128.43	S	59.19
3	− 20.24	S	S	225.65	− 250.99	− 80.03	− 85.24	S	88.43	5.25
4	S	S	45.59	− 128.58	− 67.64	154.59	S	S	3.20	127.69
5	S	143.29	45.09	69.30	165.37	S	S	− 51.11	− 6.25	− 44.26
6	− 13.72	10.83	− 92.92	8.59	S	S	− 198.59	56.79	− 69.69	5.02
7	− 43.36	− 139.67	− 77.97	84.77	S	− 16.07	28.51	− 27.73	− 123.92	S
8	53.11	50.97	78.47	S	25.77	− 51.66	305.28	− 69.41	S	S
9	1.08	32.91	S	S	− 66.88	− 16.53	− 104.41	113.38	S	38.94
10	43.00	S	S	− 24.34	− 168.97	43.46	− 97.50	S	− 127.32	− 103.23
11	S	S	36.37	18.90	178.19	− 89.13	S	S	29.45	19.14
12	S	123.22	70.25	− 25.78	63.40	S	S	122.13	25.69	− 110.77
13	64.46	− 18.54	50.07	106.82	S	S	169.74	− 47.48	− 34.42	− 49.36
14	42.11	11.95	− 39.61	− 193.87	S	56.02	188.48	− 31.43	2.13	S
15	0.73	47.39	− 76.23	S	198.41	− 4.36	− 54.46	65.32	S	S
16	9.61	− 138.88	S	S	126.79	342.95	45.53	− 34.17	S	112.17
17	52.45	S	S	− 59.85	− 164.83	32.66	63.87	S	− 105.96	79.59
18	S	S	− 45.09	− 16.52	7.54	53.16	S	S	61.60	132.57
19	S	34.21	3.74	50.44	− 150.43	S	S	− 185.58	− 30.80	28.74
20	61.32	74.58	116.83	− 20.65	S	S	− 123.58	− 2.03	0.07	− 21.28
21	− 12.56	− 12.77	− 39.11	− 37.46	S	36.18	− 123.79	25.07	29.10	S
22	41.74	− 32.56	− 17.93	S	− 84.30	− 80.68	52.17	77.59	S	S
23	− 15.88	87.78	S	S	− 120.28	− 151.73	58.20	7.36	S	51.65
24	0.74	S	S	− 174.61	113.08	16.91	− 111.82	S	− 8.31	− 19.88
25	S	H	− 150.71	− 123.58	− 211.43	− 117.05	S	S	159.19	− 45.88
26	S	H	− 150.71	171.07	− 24.68	S	S	H	− 7.73	79.80
27	H	37.50	− 27.16	− 235.23	S	S	H	179.97	95.31	4.95
28	− 53.19	− 26.18	33.63	92.81	S	H	− 122.68	11.77	− 16.75	S
29	− 35.84	− 27.05	− 70.25	S	H	33.77	− 58.54	− 81.94	S	S
30	19.58	0.86	S	S	227.89	− 166.50	− 11.35	139.08	S	H
31	− 50.23	S	S	H	− 4.80	39.30	13.56	S	H	− 75.07
Close	5643.18	7331.04	8899.95	10559.74	10522.33	10911.94	9925.25	8850.26	10188.45	10467.48
Change	74.10	322.05	− 163.42	− 229.30	− 211.58	176.97	− 20.97	370.17	− 37.12	274.97

*Was Number One month for nine straight years
But five out of the last eight have caused May tears*

First Trading Day in May Dow Up Solidly 7 of Last 8

MONDAY
D 61.9
S 61.9
N 66.7

1

The average man desires to be told specifically which particular stock to buy or sell. He wants to get something for nothing. He does not wish to work. — William Lefevre (*Reminiscences of a Stock Operator*)

TUESDAY
D 66.7
S 71.4
N 71.4

2

Every successful enterprise requires three people—a dreamer, a businessman, and a son-of-a-bitch. — Peter McArthur (1904)

WEDNESDAY
D 42.9
S 52.4
N 71.4

3

Don't worry about people stealing your ideas. If the ideas are any good, you'll have to ram them down people's throats.
— Howard Aiken (U.S. computer scientist, 1900-1973)

THURSDAY
D 38.1
S 23.8
N 42.9

4

Obstacles don't have to stop you. If you run into a wall, don't turn around and give up. Figure out how to climb it, go through it, or work around it. — Michael Jordan

FRIDAY
D 28.6
S 23.8
N 42.9

5

A realist believes that what is done or left undone in the short run determines the long run.
— Sydney J. Harris (American journalist and author, 1917-1986)

SATURDAY

6

SUNDAY

7

"BEST SIX MONTHS" STILL AN EYE-POPPING STRATEGY

Our Best Six Months Switching Strategy consistently delivers. Investing in the Dow Jones Industrial Average between November 1st and April 30th each year and then switching into fixed income for the other six months has produced reliable returns with reduced risk since 1950.

The chart on page 138 shows November, December, January, March and April to be the top months since 1950. Add February, and an excellent strategy is born! These six consecutive months gained 10764.72 Dow points in 55 years, while the remaining May through October months *lost* 786.54 points. The S&P gained 1053.79 points in the same Best Six Months versus 84.99 points in the worst six.

Percentage changes for the Dow during each six-month period since 1950 are shown along with a compounding $10,000 investment.

The November-April $489,933 gain overshadows the May-October $502 loss. (S&P results were $357,785 to $7,461.) Just two November-April losses were double-digit: April 1970 (Cambodian invasion) and 1973 (OPEC oil embargo). Similarly, Iraq muted the Best Six Months and inflated the Worst Six Months in 2003.

When we discovered this strategy in 1986, November-April outperformed May-October by $88,163 to minus $1,522. Results improved substantially these past 19 years, $401,770 to $1,020. As sensational as these results are, they are nearly tripled with a simple timing indicator, see page 52.

SIX-MONTH SWITCHING STRATEGY

	DJIA % Change May 1-Oct 31	Investing $10,000	DJIA % Change Nov 1-Apr 30	Investing $10,000
1950	5.0%	$10,500	15.2%	$11,520
1951	1.2	10,626	− 1.8	11,313
1952	4.5	11,104	2.1	11,551
1953	0.4	11,148	15.8	13,376
1954	10.3	12,296	20.9	16,172
1955	6.9	13,144	13.5	18,355
1956	− 7.0	12,224	3.0	18,906
1957	− 10.8	10,904	3.4	19,549
1958	19.2	12,998	14.8	22,442
1959	3.7	13,479	− 6.9	20,894
1960	− 3.5	13,007	16.9	24,425
1961	3.7	13,488	− 5.5	23,082
1962	− 11.4	11,950	21.7	28,091
1963	5.2	12,571	7.4	30,170
1964	7.7	13,539	5.6	31,860
1965	4.2	14,108	− 2.8	30,968
1966	− 13.6	12,189	11.1	34,405
1967	− 1.9	11,957	3.7	35,678
1968	4.4	12,483	− 0.2	35,607
1969	− 9.9	11,247	− 14.0	30,622
1970	2.7	11,551	24.6	38,155
1971	− 10.9	10,292	13.7	43,382
1972	0.1	10,302	− 3.6	41,820
1973	3.8	10,693	− 12.5	36,593
1974	− 20.5	8,501	23.4	45,156
1975	1.8	8,654	19.2	53,826
1976	− 3.2	8,377	− 3.9	51,727
1977	− 11.7	7,397	2.3	52,917
1978	− 5.4	6,998	7.9	57,097
1979	− 4.6	6,676	0.2	57,211
1980	13.1	7,551	7.9	61,731
1981	− 14.6	6,449	− 0.5	61,422
1982	16.9	7,539	23.6	75,918
1983	− 0.1	7,531	− 4.4	72,578
1984	3.1	7,764	4.2	75,626
1985	9.2	8,478	29.8	98,163
1986	5.3	8,927	21.8	119,563
1987	− 12.8	7,784	1.9	121,835
1988	5.7	8,228	12.6	137,186
1989	9.4	9,001	0.4	137,735
1990	− 8.1	8,272	18.2	162,803
1991	6.3	8,793	9.4	178,106
1992	− 4.0	8,441	6.2	189,149
1993	7.4	9,066	0.0	189,206
1994	6.2	9,628	10.6	209,262
1995	10.0	10,591	17.1	245,046
1996	8.3	11,470	16.2	284,743
1997	6.2	12,181	21.8	346,817
1998	− 5.2	11,548	25.6	435,602
1999	− 0.5	11,490	0.0	435,776
2000	2.2	11,743	− 2.2	426,189
2001	− 15.5	9,923	9.6	467,103
2002	− 15.6	8,375	1.0	471,774
2003	15.6	9,682	4.3	492,060
2004	− 1.9	9,498	1.6	499,933
Average	**0.3%**		**7.9%**	
# Up	**32**		**43**	
# Down	**23**		**12**	
55-Year Gain (Loss)		**($502)**		**$489,933**

MAY

MONDAY
D 57.1
S 52.4
N 66.7
8

The worse a situation becomes, the less it takes to turn it around, the bigger the upside.
— George Soros (Financier, philanthropist, political activist, author and philosopher, b. 1930)

TUESDAY
D 66.7
S 61.9
N 57.1
9

Make money and the whole nation will conspire to call you a gentleman. — George Bernard Shaw

FOMC Meeting

WEDNESDAY
D 61.9
S 57.1
N 42.9
10

When you get to the end of your rope, tie a knot and hang on. — Franklin D. Roosevelt (32nd U.S. President, 1882-1945)

THURSDAY
D 66.7
S 66.7
N 61.9
11

I measure what's going on, and I adapt to it. I try to get my ego out of the way. The market is smarter than I am so I bend.
— Martin Zweig

Friday Before Mother's Day Dow Up 8 of Last 11

FRIDAY
D 57.1
S 61.9
N 52.4
12

The greatest lie ever told: Build a better mousetrap and the world will beat a path to your door. — Yale Hirsch

SATURDAY
13

Mother's Day

SUNDAY
14

MACD-TIMING TRIPLES "BEST SIX MONTHS" RESULTS

Using the simple MACD (Moving Average Convergence Divergence) indicator developed by Gerald Appel (2006 Best Investment Book, page 92) to better time entries and exits into and out of the Best Six Months period nearly triples the results.

Sy Harding's *Riding the Bear* dubbed trading our Best Six Months Switching Strategy (page 50) with MACD triggers the "best mechanical system ever."

Our *Almanac Investor Newsletter* and *Platform* implement this system with quite a degree of success. Starting October 1 we look to catch the market's first hint of an uptrend after the summer doldrums, and beginning April 1 we prepare to exit these seasonal positions as soon as the market falters.

In up-trending markets MACD signals get you in earlier and keep you in longer. But if the market is trending down, entries are delayed until the market turns up and exit points can come a month earlier. Thus, our "Best Six Months" could be lengthened or shortened a month or so.

The results are astounding applying the simple MACD signals. Instead of $10,000 gaining $489,933 over the 55 recent years when invested only during the Best Six Months (page 50), the gain nearly tripled to $1,436,723. The $318 loss during the worst six months expanded to a loss of $6,629.

Impressive results for being invested during only 6½ months of the year on average! For the rest of the year you could park in a money market fund, or if a long-term holder, you could write options on your positions (sell call options).

Updated signals are e-mailed to our monthly newsletter subscribers as soon as they are triggered. For further information on how the MACD indicator is calculated, dates when signals were given, or for a FREE 1-month trial to our *Almanac Investor Platform*, please visit our website*http://www. hirschorg.com/MACD*.

SIX-MONTH SWITCHING STRATEGY+TIMING

	DJIA % Change May 1-Oct 31*	Investing $10,000	DJIA % Change Nov 1-Apr 30*	Investing $10,000
1950	7.3%	$10,730	13.3%	$11,330
1951	0.1	10,741	1.9	11,545
1952	1.4	10,891	2.1	11,787
1953	0.2	10,913	17.1	13,803
1954	13.5	12,386	16.3	16,053
1955	7.7	13,340	13.1	18,156
1956	− 6.8	12,433	2.8	18,664
1957	− 12.3	10,904	4.9	19,579
1958	17.3	12,790	16.7	22,849
1959	1.6	12,995	− 3.1	22,141
1960	− 4.9	12,358	16.9	25,883
1961	2.9	12,716	− 1.5	25,495
1962	− 15.3	10,770	22.4	31,206
1963	4.3	11,233	9.6	34,202
1964	6.7	11,986	6.2	36,323
1965	2.6	12,298	− 2.5	35,415
1966	− 16.4	10,281	14.3	40,479
1967	− 2.1	10,065	5.5	42,705
1968	3.4	10,407	0.2	42,790
1969	− 11.9	9,169	− 6.7	39,923
1970	− 1.4	9,041	20.8	48,227
1971	− 11.0	8,046	15.4	55,654
1972	− 0.6	7,998	− 1.4	54,875
1973	− 11.0	7,118	0.1	54,930
1974	− 22.4	5,524	28.2	70,420
1975	0.1	5,530	18.5	83,448
1976	− 3.4	5,342	− 3.0	80,945
1977	− 11.4	4,733	0.5	81,350
1978	− 4.5	4,520	9.3	88,916
1979	− 5.3	4,280	7.0	95,140
1980	9.3	4,678	4.7	99,612
1981	− 14.6	3,995	0.4	100,010
1982	15.5	4,614	23.5	123,512
1983	2.5	4,729	− 7.3	114,496
1984	3.3	4,885	3.9	118,961
1985	7.0	5,227	38.1	164,285
1986	− 2.8	5,081	28.2	210,613
1987	− 14.9	4,324	3.0	216,931
1988	6.1	4,588	11.8	242,529
1989	9.8	5,038	3.3	250,532
1990	− 6.7	4,700	15.8	290,116
1991	4.8	4,926	11.3	322,899
1992	− 6.2	4,621	6.6	344,210
1993	5.5	4,875	5.6	363,486
1994	3.7	5,055	13.1	411,103
1995	7.2	5,419	16.7	479,757
1996	9.2	5,918	21.9	584,824
1997	3.6	6,131	18.5	693,016
1998	− 12.4	5,371	39.9	969,529
1999	− 6.4	5,027	5.1	1,018,975
2000	− 6.0	4,725	5.4	1,074,000
2001	− 17.3	3,908	15.8	1,243,692
2002	− 25.2	2,923	6.0	1,318,314
2003	16.4	3,402	7.8	1,421,142
2004	− 0.9	3,371	1.8	1,446,723
Average	− 1.5%		9.9%	
# Up	28		48	
# Down	27		7	
55-Year Gain (Loss)	($6,629)			$1,436,723

*MACD-generated entry and exit points (earlier or later) can lengthen or shorten six-month periods.

52

Monday Before May Expiration Dow Up 16 of Last 18
Monday After Mother's Day Dow Up 13 of Last 16

MONDAY
D 52.4
S 57.1
N 61.9
15

In order to be a great writer (or "investor") a person must have a built-in, shockproof crap detector. — Ernest Hemingway

TUESDAY
D 47.6
S 42.9
N 52.4
16

The monuments of wit survive the monuments of power. — Francis Bacon (English philosopher, essayist, statesman, 1561-1626)

WEDNESDAY
D 57.1
S 66.7
N 66.7
17

Never will a man penetrate deeper into error than when he is continuing on a road that has led him to great success.
— Friedrich von Hayek (*Counterrevolution of Science*)

THURSDAY
D 57.1
S 57.1
N 47.6
18

Give me a stock clerk with a goal and I will give you a man who will make history. Give me a man without a goal, and I will give you a stock clerk. — James Cash Penney (J.C. Penney founder)

May Expiration Day Dow Down 11 of Last 18

FRIDAY
D 66.7
S 57.1
N 61.9
19

It isn't as important to buy as cheap as possible as it is to buy at the right time. — Jesse Livermore

SATURDAY
20

SUNDAY
21

TOP PERFORMING NASDAQ MONTHS PAST 34½ YEARS

NASDAQ stocks continue to run away during three consecutive months, November, December and January, with an average gain of 7.9% despite the slaughter of November 2000, down 22.9%, December 2001, up only 1.0%, January 2002, –0.8%, and December 2002, –9.7% during the three-year bear that shrank the tech-dominated index by 77.9%. Solid gains in November and December 2004 offset January 2005's 5.2% Iraq-turmoil-fueled drop.

You can see the months graphically on page 139. January by itself is impressive, up 3.7% on average. April, May and June also shine, creating our NASDAQ Best Eight Months strategy. What appears as a Death Valley abyss occurs during NASDAQ's bleakest four months: July, August, September and October. NASDAQ's Best Eight Months seasonal strategy using MACD timing is displayed on page 58.

MONTHLY CHANGES (JANUARY 1971 — JUNE 2005)

NASDAQ Composite*

Month	Total % Change	Avg. % Change	# Up	# Down
Jan	128.5%	3.7%	24	11
Feb	21.2	0.6	19	16
Mar	9.5	0.3	21	14
Apr	36.9	1.1	22	13
May	42.3	1.2	21	14
Jun	43.4	1.2	22	13
Jul	– 15.0	– 0.4	16	18
Aug	7.6	0.2	18	16
Sep	– 34.7	– 1.0	18	16
Oct	20.0	0.6	18	16
Nov	70.2	2.1	23	11
Dec	71.8	2.1	21	13

% Rank	Total % Change	Avg. % Change	# Up	# Down
Jan	128.5%	3.7%	24	11
Dec	71.8	2.1	21	13
Nov	70.2	2.1	23	11
Jun	43.4	1.2	22	13
May	42.3	1.2	21	14
Apr	36.9	1.1	22	13
Feb	21.2	0.6	19	16
Oct	20.0	0.6	18	16
Mar	9.5	0.3	21	14
Aug	7.6	0.2	18	16
Jul	– 15.0	– 0.4	16	18
Sep	– 34.7	– 1.0	18	16
Totals	**401.7%**	**11.7%**		
Average		**0.98%**		

Dow Jones Industrials

Month	Total % Change	Avg. % Change	# Up	# Down
Jan	64.9%	1.9%	23	12
Feb	17.0	0.5	20	15
Mar	29.2	0.8	22	13
Apr	68.1	1.9	19	16
May	19.0	0.5	19	16
Jun	11.9	0.3	20	15
Jul	12.5	0.4	17	17
Aug	– 5.3	– 0.2	19	15
Sep	– 54.5	– 1.6	9	25
Oct	20.2	0.6	20	14
Nov	47.6	1.4	23	11
Dec	62.5	1.8	25	9

% Rank	Total % Change	Avg. % Change	# Up	# Down
Apr	68.1	1.9%	19	16
Jan	64.9	1.9	23	12
Dec	62.5	1.8	25	9
Nov	47.6	1.4	23	11
Mar	29.2	0.8	22	13
Oct	20.2	0.6	20	14
May	19.0	0.5	19	16
Feb	17.0	0.5	20	15
Jun	11.9	0.3	20	15
Jul	12.5	0.4	17	17
Aug	– 5.3	– 0.2	19	15
Sep	– 54.5	– 1.6	9	25
Totals	**293.1%**	**8.3%**		
Average		**0.69%**		

For comparison, Dow figures are shown. During this period NASDAQ averaged a 0.97% gain per month, 39 percent more than the Dow's 0.70% per month. Between January 1971 and January 1982, NASDAQ's composite index doubled in the twelve years, while the Dow stayed flat. But while NASDAQ plummeted 77.9% from its 2000 highs to the 2002 bottom, the Dow only lost 37.8%.

*Based on NASDAQ composite, prior to February 5, 1971, based on National Quotation Bureau indices

MONDAY
D 47.6
S 52.4
N 47.6
22

Mankind is divided into three classes: Those that are immovable, those that are movable, and those that move.
— Arabian proverb (also attributed to Benjamin Franklin)

 TUESDAY
D 33.3
S 33.3
N 42.9
23

You know a country is falling apart when even the government will not accept its own currency.
— Jim Rogers (Financier, *Adventure Capitalist*, b. 1942)

WEDNESDAY
D 71.4
S 76.2
N 61.9
24

Some people are so boring they make you waste an entire day in five minutes. — Jules Renard (French author, 1864-1910)

THURSDAY
D 42.9
S 52.4
N 47.6
25

Big money is made in the stock market by being on the right side of major moves. I don't believe in swimming against the tide.
— Martin Zweig

Friday Before Memorial Day Tends to be Lackluster with Light Trading

FRIDAY
D 52.4
S 52.4
N 61.9
26

You don't learn to hold your own in the world by standing on guard, but by attacking and getting well hammered yourself.
— George Bernard Shaw (Irish dramatist, 1856-1950)

SATURDAY
27

June Bullish Seasonalities: see pages 80 and 116.

SUNDAY
28

JUNE ALMANAC

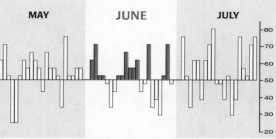

JUNE								JULY						
S	M	T	W	T	F	S		S	M	T	W	T	F	S
				1	2	3								1
4	5	6	7	8	9	10		2	3	4	5	6	7	8
11	12	13	14	15	16	17		9	10	11	12	13	14	15
18	19	20	21	22	23	24		16	17	18	19	20	21	22
25	26	27	28	29	30			23	24	25	26	27	28	29
								30	31					

Market Probability Chart above is a graphic representation of the S&P 500 Recent Market Probability Calendar on page 121.

◆ The "summer rally" in most years is the weakest rally of all four seasons (page 70) ◆ Week after June Triple-Witching Day Dow down 14 of last 16 (page 76) ◆ RECENT RECORD: S&P 14 up, 8 down, average gain 0.7%, ranks eighth ◆ Much stronger for NASDAQ, average gain 1.6% last 22 years ◆ Watch out for end-of-quarter "portfolio pumping" on last day of June, Dow down 12 of last 18, but NASDAQ up 14 of last 18 ◆ Midterm Election Year Junes worst S&P month, down 10 of 14, average loss –2.0% ◆ June ends NASDAQ's Best Eight Months.

JUNE DAILY POINT CHANGES DOW JONES INDUSTRIALS

	1996	1997	1998	1999	2000	2001	2002	2003	2004	2005
Previous Month Close	5643.18	7331.04	8899.95	10559.74	10522.33	10911.94	9925.25	8850.26	10188.45	10467.48
1	S	S	22.42	36.52	129.87	78.47	S	S	14.20	82.39
2	S	− 41.64	− 31.13	− 18.37	142.56	S	S	47.55	60.32	3.62
3	− 18.47	22.75	− 87.44	85.80	S	S	− 215.46	25.14	− 67.06	− 92.52
4	41.00	− 42.49	66.76	136.15	S	71.11	− 21.95	116.03	46.91	S
5	31.77	35.63	167.15	S	20.54	114.32	108.96	2.32	S	S
6	− 30.29	130.49	S	S	− 79.73	− 105.60	− 172.16	21.49	S	6.06
7	29.92	S	S	109.54	77.29	20.50	− 34.97	S	148.26	16.04
8	S	S	31.89	− 143.74	− 144.14	− 113.74	S	S	41.44	− 6.21
9	S	42.72	− 19.68	− 75.35	− 54.66	S	S	− 82.79	− 64.08	26.16
10	− 9.24	60.77	− 78.22	− 69.02	S	S	55.73	74.89	41.66	9.61
11	− 19.21	36.56	− 159.93	− 130.76	S	− 54.91	− 128.14	128.33	H*	S
12	− 0.37	135.64	23.17	S	− 49.85	26.29	100.45	13.33	S	S
13	− 10.34	70.57	S	S	57.63	− 76.76	− 114.91	− 79.43	S	9.93
14	− 8.50	S	S	72.82	66.11	− 181.49	− 28.59	S	− 75.37	25.01
15	S	S	− 207.01	31.66	26.87	− 66.49	S	S	45.70	18.80
16	S	9.95	37.36	189.96	− 265.52	S	S	201.84	− 0.85	12.28
17	3.33	11.31	164.17	56.68	S	S	213.21	4.06	− 2.06	44.42
18	− 24.75	42.07	− 16.45	13.93	S	21.74	18.70	− 29.22	38.89	S
19	20.32	58.35	− 100.14	S	108.54	− 48.71	− 144.55	− 114.27	S	S
20	11.08	19.45	S	S	− 122.68	50.66	− 129.80	21.22	S	− 13.96
21	45.80	S	S	− 39.58	62.58	68.10	− 177.98	S	− 44.94	− 9.44
22	S	S	− 1.74	− 94.35	− 121.62	− 110.84	S	S	23.60	− 11.74
23	S	− 192.25	117.33	− 54.77	28.63	S	S	− 127.80	84.50	− 166.49
24	12.56	153.80	95.41	− 132.03	S	S	28.03	36.90	− 35.76	− 123.60
25	1.48	− 68.08	11.71	17.73	S	− 100.37	− 155.00	− 98.32	− 71.97	S
26	− 36.57	− 35.73	8.96	S	138.24	− 31.74	6.71	67.51	S	S
27	− 5.17	33.47	S	S	− 38.53	− 37.64	149.81	− 89.99	S	− 7.06
28	− 22.90	S	S	102.59	23.33	131.37	− 26.66	S	− 14.75	114.85
29	S	S	52.82	160.20	− 129.75	63.81	S	S	56.34	− 31.15
30	S	− 14.93	− 45.34	155.45	49.85	S	S	− 3.61	22.05	− 99.51
Close	5654.63	7672.79	8952.02	10970.80	10447.89	10502.40	9243.26	8985.44	10435.48	10274.97
Change	11.45	341.75	52.07	411.06	− 74.44	− 409.54	− 681.99	135.18	247.03	− 192.51

*Reagan funeral

Last day of June not hot for the Dow
But for stocks on NASDAQ, WOW!

Memorial Day (Market Closed)

MONDAY
29

The highest reward for a person's toil is not what they get for it, but what they become by it. — John Ruskin (English writer)

Memorial Day Week Dow Down 6 of Last 10,
Up 240 Dow Points in 1999, 495 Points in 2000, 249 Points in 2003

TUESDAY
D 66.7
S 57.1
N 61.9
30

We pay the debts of the last generation by issuing bonds payable by the next generation. — Lawrence J. Peter

WEDNESDAY
D 57.1
S 57.1
N 76.2
31

I have a love affair with America, because there are no built-in barriers to anyone in America. I come from a country where there were barriers upon barriers. — Michael Caine (Actor, quoted in *Parade Magazine*, February 16, 2003)

First Trading Day in June Dow Up 7 of Last 8, Down 215 Points in 2002

THURSDAY
D 71.4
S 61.9
N 61.9
1

Cheapening the cost of necessities and conveniences of life is the most powerful agent of civilization and progress.
— Thomas Elliott Perkins (1888)

FRIDAY
D 57.1
S 71.4
N 81.0
2

There have been three great inventions since the beginning of time: the fire, the wheel, and central banking. — Will Rogers

SATURDAY
3

SUNDAY
4

GET MORE OUT OF NASDAQ'S "BEST EIGHT MONTHS" WITH MACD TIMING

NASDAQ's amazing eight-month run from November through June is hard to miss on pages 54 and 139. A $10,000 investment in these eight months since 1971 gained $323,367 versus a loss of $4,277 during the void that is the four-month period July-October. Notice how October has moved up in the ranks, though.

Using the same MACD timing indicators on the NASDAQ as is done for the Dow (page 52) has enabled us to capture much of October's improved performance, pumping up NASDAQ's results considerably. Over the 34 years since NASDAQ began, the gain on the same $10,000 more than doubles to $671,954 and the loss during the four-month void increases to $7,243. Only four sizeable losses occur during the favorable period and the bulk of NASDAQ's bear markets were avoided including the worst of the 2000-2002 bear.

Updated signals are e-mailed to our monthly newsletter subscribers as soon as they are triggered. For further information on how the MACD indicator is calculated or for a FREE 1-month trial to our *Almanac Investor Platform*, visit *http://www.hirschorg.com/MACD*.

BEST EIGHT MONTHS STRATEGY + TIMING

MACD Signal Date	Worst 4 Months July 1-Oct 31* NASDAQ	% Change	Investing $10,000	MACD Signal Date	Best 8 Months Nov 1-June 30* NASDAQ	% Change	Investing $10,000
22-Jul-71	109.54	− 3.6	$9,640	4-Nov-71	105.56	24.1	$12,410
7-Jun-72	131.00	− 1.8	9,466	23-Oct-72	128.66	−22.7	9,593
25-Jun-73	99.43	− 7.2	8,784	7-Dec-73	92.32	−20.2	7,655
3-Jul-74	73.66	−23.2	6,746	7-Oct-74	56.57	47.8	11,314
11-Jun-75	83.60	− 9.2	6,125	7-Oct-75	75.88	20.8	13,667
22-Jul-76	91.66	− 2.4	5,978	19-Oct-76	89.45	13.2	15,471
27-Jul-77	101.25	− 4.0	5,739	4-Nov-77	97.21	26.6	19,586
7-Jun-78	123.10	− 6.5	5,366	6-Nov-78	115.08	19.1	23,327
3-Jul-79	137.03	− 1.1	5,307	30-Oct-79	135.48	15.5	26,943
20-Jun-80	156.51	26.2	6,697	9-Oct-80	197.53	11.2	29,961
4-Jun-81	219.68	−17.6	5,518	1-Oct-81	181.09	− 4.0	28,763
7-Jun-82	173.84	12.5	6,208	7-Oct-82	195.59	57.4	45,273
1-Jun-83	307.95	−10.7	5,544	3-Nov-83	274.86	−14.2	38,844
1-Jun-84	235.90	5.0	5,821	15-Oct-84	247.67	17.3	45,564
3-Jun-85	290.59	− 3.0	5,646	1-Oct-85	281.77	39.4	63,516
10-Jun-86	392.83	−10.3	5,064	1-Oct-86	352.34	20.5	76,537
30-Jun-87	424.67	−22.7	3,914	2-Nov-87	328.33	20.1	91,921
8-Jul-88	394.33	-6.6	3,656	29-Nov-88	368.15	22.4	112,511
13-Jun-89	450.73	0.7	3,682	9-Nov-89	454.07	1.9	114,649
11-Jun-90	462.79	−23.0	2,835	2-Oct-90	356.39	39.3	159,706
11-Jun-91	496.62	6.4	3,016	1-Oct-91	528.51	7.4	171,524
11-Jun-92	567.68	1.5	3,061	14-Oct-92	576.22	20.5	206,686
7-Jun-93	694.61	9.9	3,364	1-Oct-93	763.23	− 4.4	197,592
17-Jun-94	729.35	5.0	3,532	11-Oct-94	765.57	13.5	224,267
1-Jun-95	868.82	17.2	4,140	13-Oct-95	1018.38	21.6	272,709
3-Jun-96	1238.73	1.0	4,181	7-Oct-96	1250.87	10.3	300,798
4-Jun-97	1379.67	24.4	5,201	3-Oct-97	1715.87	1.8	306,212
1-Jun-98	1746.82	− 7.8	4,795	15-Oct-98	1611.01	49.7	458,399
1-Jun-99	2412.03	· 18.5	5,682	6-Oct-99	2857.21	35.7	622,047
29-Jun-00	3877.23	−18.2	4,648	18-Oct-00	3171.56	−32.2	421,748
1-Jun-01	2149.44	−31.1	3,202	1-Oct-01	1480.46	5.5	444,944
3-Jun-02	1562.56	−24.0	2,434	2-Oct-02	1187.30	38.5	616,247
20-Jun-03	1644.72	15.1	2,802	6-Oct-03	1893.46	4.3	642,746
21-Jun-04	1974.38	− 1.6	2,757	1-Oct-04	1942.20	6.1	681,954
8-Jun-05	2060.18						
	34-Year Loss	**($7,243)**			**34-Year Gain**	**$671,954**	

* MACD-generated entry and exit points (earlier or later) can lengthen or shorten eight-month periods.

JUNE

Start Looking for NASDAQ MACD Sell Signal (Page 58)
Almanac Investor *Subscribers Are E-mailed Alert When It Triggers*

MONDAY
D 57.1
S 52.4
N 57.1
5

We spend $500 million a year just in training our people. We've developed some technology that lets us do simulations. Think of Flight Simulation. What we've found is that the retention rate from simulation is about 75%, opposed to 25% from classroom work. — Joe Forehand (CEO, Accenture, *Forbes*, July 7, 2003)

TUESDAY
D **61.9**
S 52.4
N **61.9**
6

The test of success is not what you do when you are on top. Success is how high you bounce when you hit bottom.
— General George S. Patton, Jr. (1885-1945)

WEDNESDAY
D 47.6
S 47.6
N 52.4
7

I always keep these seasonal patterns in the back of my mind. My antennae start to purr at certain times of the year.
— Kenneth Ward

THURSDAY
D 42.9
S **33.3**
N 42.9
8

The mind is not a vessel to be filled but a fire to be kindled. — Plutarch (Greek biographer and philosopher, *Parallel Lives*, 46-120 AD)

FRIDAY
D **33.3**
S 42.9
N 47.6
9

To me, the "tape" is the final arbiter of any investment decision. I have a cardinal rule: Never fight the tape! — Martin Zweig

SATURDAY
10

SUNDAY
11

DOW GAINS MOST FIRST TWO DAYS OF WEEK

Since 1989, Monday* and Tuesday have been the most consistently bullish days of the week for the Dow, Thursday and Friday** the most bearish, as traders have become reluctant to stay long going into the weekend. Since 1989 Mondays and Tuesdays gained 8696.37 Dow points, while Thursday and Friday combined for a total loss of 1845.36 points. In past flat and bear market years Friday was the worst day of the week and Monday second worst. In bull years Monday is best and Friday number two. See pages 66 and 132-135 for more.

ANNUAL DOW POINT CHANGES FOR DAYS OF THE WEEK SINCE 1953

Year	Monday*	Tuesday	Wednesday	Thursday	Friday**	Year's DJIA Closing	Year's Point Change
1953	− 36.16	− 7.93	19.63	5.76	7.70	280.90	− 11.00
1954	15.68	3.27	24.31	33.96	46.27	404.39	123.49
1955	− 48.36	26.38	46.03	− 0.66	60.62	488.40	84.01
1956	− 27.15	− 19.36	− 15.41	8.43	64.56	499.47	11.07
1957	− 109.50	− 7.71	64.12	3.32	− 14.01	435.69	− 63.78
1958	17.50	23.59	29.10	22.67	55.10	583.65	147.96
1959	− 44.48	29.04	4.11	13.60	93.44	679.36	95.71
1960	− 111.04	− 3.75	− 5.62	6.74	50.20	615.89	− 63.47
1961	− 23.65	10.18	87.51	− 5.96	47.17	731.14	115.25
1962	− 101.60	26.19	9.97	− 7.70	− 5.90	652.10	− 79.04
1963	− 8.88	47.12	16.23	22.39	33.99	762.95	110.85
1964	− 0.29	− 17.94	39.84	5.52	84.05	874.13	111.18
1965	− 73.23	39.65	57.03	3.20	68.48	969.26	95.13
1966	− 153.24	− 27.73	56.13	− 46.19	− 12.54	785.69	− 183.57
1967	68.65	31.50	25.42	92.25	38.90	905.11	119.42
1968†	6.41	34.94	25.16	− 72.06	44.19	943.75	38.64
1969	− 164.17	− 36.70	18.33	23.79	15.36	800.36	− 143.39
1970	− 100.05	− 46.09	116.07	− 3.48	72.11	838.92	38.56
1971	2.99	9.56	13.66	8.04	23.01	890.20	51.28
1972	− 87.40	− 1.23	65.24	8.46	144.75	1020.02	129.82
1973	− 174.11	10.52	− 5.94	36.67	− 36.30	850.86	− 169.16
1974	− 149.37	47.51	− 20.31	− 13.70	− 98.75	616.24	− 234.62
1975	39.46	− 109.62	56.93	124.00	125.40	852.41	236.17
1976	70.72	71.76	50.88	− 33.70	− 7.42	1004.65	152.24
1977	− 65.15	− 44.89	− 79.61	− 5.62	21.79	831.17	− 173.48
1978	− 31.29	− 70.84	71.33	− 64.67	69.31	805.01	− 26.16
1979	− 32.52	9.52	− 18.84	75.18	0.39	838.74	33.73
1980	− 86.51	135.13	137.67	− 122.00	60.96	963.99	125.25
1981	− 45.68	− 49.51	− 13.95	− 14.67	34.82	875.00	− 88.99
1982	5.71	86.20	28.37	− 1.47	52.73	1046.54	171.54
1983	30.51	− 30.92	149.68	61.16	1.67	1258.64	212.10
1984	− 73.80	78.02	− 139.24	92.79	− 4.84	1211.57	− 47.07
1985	80.36	52.70	51.26	46.32	104.46	1546.67	335.10
1986	− 39.94	97.63	178.65	29.31	83.63	1895.95	349.28
1987	− 559.15	235.83	392.03	139.73	− 165.56	1938.83	42.88
1988	268.12	166.44	− 60.48	− 230.84	86.50	2168.57	229.74
1989	− 53.31	143.33	233.25	90.25	171.11	2753.20	584.63
Subtotal	− 1937.20	941.79	1708.54	330.82	1417.35		2461.30
1990	219.90	− 25.22	47.96	− 352.55	− 9.63	2633.66	− 119.54
1991	191.13	47.97	174.53	254.79	− 133.25	3168.83	535.17
1992	237.80	− 49.67	3.12	108.74	− 167.71	3301.11	132.28
1993	322.82	− 37.03	243.87	4.97	− 81.65	3754.09	452.98
1994	206.41	− 95.33	29.98	− 168.87	108.16	3834.44	80.35
1995	262.97	210.06	357.02	140.07	312.56	5117.12	1282.68
1996	626.41	155.55	− 34.24	268.52	314.91	6448.27	1331.15
1997	1136.04	1989.17	− 590.17	− 949.80	− 125.26	7908.25	1459.98
1998	649.10	679.95	591.63	− 1579.43	931.93	9181.43	1273.18
1999	980.49	− 1587.23	826.68	735.94	1359.81	11497.12	2315.69
2000	2265.45	306.47	− 1978.34	238.21	− 1542.06	10786.85	− 710.27
2001	− 389.33	336.86	− 396.53	976.41	− 1292.76	10021.50	− 765.35
2002	− 1404.94	− 823.76	1443.69	− 428.12	− 466.74	8341.63	− 1679.87
2003	978.87	482.11	− 425.46	566.22	510.55	10453.92	2112.29
2004	201.12	523.28	358.76	− 409.72	− 344.35	10783.01	329.09
2005 ‡	77.37	21.58	46.73	− 344.84	− 280.41	10303.44	− 479.57
Subtotal	6561.61	2134.76	699.23	− 939.46	− 905.90		7550.24
Totals	4624.41	3076.55	2407.77	− 608.64	511.45		10011.54

* On Monday holidays, following Tuesday included in Monday figures
** On Friday holidays, preceding Thursday included in Friday figures
† Most Wednesdays closed last 7 months of 1968   ‡ Partial year through July 1, 2005

JUNE

Monday Before June Triple Witching Dow Down 5 of Last 9, But Back-to-Back 200+ Point Gains 2002-2003

MONDAY
D 57.1
S 52.4
N 52.4
12

Any human anywhere will blossom in a hundred unexpected talents and capacities simply by being given the opportunity to do so.
— Doris Lessing (British novelist, born in Persia 1919)

TUESDAY
D 42.9
S 52.4
N 52.4
13

You must automate, emigrate, or evaporate. — James A. Baker (*General Electric*)

WEDNESDAY
D 66.7
S 66.7
N 57.1
14

The incestuous relationship between government and big business thrives in the dark.
— Jack Anderson (Washington journalist and author, *Peace, War and Politics*, b. 1922)

THURSDAY
D 47.6
S 57.1
N 57.1
15

Life does not consist mainly of facts and happenings. It consists mainly of the storm of thoughts that are forever blowing through one's mind. — Mark Twain (1835-1910, pen name of Samuel Longhorne Clemens, American novelist and satirist)

June Triple Witching Up 8 Straight 1985-1992, Up 7 Down 6 Since

FRIDAY
D 57.1
S 57.1
N 47.6
16

If I had my life to live over again, I would elect to be a trader of goods rather than a student of science. I think barter is a noble thing. — Albert Einstein (German/American physicist, 1921 Nobel Prize, 1934, 1879-1955)

SATURDAY
17

Father's Day

SUNDAY
18

FIRST-TRADING-DAY-OF-THE-MONTH PHENOMENON
DOW GAINS MORE ONE DAY THAN ALL OTHER DAYS

Over the last eight years the Dow Jones Industrial Average has gained more points on the first trading days of all months than all other days combined. While the Dow gained 2781.88 points between September 2, 1997 (7622.42) and April 1, 2005 (10404.30), it is incredible that 3867.28 points were gained on the first trading days of these 92 months. The remaining 1815 trading days combined saw the Dow lose 1085.40 points during the period. This averages out to gains of 42.04 points on first days, in contrast to a 0.60-point loss on all others.

Note September 1997 through October 2000 racked up a total gain of 2632.39 Dow points on the first trading days of these 38 months (winners except for seven occasions). But between November 2000, when the last two cyclical bear markets did the bulk of their damage, and September 2002, frightened investors switched from pouring money into the market on that day to pulling it out, fourteen months out of twenty-three, netting a 404.80 Dow point loss.

First days of August have performed worst, falling five times out of seven. January's first day has also deteriorated; down four of the last six, as profit taking shifts to the opening of the New Year. In rising market trends first days perform much better as institutions are likely anticipating strong performance at each month's outset. S&P 500 first days track the Dow's pattern closely but NASDAQ first days are not as strong with weakness in January, April, July, August and October.

As the two-and-half-year bull market appears to have ended in the spring of 2005, first days of the month could be prone to weakness until a new bull market emerges.

DOW POINTS GAINED ON FIRST DAY OF MONTH
FROM SEPTEMBER 1997 TO APRIL 1, 2005

	1997	1998	1999	2000	2001	2002	2003	2004	2005	Totals
Jan		56.79	2.84	− 139.61	− 140.70	51.90	265.89	− 44.07	− 53.58	− 0.54
Feb		201.28	− 13.13	100.52	96.27	− 12.74	56.01	11.11	62.00	501.32
Mar		4.73	18.20	9.62	− 45.14	262.73	− 53.22	94.22	63.77	354.91
Apr		68.51	46.35	300.01	− 100.85	− 41.24	77.73	15.63	− 99.46	266.68
May		83.70	225.65	77.87	163.37	113.41	− 25.84	88.43		726.59
Jun		22.42	36.52	129.87	78.47	− 215.46	47.55	14.20		113.57
Jul		96.65	95.62	112.78	91.32	− 133.47	55.51	− 101.32		217.09
Aug		− 96.55	− 9.19	84.97	− 12.80	− 229.97	− 79.83	39.45		− 303.92
Sep	257.36	288.36	108.60	23.68	47.74	− 355.45	107.45	− 5.46		472.28
Oct	70.24	− 210.09	− 63.95	49.21	− 10.73	346.86	194.14	112.38		488.06
Nov	232.31	114.05	− 81.35	− 71.67	188.76	120.61	57.34	26.92		586.97
Dec	189.98	16.99	120.58	− 40.95	− 87.60	− 33.52	116.59	162.20		444.27
Totals	749.89	646.84	486.74	636.30	268.11	− 126.34	819.32	413.69	− 27.27	3867.28

SUMMARY FIRST DAYS VS. OTHER DAYS OF MONTH

	# of Days	Total Points Gained	Average Daily Point Gain
First days	92	3867.28	42.04
Other days	1815	− 1085.40	− 0.60

JUNE

🐂 **MONDAY**
D 52.4
S 61.9
N 47.6
19

In a bear market everyone loses. And the winner is the one who loses the least. — Richard Russell (*Dow Theory Letters*)

TUESDAY
D 38.1
S 42.9
N 47.6
20

In an uptrend, if a higher high is made but fails to carry through, and prices dip below the previous high, the trend is apt to reverse. The converse is true for downtrends. — Victor Sperandeo (*Trader Vic—Methods of a Wall Street Master*)

WEDNESDAY
D 47.6
S 47.6
N 57.1
21

Become more humble as the market goes your way. — Bernard Baruch

🐂 **THURSDAY**
D 61.9
S 71.4
N 57.1
22

Towering genius disdains a beaten path. It scorns to tread in the footsteps of any predecessor, however illustrious. It thirsts for distinction. — Abraham Lincoln (16th U.S. President, 1809-1865)

🐻 **FRIDAY**
D 42.9
S 33.3
N 42.9
23

Knowledge born from actual experience is the answer to why one profits; lack of it is the reason one loses. — Gerald M. Loeb

SATURDAY
24

SUNDAY
25

JULY ALMANAC

JULY						
S	M	T	W	T	F	S
						1
2	3	4	5	6	7	8
9	10	11	12	13	14	15
16	17	18	19	20	21	22
23	24	25	26	27	28	29
30	31					

AUGUST						
S	M	T	W	T	F	S
		1	2	3	4	5
6	7	8	9	10	11	12
13	14	15	16	17	18	19
20	21	22	23	24	25	26
27	28	29	30	31		

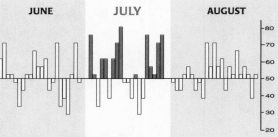

Market Probability Chart above is a graphic representation of the S&P 500 Recent Market Probability Calendar on page 121.

◆ July is the best month of the third quarter except for NASDAQ (page 72) ◆ Start of 2nd half brings an inflow of retirement funds ◆ First trading day Dow up 13 of last 16 ◆ RECENT RECORD: S&P 9 up, 13 down, average gain 0.4%, ranks ninth ◆ Graph above shows strength through most of July except middle ◆ NASDAQ's 12-day mid-year rally gains 3.2% on average since 1987 v. 0.1% for the month of July ◆ July closes well except if bear market in progress ◆ Huge gain in July usually provides better buying opportunity over next 4 months ◆ Start of NASDAQ's worst four months of the year (page 54) ◆ Midterm Election Julys worst for NASDAQ –3.4%, up 2 down 6.

JULY DAILY POINT CHANGES DOW JONES INDUSTRIALS

Previous Month	1995	1996	1997	1998	1999	2000	2001	2002	2003	2004
Close	4556.10	5654.63	7672.79	8952.02	10970.80	10447.89	10502.40	9243.26	8985.44	10435.48
1	S	75.35	49.54	96.65	95.62	S	S	– 133.47	55.51	– 101.32
2	S	– 9.60	73.05	– 23.41	72.82	S	91.32	– 102.04	101.89	– 51.33
3	29.05	– 17.36	100.43	H	S	112.78*	– 22.61*	47.22*	– 72.63*	S
4	H	H	H	S	S	H	H	H	H	S
5	30.08	– 114.88	S	S	H	– 77.07	– 91.25	324.53	S	H
6	48.77	S	S	66.51	– 4.12	– 2.13	– 227.18	S	S	– 63.49
7	38.73	S	– 37.32	6.73	52.24	154.51	S	S	146.58	20.95
8	S	– 37.31	103.82	89.93	– 60.47	S	S	– 104.60	6.30	– 68.73
9	S	31.03	– 119.88	– 85.19	66.81	S	46.72	– 178.81	– 66.88	41.66
10	– 0.34	21.79	44.33	15.96	S	10.60	– 123.76	– 282.59	– 120.17	S
11	– 21.79	– 83.11	35.06	S	S	80.61	65.38	– 11.97	83.55	S
12	46.69	– 9.98	S	S	7.28	56.22	237.97	– 117.00	S	25.00
13	0.19	S	S	– 9.53	– 25.96	5.30	60.07	S	S	9.37
14	– 18.66	S	1.16	149.33	– 26.92	24.04	S	S	57.56	– 38.79
15	S	– 161.05	52.73	– 11.07	38.31	S	S	– 45.34	– 48.18	– 45.64
16	S	9.25	63.17	93.72	23.43	S	– 66.94	– 166.08	– 34.38	– 23.38
17	27.47	18.12	– 18.11	9.78	S	– 8.48	134.27	69.37	– 43.77	S
18	– 50.01	87.30	– 130.31	S	S	– 64.35	– 36.56	– 132.99	137.33	S
19	– 57.41	– 37.36	S	S	– 22.16	– 43.84	40.17	– 390.23	S	45.72
20	12.68	S	16.26	– 42.22	– 191.55	147.79	– 33.35	S	S	55.01
21	N/C	S	16.26	– 105.56	6.65	– 110.31	S	S	– 91.46	– 102.94
22	S	– 35.88	154.93	– 61.28	– 33.56	S	S	– 234.68	61.76	4.20
23	S	– 44.39	26.71	– 195.93	– 58.26	S	– 152.23	– 82.24	35.79	– 88.11
24	27.12	8.14	28.57	4.38	S	– 48.44	– 183.30	488.95	– 81.73	S
25	45.78	67.32	– 3.49	S	S	14.85	164.55	– 4.98	172.06	S
26	– 7.39	51.05	S	S	– 47.80	– 183.49	49.96	78.08	S	0.30
27	25.71	S	S	90.88	115.88	69.65	– 38.96	S	S	123.22
28	– 17.26	S	7.67	– 93.46	– 6.97	– 74.96	S	S	– 18.06	31.93
29	S	– 38.47	53.42	– 19.82	– 180.78	S	S	447.49	– 62.05	12.17
30	S	47.34	80.36	111.99	– 136.14	S	– 14.95	– 31.85	– 4.41	10.47
31	– 7.04	46.98	– 32.28	– 143.66	S	10.81	121.09	56.56	33.75	S
Close	4708.47	5528.91	8222.61	8883.29	10655.15	10521.98	10522.81	8736.59	9233.80	10139.71
Change	152.37	– 125.72	549.82	– 68.73	– 315.65	74.09	20.41	– 506.67	248.36	– 295.77

* Shortened trading day

When Dow and S&P in July are inferior
NASDAQ days tend to be even drearier

Receive the *Stock Trader's Almanac 2007* FREE!
Subscribe to the *Almanac Investor Platform*

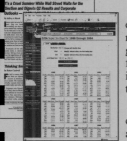

The *Almanac Investor Platform* includes our *Almanac Investor Newsletter*, Email Alerts, *Online Almanac Research Tool* and a free copy of the annual *Stock Trader's Almanac*.

Almanac Investor Newsletter is specifically designed to update and expand the proven strategies outlined in the *Stock Trader's Almanac*. Each monthly issue provides market timing, seasonal strategies, exciting small-cap growth stocks and seasoned undervalued equities, and investment strategies focusing on Exchange Traded Funds (see page 80). As of the September 2005 issue, the Almanac Investor Stock Portfolio has gained 212.5% since inception in July 2001.

Monthly newsletters are available to *Almanac Investors* immediately upon completion in the subscriber's area of *stocktradersalmanac.com*. Subscribers also receive an *Almanac Investor* Email Alert to notify them about the new issue.

Subscribers receive important Email Alerts such as the January Barometer, MACD Seasonal Buy and Sell Signals, stock and strategy updates, the yearend FREE-LUNCH Menu, and so much more!

Our *Online Almanac Research Tool* allows *Almanac Investors* to do their own historical research, update *Almanac* market indicators and strategies as well as create their own.

Subscribe to the *Almanac Investor Platform* at the Special Introductory Rate of $179 for one year, or $17.50 per month and receive 12-issues of *Almanac Investor Newsletter* (regularly $295) plus, the *2007 Stock Trader's Almanac* (retail $34.95 + $5 shipping) and full access to our *Online Almanac Research Tool* ($295/year) as free bonuses!

Subscribe today at *stocktradersalmanac.com* using promotion code STA6, call Toll-Free 800-477-3400, mail the money-saving coupon below, or fax it to 845-358-4223.

All prices are in US Dollars. • The Hirsch Organization offers a pro rated refund for annual subscriptions. Monthly subscribers can cancel anytime. Monthly subscribers who cancel within the first three months of their subscription will be charged $34.95 + $5 shipping and handling for their copy of the *2007 Stock Trader's Almanac*.

JUNE/JULY

June Ends NASDAQ's "Best Eight Months" (Pages 54, 58 & 139)

MONDAY
D 42.9
S 38.1
N 47.6
26

There's nothing wrong with cash. It gives you time to think. — Robert Prechter, Jr. (*Elliott Wave Theorist*)

TUESDAY
D 42.9
S 28.6
N 33.3
27

Good judgment is usually the result of experience and experience frequently is the result of bad judgment.
— Robert Lovell (Quoted by Robert Sobel, *Panic on Wall Street*)

FOMC Meeting (2 Days)

WEDNESDAY
D 47.6
S 52.4
N 57.1
28

When I talk to a company that tells me the last analyst showed up three years ago, I can hardly contain my enthusiasm.
— Peter Lynch

THURSDAY
D 61.9
S 71.4
N 71.4
29

A committee is a cul de sac down which ideas are lured and then quietly strangled. — Sir Barnett Cocks (Member of Parliament)

Last Day of Second Quarter Dow Down 12 of Last 18 — NASDAQ Up 14 of 18

FRIDAY
D 42.9
S 47.6
N 81.0
30

The symbol of all relationships among...men, the moral symbol of respect for human beings, is the trader.
— Ayn Rand (Russian-born American novelist and philosopher, from Galt's Speech, *Atlas Shrugged*, 1957, 1905-1982)

SATURDAY
1

July Bullish Seasonalities: see pages 80 and 116.

SUNDAY
2

2004 DAILY DOW POINT CHANGES
(DOW JONES INDUSTRIAL AVERAGE)

Week #		Monday**	Tuesday	Wednesday	Thursday	Friday**	Weekly Dow Close	Net Point Change
						2003 Close	10453.92	
1					Holiday	− 44.07	10409.85	− 44.07†
2	J	134.22	− 5.41	− 9.63	63.41	− 133.55	10458.89	49.04
3	A	26.29	− 58.00	111.19	15.48	46.66	10600.51	141.62
4	N	Holiday	− 71.85	94.96	− 0.44	− 54.89	10568.29	− 32.22
5		134.22	− 92.59	− 141.55	41.92	− 22.22	10488.07	− 80.22
6		11.11	6.00	− 34.44	24.81	97.48	10593.03	104.96
7	F	− 14.00	34.82	123.85	− 43.63	− 66.22	10627.85	34.82
8	E	Holiday	87.03	− 42.89	− 7.26	− 45.70	10619.03	− 8.82
9	B	− 9.41	− 43.25	35.25	− 21.48	3.78	10583.92	− 35.11
10		94.22	− 86.66	1.63	− 5.11	7.55	10595.55	11.63
11	M	− 66.07	− 72.52	− 160.07	− 168.51	111.70	10240.08	− 355.47
12	A	− 137.19	81.78	115.63	− 4.52	− 109.18	10186.60	− 53.48
13	R	− 121.85	− 1.11	− 15.41	170.59	− 5.85	10212.97	26.37
14		116.66	52.07	− 24.00	15.63	97.26	10470.59	257.62
15		87.78	12.44	− 90.66	− 38.12	Holiday	10442.03	− 28.56
16	A	73.53	− 134.28	3.33	19.51	54.51	10451.97	9.94
17	P	− 14.12	− 123.35	2.77	143.93	11.64	10472.84	20.87
18	R	− 28.11	33.43	− 135.56	− 70.33	− 46.70	10225.57	− 247.27
19		88.43	3.20	− 6.25	− 69.69	− 123.92	10117.34	− 108.23
20	M	− 127.32	29.45	25.69	− 34.42	2.13	10012.87	− 104.47
21	A	− 105.96	61.60	− 30.80	− 0.07	29.10	9966.74	− 46.13
22	Y	− 8.31	159.19	− 7.73	95.31	− 16.75	10188.45	221.71
23		Holiday	14.20	60.32	− 67.06	46.91	10242.82	54.37
24	J	148.26	41.44	− 64.08	41.66	Holiday ‡	10410.10	167.28
25	U	− 75.37	45.70	− 0.85	− 2.06	38.89	10416.41	6.31
26	N	− 44.94	23.60	84.50	− 35.76	− 71.97	10371.84	− 44.57
27		− 14.75	56.34	22.05	− 101.32	− 51.33	10282.83	− 89.01
28	J	Holiday	− 63.49	20.95	− 68.73	41.66	10213.22	− 69.61
29	U	25.00	9.37	− 38.79	− 45.64	− 23.38	10139.78	− 73.44
30	L	− 45.72	55.01	− 102.94	4.20	− 88.11	9962.22	− 177.56
31		0.30	123.22	31.93	12.17	10.47	10139.71	177.49
32		39.45	− 58.92	6.27	− 163.48	− 147.70	9815.33	− 324.38
33	A	− 0.67	130.01	− 6.35	− 123.73	10.76	9825.35	10.02
34	U	129.20	18.28	110.32	− 42.33	69.32	10110.14	284.79
35	G	− 37.09	25.58	83.11	− 8.33	21.60	10195.01	84.87
36		− 72.49	51.40	− 5.46	121.82	− 30.08	10260.20	65.19
37	S	Holiday	82.59	− 29.43	− 24.26	23.97	10313.07	52.87
38	E	1.69	3.40	− 86.80	13.13	39.97	10284.46	− 28.61
39	P	− 79.57	40.04	− 135.75	− 70.28	8.34	10047.24	− 237.22
40		− 58.70	88.86	58.84	− 55.97	112.38	10192.65	145.41
41		23.89	− 38.86	62.24	− 114.52	− 70.20	10055.20	− 137.45
42	O	26.77	− 4.79	− 74.85	− 107.88	38.93	9933.38	− 121.82
43	C	22.94	− 58.70	− 10.69	− 21.17	− 107.95	9757.81	− 175.57
44	T	− 7.82	138.49	113.55	2.51	22.93	10027.47	269.66
45		26.92	− 18.66	101.32	177.71	72.78	10387.54	360.07
46	N	3.77	− 4.94	− 0.89	84.36	69.17	10539.01	151.47
47	O	11.23	− 62.59	61.92	22.98	− 115.64	10456.91	− 82.10
48	V	32.51	3.18	27.71	Holiday	1.92*	10522.23	65.32
49		− 46.33	− 47.88	162.20	− 5.10	7.09	10592.21	69.98
50	D	− 45.15	− 106.48	53.65	58.59	− 9.60	10543.22	− 48.99
51	E	95.10	38.13	15.00	14.19	− 55.72	10649.92	106.70
52	C	11.68	97.83	56.46	11.23	Holiday	10827.12	177.20
53		− 50.99	78.41	− 25.35	− 28.89	− 17.29	10783.01	− 44.11
TOTALS		**201.12****	**523.28**	**358.76**	**409.72**	**− 344.35****		**329.09**

Bold Color: Down Friday, Down Monday   *Shortened trading day: Nov. 26, ‡Reagan Funeral   †Partial week*

** On Monday holidays, the following Tuesday is included in the Monday total.
** On Friday holidays, the preceding Thursday is included in the Friday total.

66

(Shortened Trading Day)

First Trading Day in July Dow Up 13 of Last 16

MONDAY

3

D 71.4
S 76.2
N 61.9

Whom the gods would destroy, they first put on the cover of Business Week. — Paul Krugman (*Economist*, referring to CEO of Enron, *New York Times* Op-Ed August 17, 2001, On cover February 12, gets pie in the face June 23, and quits August 16)

Independence Day (Market Closed)

TUESDAY

4

It's a lot of fun finding a country nobody knows about. The only thing better is finding a country everybody's bullish on and shorting it. — Jim Rogers

WEDNESDAY

5

D 57.1
S 52.4
N 52.4

During the first period of a man's life, the greatest danger is: not to take the risk. — Soren Kierkegaard

THURSDAY

6

D 33.3
S 33.3
N 38.1

Unless you love EVERYBODY, you can't sell ANYBODY. — (From *Jerry Maguire*, 1996)

July Begins NASDAQ's "Worst Four Months" (Pages 54, 58 & 139)

FRIDAY

7

D 57.1
S 61.9
N 52.4

A good manager is a man who isn't worried about his own career but rather the careers of those who work for him...Don't worry about yourself! Take care of those who work for you and you'll float to greatness on their achievements. — H.S.M. Burns

SATURDAY

8

SUNDAY

9

MID-YEAR RALLY: CHRISTMAS IN JULY

What's old is often new in the stock market. Nothing excites Wall Street more than the prospects for a "summer rally." Every year when the weather heats up, anticipation of an upward spike in stock prices swells. On page 70 we illustrate that the "summer rally" is the weakest of all seasonal rallies.

However, a short, tradable mid-year rally for NASDAQ has emerged in recent years. In the 1969 Almanac we quoted a *Wall Street Journal* article from June 27, 1900 (106 years ago!): "The market is more likely to advance in midsummer than at any other time. The market has in the past been essentially a railway market, controlled in summer by the outlook for crops." As the U.S. has drifted away from being an agrarian society with less than 2% farming this "midsummer" rally faded.

But in the mid-1980s the market began to evolve into a tech-driven market and control in summer shifted to the outlook for second quarter earnings of technology companies. NASDAQ's mid-year rally from the end of June through mid-July is strongest. The accompanying table shows NASDAQ averaging a 3.2% gain since 1987 during the 12-day period from June's fourth-to-last trading day through July's ninth trading day versus 0.1% for the month of July.

NASDAQ COMPOSITE 12-DAY MID-YEAR RALLY

	June Close	4th Last June Trading Day	9th July Trading Day	July Close	12-Day % Change	July Change
1985	296.20	292.30	302.39	301.29	3.5%	1.7%
1986	405.51	402.22	384.80	371.37	− 4.3	− 8.4
1987	424.67	427.20	431.14	434.93	0.9	2.4
1988	394.66	389.00	394.67	387.33	1.5	− 1.9
1989	435.29	448.55	448.90	453.84	0.1	4.3
1990	462.29	455.38	468.44	438.24	2.9	− 5.2
1991	475.92	473.30	492.71	502.04	4.1	5.5
1992	563.60	548.20	575.21	580.83	4.9	3.1
1993	703.95	694.81	712.49	704.70	2.5	0.1
1994	705.96	702.68	721.56	722.16	2.7	2.3
1995	933.45	919.56	999.33	1001.21	8.7	7.3
1996	1185.02	1172.58	1103.49	1080.59	− 5.9	− 8.8
1997	1442.07	1446.24	1523.88	1593.81	5.4	10.5
1998	1894.74	1863.25	1968.41	1872.39	5.6	− 1.2
1999	2686.12	2552.65	2818.13	2638.49	10.4	− 1.8
2000	3966.11	3858.96	4246.18	3766.99	10.0	− 5.0
2001	2160.54	2064.62	2084.79	2027.13	1.0	− 6.2
2002	1463.21	1423.99	1373.50	1328.26	− 3.5	− 9.2
2003	1622.80	1602.66	1754.82	1735.02	9.5	6.9
2004	2047.79	2025.47	1914.88	1887.36	− 5.5	− 7.8
2005	2056.96	2045.20	2152.82	2184.83	5.3	6.2
			1985 Average		2.8%	− 0.2%
			1987 Average		3.2%	0.1%

MONDAY
D 57.1
S **61.9**
N **66.7**
10

Whenever you see a successful business, someone once made a courageous decision.
— Peter Drucker (Management consultant, "The man who invented the corporate society," born in Austria 1909)

July Is the Best Performing Dow and S&P Month of the Third Quarter

TUESDAY
D 42.9
S **38.1**
N 57.1
11

A man will fight harder for his interests than his rights. — Napoleon Bonaparte (Emperor of France 1804-1815, 1769-1821)

WEDNESDAY
D **71.4**
S **61.9**
N **61.9**
12

By the law of nature the father continues master of his child no longer than the child stands in need of his assistance; after that term they become equal, and then the son entirely independent of the father, owes him no obedience, but only respect.
— Jean-Jacques Rousseau (*The Social Contract*)

THURSDAY
D **61.9**
S **71.4**
N **76.2**
13

The wisdom of the ages is the fruits of freedom and democracy.
— Lawrence Kudlow (Economist, 24th Annual Paulson SmallCap Conference, Waldorf Astoria NYC, November 8, 2001)

12-Day Mid-Year NASDAQ Rally Ends July 14th, Averages 3.2% Since 1987 v. 0.1% for July

FRIDAY
D **71.4**
S **81.0**
N **81.0**
14

It is the mark of many famous people that they cannot part with their brightest hour.
— Lillian Hellman, (Playwright, *The Children's Hour* and *Little Foxes*, 1905-1984)

SATURDAY
15

SUNDAY
16

A RALLY FOR ALL SEASONS

Most years, especially when the market sells off during the first half, prospects for the perennial summer rally become the buzz on the street. Parameters for this "rally" were defined by the late Ralph Rotnem as the lowest close in the Dow Jones Industrials in May or June to the highest close in July, August, or September. Such a big deal is made of the "summer rally" that one might get the impression the market puts on its best performance in the summertime. Nothing could be further from the truth! Not only does the market "rally" in every season of the year, but it does so with more gusto in the winter, spring, and fall than in the summer.

Winters in 42 years averaged a 13.4% gain as measured from the low in November or December to the first quarter closing high. Spring rose 11.1% followed by fall with 10.9%. Last and least was the average 9.3% "summer rally." Even 2003's impressive 14.3% "summer rally" was outmatched by spring and fall. Nevertheless, no matter how thick the gloom or grim the outlook, don't despair! There's always a rally for all seasons, statistically. NASDAQ's 12-day mid-year rally on page 68 is tradable.

SEASONAL GAINS IN DOW JONES INDUSTRIALS

	WINTER RALLY Nov/Dec Low to Q1 High	SPRING RALLY Feb/Mar Low to Q2 High	SUMMER RALLY May/Jun Low to Q3 High	FALL RALLY Aug/Sep Low to Q4 High
1964	15.3%	6.2%	9.4%	8.3%
1965	5.7	6.6	11.6	10.3
1966	5.9	4.8	3.5	7.0
1967	11.6	8.7	11.2	4.4
1968	7.0	11.5	5.2	13.3
1969	0.9	7.7	1.9	6.7
1970	5.4	6.2	22.5	19.0
1971	21.6	9.4	5.5	7.4
1972	19.1	7.7	5.2	11.4
1973	8.6	4.8	9.7	15.9
1974	13.1	8.2	1.4	11.0
1975	36.2	24.2	8.2	8.7
1976	23.3	6.4	5.9	4.6
1977	8.2	3.1	2.8	2.1
1978	2.1	16.8	11.8	5.2
1979	11.0	8.9	8.9	6.1
1980	13.5	16.8	21.0	8.5
1981	11.8	9.9	0.4	8.3
1982	4.6	9.3	18.5	37.8
1983	15.7	17.8	6.3	10.7
1984	5.9	4.6	14.1	9.7
1985	11.7	7.1	9.5	19.7
1986	31.1	18.8	9.2	11.4
1987	30.6	13.6	22.9	5.9
1988	18.1	13.5	11.2	9.8
1989	15.1	12.9	16.1	5.7
1990	8.8	14.5	12.4	8.6
1991	21.8	11.2	6.6	9.3
1992	14.9	6.4	3.7	3.3
1993	8.9	7.7	6.3	7.3
1994	9.7	5.2	9.1	5.0
1995	13.6	19.3	11.3	13.9
1996	19.2	7.5	8.7	17.3
1997	17.7	18.4	18.4	7.3
1998	20.3	13.6	8.2	24.3
1999	15.1	21.6	8.2	12.6
2000	10.8	15.2	9.8	3.5
2001	6.4	20.8	1.7	23.1
2002	14.8	7.9	2.8	17.6
2003	6.5	23.9	14.3	15.7
2004	11.6	5.2	4.4	10.6
2005	9.0	2.1		
Totals	**562.2%**	**466.0%**	**379.8%**	**448.3%**
Average	**13.4%**	**11.1%**	**9.3%**	**10.9%**

Monday Before July Expiration Dow Down 6 of 9 1994-2002, Up Last 3

MONDAY

D 47.6
S 47.6
N 57.1

17

Major bottoms are usually made when analysts cut their earnings estimates and companies report earnings which are below expectations. — Edward Babbitt, Jr. (Avatar Associates)

TUESDAY

D 52.4
S 47.6
N 47.6

18

There are no secrets to success. Don't waste your time looking for them. Success is the result of perfection, hard work, learning from failure, loyalty to those for whom you work, and persistence. — General Colin Powell

Historically One of the Worst Weeks of the Year

WEDNESDAY

D 38.1
S 38.1
N 38.1

19

I am sorry to say that there is too much point to the wisecrack that life is extinct on other planets because their scientists were more advanced than ours. — John F. Kennedy (35th U.S. President, 1917-1963)

THURSDAY

D 47.6
S 52.4
N 47.6

20

It is not how right or how wrong you are that matters, but how much money you make when right and how much you do not lose when wrong. — George Soros (Financier, philanthropist, political activist, author and philosopher, b. 1930)

July Expiration Day Dow Down 9 of Last 14 — Off 390 Dow Points in 2002

FRIDAY

D 38.1
S 28.6
N 33.3

21

Success isn't measured by the position you reach in life; it's measured by the obstacles you overcome.
— Booker T. Washington (Founder of Tuskegee Institute, 1856-1915)

SATURDAY

22

SUNDAY

23

FIRST MONTH OF QUARTERS IS THE MOST BULLISH

We have observed over the years that the investment calendar reflects the annual, semi-annual and quarterly operations of institutions during January, April and July. The opening month of the first three quarters produces the greatest gains in the Dow Jones Industrials and the S&P 500. NASDAQ's record differs slightly.

The fourth quarter had behaved quite differently since it is affected by year-end portfolio adjustments and Presidential and Congressional elections in even-numbered years. But in recent years, with October 1987 not factored in, October has transformed into a bear-killing-turnaround month, posting some mighty gains in six of the last seven years. (See pages 147, 151, 157.)

After experiencing the most powerful bull market of all time during the 1990s, followed by the ferocious bear market early in the millennium, we divided the monthly average percent changes into two groups: before 1991 and after. Comparing the month-by-month quarterly behavior of the three major U.S. averages in the table, you'll see that first months of the first three quarters perform best overall. Nasty sell-offs in April 2000, 2002, 2004 and 2005 and July 2000-2002 and 2004, hit the NASDAQ hardest. (See pages 146-147, 150-151, 156-157.)

Between 1950 and 1990, the S&P 500 gained 1.3% (Dow, 1.4%) on average in first months of the first three quarters. Second months barely eked out any gain, while third months, thanks to March, moved up 0.23% (Dow, 0.07%) on average. NASDAQ's first month of the first three quarters averages 1.67% from 1971-1990 with July being a negative drag.

The bear spread out much of its damage during 2000-2003 in the first three quarters staging turnarounds for the most part in October. The once-feared month has been the bulls' latter-day savior.

DOW JONES INDUSTRIALS, S&P 500 & NASDAQ
AVERAGE MONTHLY % CHANGES BY QUARTER

	DJIA 1950-1990			S&P 500 1950-1990			NASDAQ 1971-1990		
	1st Mo	2nd Mo	3rd Mo	1st Mo	2nd Mo	3rd Mo	1st Mo	2nd Mo	3rd Mo
1Q	1.5%	−0.01%	1.0%	1.5%	−0.1%	1.1%	3.8%	1.2%	0.9%
2Q	1.6	−0.4	0.1	1.3	−0.1	0.3	1.7	0.8	1.1
3Q	1.1	0.3	−0.9	1.1	0.3	−0.7	−0.5	0.1	−1.6
Tot	4.2%	−0.1%	0.2%	3.9%	0.1%	0.7%	5.0%	2.1%	0.4%
Avg	1.40%	−0.04%	0.07%	1.30%	0.03%	0.23%	1.67%	0.70%	0.13%
4Q	−0.1%	1.4%	1.7%	0.4%	1.7%	1.6%	−1.4%	1.6%	1.4%
	DJIA 1991-June 2005			S&P 500 1991-June 2005			NASDAQ 1991-June 2005		
1Q	1.0%	0.8%	0.5%	1.1%	0.2%	0.7%	3.5%	−0.2%	−0.6%
2Q	2.1	1.5	−0.5	1.3	1.4	0.2	0.2	1.7	1.5
3Q	0.8	−1.1	−1.7	0.04	−0.7	−0.8	−0.3	0.4	0.2
Tot	3.9%	1.2%	−1.7%	2.4%	0.9%	0.1%	3.4%	1.9%	0.7%
Avg	1.30%	0.40%	−0.57%	0.80%	0.30%	0.03%	1.13%	0.62%	0.23%
4Q	2.6%	2.4%	2.2%	2.5%	1.9%	2.2%	3.4%	2.8%	3.1%
	DJIA 1950-June 2005			S&P 500 1950-June 2005			NASDAQ 1971-June 2005		
1Q	1.3%	0.2%	0.9%	1.4%	−0.02%	1.0%	3.7%	0.6%	0.3%
2Q	1.8	0.1	−0.1	1.3	0.3	0.2	1.1	1.2	1.2
3Q	1.0	−0.04	−1.1	0.8	0.02	−0.7	−0.4	0.2	−1.0
Tot	4.1%	0.3%	−0.3%	3.5%	0.3%	0.5%	4.4%	2.0%	0.5%
Avg	1.37%	0.09%	−0.10%	1.17%	0.11%	0.17%	1.47%	0.67%	0.17%
4Q	0.6%	1.7%	1.8%	0.9%	1.7%	1.7%	0.6%	2.1%	2.1%

JULY

July Closes Well Unless There Is a Bear Market in Progress

MONDAY
24

D 42.9
S 38.1
N 38.1

Regret for the things we did can be tempered by time; it is regret for the things we did not do that is inconsolable.
— Sydney J. Harris (American journalist and author, 1917-1986)

TUESDAY
25

D 71.4
S 76.2
N 66.7

The soul is dyed the color of its thoughts. Think only on those things that are in line with your principles and can bear the light of day. The content of your character is your choice. Day by day, what you do is who you become.
— Heraclitus (Greek philosopher, 535-475 BC)

WEDNESDAY
26

D 57.1
S 57.1
N 61.9

The secret to business is to know something that nobody else knows. — Aristotle Onassis (Greek shipping billionaire)

THURSDAY
27

D 47.6
S 52.4
N 52.4

To affect the quality of the day, that is the highest of the arts. — Henry David Thoreau

FRIDAY
28

D 61.9
S 71.4
N 57.1

If we hire people bigger than ourselves, we will become a company of giants—smaller than ourselves, a company of midgets.
— David Oglivy (*Forbes ASAP*)

SATURDAY
29

August Bullish Seasonalities: see pages 80 and 116.

SUNDAY
30

AUGUST ALMANAC

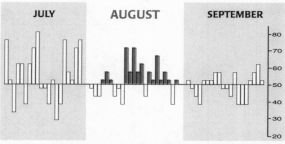

Market Probability Chart above is a graphic representation of the S&P 500 Recent Market Probability Calendar on page 121.

AUGUST							SEPTEMBER					
S	M	T	W	T	F	S	S	M	T	W	T	F	S
		1	2	3	4	5						1	2
6	7	8	9	10	11	12	3	4	5	6	7	8	9
13	14	15	16	17	18	19	10	11	12	13	14	15	16
20	21	22	23	24	25	26	17	18	19	20	21	22	23
27	28	29	30	31			24	25	26	27	28	29	30

◆ Harvesting made August the best stock market month 1901-1951 ◆ Now that less than 2% farm, August has become the worst S&P month in the past 18 years, second worst Dow and NASDAQ month (NAS up 11.7% in 2000 but down 10.9 in 2001 ◆ Shortest bear in history (45 days) caused by turmoil in Russia, currency crisis and hedge fund debacle ended here in 1998, with a record 1344.22 point drop in the Dow, off 15.1% ◆ Saddam Hussein triggered a 10.0% slide in 1990 ◆ Best Dow gains: 1982 (11.5%) and 1984 (9.8%) as bear markets ended ◆ End of August merciless 6 of the last 9 years average loss last 5 days: Dow –2.9%, S&P –2.7%, NASDAQ –2.4%.

AUGUST DAILY POINT CHANGES DOW JONES INDUSTRIALS

Previous Month Close	1995 4708.47	1996 5528.91	1997 8222.61	1998 8883.29	1999 10655.15	2000 10521.98	2001 10522.81	2002 8736.59	2003 9233.80	2004 10139.71
1	– 8.10	65.84	– 28.57	S	S	84.97	– 12.80	– 229.97	– 79.83	S
2	– 10.22	85.08	S	S	– 9.19	80.58	41.17	– 193.49	S	39.45
3	11.27	S	S	– 96.55	31.35	19.05	– 38.40	S	S	– 58.92
4	– 17.96	S	4.41	– 299.43	– 2.54	61.17	S	S	32.07	6.27
5	S	– 5.55	– 10.91	59.47	119.05	S	S	– 269.50	– 149.72	– 163.48
6	S	21.83	71.77	30.90	– 79.79	S	– 111.47	230.46	25.42	– 147.70
7	9.86	22.56	– 71.31	20.34	S	99.26	57.43	182.06	64.71	S
8	N/C	– 5.18	– 156.78	S	S	109.88	– 165.24	255.87	64.64	S
9	– 21.83	– 32.18	S	S	– 6.33	– 71.06	5.06	33.43	S	– 0.67
10	– 27.83	S	S	– 23.17	– 52.55	2.93	117.69	S	S	130.01
11	– 25.36	S	30.89	– 112.00	132.65	119.04	S	S	26.26	– 6.35
12	S	23.67	– 101.27	90.11	1.59	S	S	– 56.56	92.71	– 123.73
13	S	– 57.70	– 32.52	– 93.46	184.26	S	– 0.34	– 206.50	– 38.30	10.76
14	41.56	19.60	13.71	– 34.50	S	148.34	3.74	260.92	38.80	S
15	– 19.02	– 1.10	– 247.37	S	S	– 109.14	– 66.22	74.83	11.13	S
16	– 1.76	23.67	S	S	73.14	– 58.61	46.57	– 40.08	S	129.20
17	– 8.45	S	S	149.85	70.29	47.25	– 151.74	S	S	18.28
18	– 13.03	S	108.70	139.80	– 125.70	– 9.16	S	S	90.76	110.32
19	S	9.99	114.74	– 21.37	– 27.54	S	S	212.73	16.45	– 42.33
20	S	21.82	103.13	– 81.87	136.77	S	79.29	– 118.72	– 31.39	69.32
21	– 2.82	– 31.44	– 127.28	77.76	S	33.33	– 145.93	85.16	26.17	S
22	5.64	43.65	– 6.04	S	199.15	59.34	102.76	96.41	– 74.81	S
23	– 35.57	– 10.73	S	32.96	– 16.46	5.50	– 47.75	– 180.68	S	– 37.09
24	– 4.23	S	– 28.34	36.04	42.74	38.09	194.02	S	S	25.58
25	20.78	S	77.35	– 79.30	– 127.59	9.89	S	46.05	– 31.23	83.11
26	S	– 28.85	5.11	– 357.36	– 108.28	S	– 40.82	22.81	– 8.33
27	S	17.38	5.11	– 357.36	– 108.28	S	– 40.82	– 94.60	– 6.66	21.60
28	– 7.40	1.11	– 92.90	– 114.31	S	60.21	– 160.32	– 130.32	40.42	S
29	14.44	– 64.73	– 72.01	S	S	– 37.74	– 131.13	– 23.10	41.61	S
30	– 3.87	– 31.44	S	S	– 176.04	– 112.09	– 171.32	7.49	S	– 72.49
31	5.99	S	S	– 512.61	– 84.85	112.09	30.17	S	S	51.40
Close	4610.56	5616.21	7622.42	7539.07	10829.28	11215.10	9949.75	8663.50	9415.82	10173.92
Change	– 97.91	87.30	– 600.19	– 1344.22	174.13	693.12	– 573.06	– 73.09	182.02	34.21

August's a good month to go on vacation
Trading stocks will likely lead to frustration

MONDAY
D 66.7
S 76.2
N 71.4
31

The market is a voting machine, whereon countless individuals register choices which are the product partly of reason and partly of emotion.
— Graham & Dodd

First Trading Day in August Atrocious Dow Down 12 of Last 19 With Major Losses

TUESDAY
D 42.9
S 47.6
N 52.4
1

Make sure you have a jester because people in high places are seldom told the truth. — Radio caller to President Ronald Reagan

WEDNESDAY
D 52.4
S 42.9
N 38.1
2

The two most abundant elements in the universe are Hydrogen and Stupidity. — Harlan Ellison (Science fiction writer, b. 1934)

August Is the Worst S&P Month Last 15 Years
Harvesting Made August the Best Stock Market Month 1901-1951

THURSDAY
D 42.9
S 42.9
N 42.9
3

Marketing is our No. 1 priority… A marketing campaign isn't worth doing unless it serves three purposes.
It must grow the business, create news, and enhance our image. — James Robinson III (American Express)

FRIDAY
D 52.4
S 52.4
N 61.9
4

The punishment of wise men who refuse to take part in the affairs of government
is to live under the government of unwise men. — Plato

SATURDAY
5

SUNDAY
6

AURA OF THE TRIPLE WITCH – 4TH QUARTER MOST BULLISH DOWN WEEKS TRIGGER MORE WEAKNESS WEEK AFTER

Options expire the third Friday of every month but in March, June, September and December a powerful coven gathers. Since the S&P index futures began trading on April 21, 1982, stock options, index options as well as index futures all expire at the same time four times each year — known as Triple Witching. Traders have long sought to understand and master the magic of this quarterly phenomenon.

The market is still small for fledgling single-stock futures (160 at this writing) so we do not believe the term "quadruple witching" is applicable just yet.

We have analyzed what the market does prior, during and following Triple Witching expirations in search of consistent trading patterns. This is never easy. For as soon as a pattern becomes obvious, the market almost always starts to anticipate it, and the pattern tends to shift. These are some of our findings of how the Dow Jones Industrials perform around Triple-Witching Week (TWW).

* TWWs became more bullish since 1990, except in the second quarter.
* Following weeks became more bearish. Since Q1 2000 only 6 of 20 were up and 4 occurred in December.
* TWWs have tended to be down in flat periods and dramatically so during the 2000-2002 bear market.
* DOWN WEEKS TEND TO FOLLOW DOWN TWWs is a most interesting pattern. Since 1991, of 20 down TWWs, 16 following weeks were also down. This is surprising inasmuch as the previous decade had an exactly opposite pattern: There were 13 down TWWs then, but 12 up weeks followed them.
* TWWs in the second and third quarter (Worst Six Months May through October) are much weaker and the weeks following, horrendous. But in the first and fourth quarter (Best Six Months period November through April) a solid bullish bias is evident.

Throughout the Almanac you will also see notations on the performance of Mondays and Fridays of TWW as we place considerable significance on the beginnings and ends of weeks (pages 60, 66, 131-135). See more in our March 2004 *Almanac Investor Newsletter* at *stocktradersalmanac.com*.

TRIPLE-WITCHING WEEK & WEEK AFTER DOW POINT CHANGES

	Expiration Week Q1	Week After	Expiration Week Q2	Week After	Expiration Week Q3	Week After	Expiration Week Q4	Week After
1991	− 6.93	− 89.36	− 34.98	− 58.81	33.54	− 13.19	20.12	167.04
1992	40.48	− 44.95	− 69.01	− 2.94	21.35	− 76.73	9.19	12.97
1993	43.76	− 31.60	− 10.24	− 3.88	− 8.38	− 70.14	10.90	6.15
1994	32.95	−120.92	3.33	−139.84	58.54	−101.60	116.08	26.24
1995	38.04	65.02	86.80	75.05	96.85	− 33.42	19.87	− 78.76
1996	114.52	51.67	55.78	− 50.60	49.94	− 15.54	179.53	76.51
1997	−130.67	− 64.20	14.47	−108.79	174.30	4.91	− 82.01	− 76.98
1998	303.91	−110.35	−122.07	231.67	100.16	133.11	81.87	314.36
1999	27.20	− 81.31	365.05	−303.00	− 224.80	−524.30	32.73	148.33
2000	666.41	517.49	−164.76	− 44.55	− 293.65	− 79.63	−277.95	200.60
2001	−821.21	−318.63	−353.36	− 19.05	−1369.70	611.75	224.19	101.65
2002	34.74	−179.56	−220.42	− 10.53	− 326.67	−284.57	77.61	−207.54
2003	662.26	−376.20	83.63	−211.70	173.27	−331.74	236.06	46.45
2004	− 53.48	26.37	6.31	− 44.57	− 28.61	−237.22	106.70	177.20
2005	−144.69	−186.80	110.44	−325.23				
Up	10	4	8	2	8	3	12	11
Down	5	11	7	13	6	11	2	3

AUGUST

First Nine Days of August Are Historically Weak

MONDAY
7

D 52.4
S 57.1
N 52.4

Why is it right-wing [conservatives] always stand shoulder to shoulder in solidarity, while liberals always fall out among themselves? — Yevgeny Yevtushenko (Russian poet, Babi Yar, quoted in London *Observer* December 15, 1991, b. 1933)

FOMC Meeting

TUESDAY
8

D 47.6
S 52.4
N 47.6

If you don't profit from your investment mistakes, someone else will. — Yale Hirsch

WEDNESDAY
9

D 47.6
S 42.9
N 47.6

Every man who knows how to read has it in his power to magnify himself, to multiply the ways in which he exists, to make his life full, significant and interesting. — Aldous Huxley (*Forbes*)

THURSDAY
10

D 52.4
S 47.6
N 52.4

A good new chairman of the Federal Reserve Bank is worth a $10 billion tax cut. — Paul H. Douglas (U.S. Senator 1949-1967)

FRIDAY
11

D 42.9
S **38.1**
N 47.6

Bill [Gates] isn't afraid of taking long-term chances. He also understands that you have to try everything because the real secret to innovation is failing fast. — Gary Starkweather (Inventor of laser printer in 1969 at Xerox, *Fortune*, July 8, 2002)

SATURDAY
12

SUNDAY
13

WHY A 50% GAIN IN THE DOW IS POSSIBLE FROM ITS 2006 LOW TO ITS 2007 HIGH

Normally, major corrections occur sometime in the first or second years following presidential elections. In the last eleven midterm election years, bear markets began or were in progress nine times — we experienced a bull year in 1986 and a flat year in 1994.

The puniest midterm advance, 14.5% from the 1946 low, was during the industrial contraction after World War II. The next four smallest advances were: 1978 (OPEC–Iran) 20.9%, 1930 (economic collapse) 23.4%, 1966 (Vietnam) 26.7%, and 1990 (Persian Gulf War) 34.0%.

Since 1914 the Dow has gained 50% on average from its midterm election year low to its subsequent high in the following pre-election year. A swing of such magnitude is equivalent to a move from 7300 to 10950 or from 10000 to 15000.

POST-ELECTION HIGH TO MIDTERM LOW: −22.2%

Conversely, since 1913 the Dow has dropped −22.2% on average from its post-election-year high to its subsequent low in the following midterm year. At press-time the Dow's 2005 post-election year high is 10940.55. A 22.2% decline would put the Dow at 8511.75 at the 2006 midterm bottom. Whatever the level, the rally off the 2006 midterm low will likely provide one of the best buying opportunities of the 21st century.

Pretty impressive seasonality! There is no reason to think the quadrennial Presidential Election/Stock Market Cycle will not continue. Page 127 shows how effectively presidents "managed" to have much stronger economies in the third and fourth years of their terms than in their first two.

% CHANGE IN DOW JONES INDUSTRIALS BETWEEN THE MIDTERM YEAR LOW AND THE HIGH IN THE FOLLOWING YEAR

	Midterm Year Low				Pre-Election Year High			
	Date of Low			Dow	Date of High		Dow	% Gain
1	Jul	30	1914 *	52.32	Dec	27	1915	99.21	89.6%
2	Jan	15	1918 **	73.38	Nov	3	1919	119.62	63.0
3	Jan	10	1922 **	78.59	Mar	20	1923	105.38	34.1
4	Mar	30	1926 *	135.20	Dec	31	1927	202.40	49.7
5	Dec	16	1930 *	157.51	Feb	24	1931	194.36	23.4
6	Jul	26	1934 *	85.51	Nov	19	1935	148.44	73.6
7	Mar	31	1938 *	98.95	Sep	12	1939	155.92	57.6
8	Apr	28	1942 *	92.92	Jul	14	1943	145.82	56.9
9	Oct	9	1946	163.12	Jul	24	1947	186.85	14.5
10	Jan	13	1950 **	196.81	Sep	13	1951	276.37	40.4
11	Jan	11	1954 **	279.87	Dec	30	1955	488.40	74.5
12	Feb	25	1958 **	436.89	Dec	31	1959	679.36	55.5
13	Jun	26	1962 *	535.74	Dec	18	1963	767.21	43.2
14	Oct	7	1966 *	744.32	Sep	25	1967	943.08	26.7
15	May	26	1970 *	631.16	Apr	28	1971	950.82	50.6
16	Dec	6	1974 *	577.60	Jul	16	1975	881.81	52.7
17	Feb	28	1978 *	742.12	Oct	5	1979	897.61	21.0
18	Aug	12	1982 *	776.92	Nov	29	1983	1287.20	65.7
19	Jan	22	1986	1502.29	Aug	25	1987	2722.42	81.2
20	Oct	11	1990 *	2365.10	Dec	31	1991	3168.84	34.0
21	Apr	4	1994	3593.35	Dec	13	1995	5216.47	45.2
22	Aug	31	1998 *	7539.07	Dec	31	1999	11497.12	52.5
23	Oct	9	2002 *	7286.27	Dec	31	2003	10453.92	43.5
	*Bear market ended		**Bear previous year				**Average**	**50.0%**

Monday Before August Expiration Dow Up 8 of Last 10

MONDAY
D **66.7**
S **71.4**
N **76.2**
14

Those who are of the opinion that money will do everything may very well be suspected to do everything for money.
— Sir George Savile

TUESDAY
D 52.4
S 57.1
N **61.9**
15

The higher a people's intelligence and moral strength, the lower will be the prevailing rate of interest.
— Eugen von Bohm-Bawerk (Austrian economist, *Capital and Interest*, 1851-1914)

Mid-August Stronger than Beginning and End

WEDNESDAY
D **66.7**
S **71.4**
N **61.9**
16

Fight until death over taxes? Oh, no. Women, country, God, things like that. Taxes? No. — Daniel Patrick Moynihan (U.S. Senator New York 1976-2001, in response to Tim Russert on "Meet The Press" May 23, 1993, 1927- March 26, 2003)

THURSDAY
D 47.6
S 57.1
N 57.1
17

You can't grow long-term if you can't eat short-term. Anybody can manage short. Anybody can manage long. Balancing those two things is what management is. — Jack Welch (CEO of General Electric, *Business Week*, June 8, 1998)

August Expiration Day Dow Down 10 of 13 From 1990-2002, Up Last 2

FRIDAY
D 57.1
S **61.9**
N 47.6
18

If you have an important point to make, don't try to be subtle or clever. Use a pile driver. Hit the point once. Then come back and hit it again. Then hit it a third time—a tremendous whack. — Winston Churchill (British statesman, 1874-1965)

SATURDAY
19

SUNDAY
20

ALMANAC INVESTOR ETF STRATEGY

We first featured Exchange Traded Funds (ETFs) in the *2002 Stock Traders Almanac*. Only a few investors knew anything about this strange new investment vehicle. It was autumn 2001; the bubble had burst and scandal was brewing on Wall Street. No one wanted anything to do with some newfangled investment.

Fast-forward 4 years: The ETF "fad" has matured into full blown industry and now many market professionals, including us, think that ETFs are not only here to stay, but that they are the future. Almost everyone has heard of ETFs thanks to aggressive marketing from AMEX as well as the issuers. The number of ETFs has quadrupled with no end of growth is sight. The scope of ETFs has grown from broad index trackers (like the Diamonds, Spiders and QQQQs) and major indices (like Biotech, Financial Services and Semiconductors) to niche investments like the PowerShares WilderHill Clean Energy and the PowerShares Dynamic Food & Beverage Portfolio to name just two. But the most striking fact about the popularity of ETFs is that at press-time for the *2006 Almanac*, the total market cap of ETFs outstanding is in the area of a **quarter-trillion dollars!**

ETFs are basically mutual funds that trade like stocks. There are, however several major differences. You can buy ETFs throughout the day, short them and buy and sell options, none of which is possible with mutual funds. Before buying any ETF, get more information from the issuers' websites, all of which are excellent.

As ETFs have evolved and matured, we have refined and revamped our strategies. Now that we have more historical information to analyze as well as a better understanding of their tendencies, we have been able to improve our results with ETFs.

Using the table of Sector Seasonalities on page 116 as a basic guide, when a sector is coming into favor, we look for a corresponding ETF from page 189 to track the seasonality. Some sectors have only a few ETFs associated with them while several have a wide array of investment options. ETFs in the same sector don't necessarily move together. A good starting point in your research is to look at the top holdings in the fund.

Almanac Investor ETF Trading Rules

We advocate setting a Buy Limit based on the recent performance of not only the ETF, but the sector as well. Seasonalities don't always repeat, and if an ETF looks too rich, it probably is.

Stop Losses are a must, especially for the volatile sectors. Move your Stop Losses up as the price rises to lock in gains. But keep in mind it is also important to not get whipsawed. Setting the Buy Limit and the Stop Loss takes skill and is somewhat of an art.

After establishing a position, we have a target price in mind based on the historical performance of the correlating index. If the ETF moves 10% above this level, we recommend selling at what we have dubbed the "automatic sell point." Take your gains and move on! It is okay to miss a trade. It is okay to buy above the low and sell below the high. The purpose of this strategy is to get maximum returns in a short, well-defined time frame.

We invite you to peruse our *Almanac Investor* newsletter archives at *stocktradersalmanac.com* for updates and revisions to the strategy. The ETF Portfolio is at the bottom of page 15. Check the "In This Issue..." box on the bottom right of the front page to locate the articles about ETFs. The May 2005 issue is especially informative. We provide entry and exit points to newsletter subscribers. Our new book *Almanac Investor* details sector seasonality and ETFs at length.

AUGUST

MONDAY
D 42.9
S 42.9
N 42.9
21

Drawing on my fine command of language, I said nothing. — Robert Benchley

Beware the "Summer Rally" Hype — Historically the Weakest Rally (Page 70)

TUESDAY
D 61.9
S 57.1
N 76.2
22

Learn from the mistakes of others; you can't live long enough to make them all yourself. — Eleanor Roosevelt (First Lady, 1884-1962)

WEDNESDAY
D 47.6
S 52.4
N 61.9
23

Thomas Alva Edison said, "Genius is 1% inspiration and 99% perspiration!" Unfortunately, many startup "genius" entrepreneurs mistakenly switch the two percentages around, and then wonder why they can't get their projects off the ground. — Yale Hirsch

THURSDAY
D 61.9
S 66.7
N 52.4
24

The heights by great men reached and kept, were not attained by sudden flight, but they, while their companions slept, were toiling upward in the night. — Henry Wadsworth Longfellow

FRIDAY
D 47.6
S 52.4
N 47.6
25

One determined person can make a significant difference; a small group of determined people can change the course of history. — Sonia Johnson (Author, lecturer)

SATURDAY
26

September Bullish Seasonalities: see pages 80 and 116.

SUNDAY
27

SEPTEMBER ALMANAC

SEPTEMBER						
S	M	T	W	T	F	S
					1	2
3	4	5	6	7	8	9
10	11	12	13	14	15	16
17	18	19	20	21	22	23
24	25	26	27	28	29	30

OCTOBER						
S	M	T	W	T	F	S
1	2	3	4	5	6	7
8	9	10	11	12	13	14
15	16	17	18	19	20	21
22	23	24	25	26	27	28
29	30	31				

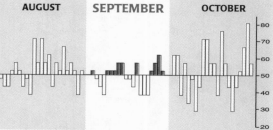

Market Probability Chart above is a graphic representation of the S&P 500 Recent Market Probability Calendar on page 121.

◆ Start of business year, end of vacations, and back to school made September a leading barometer month in first 60 years of the century, now portfolio managers back after Labor Day tend to clean house ◆ Biggest % loser on the S&P, Dow and NASDAQ (pages 46 & 54) ◆ Streak of four great Septembers averaging 4.2% gains ended with five losers in a row averaging –5.9% losses (see below) ◆ Day after Labor Day Dow up 9 of last 11 ◆ Opened strong eight of last ten years but tends to close weak due to end-of-quarter mutual fund portfolio restructuring ◆ September Triple-Witching Week is dangerous, week after pitiful (see page 76).

SEPTEMBER DAILY POINT CHANGES DOW JONES INDUSTRIALS

Previous Month Close	1995 4610.56	1996 5616.21	1997 7622.42	1998 7539.07	1999 10829.28	2000 11215.10	2001 9949.75	2002 8663.50	2003 9415.82	2004 10173.92
1	36.98	S	H	288.36	108.60	23.68	S	S	H –	5.46
2	S	257.36	– 45.06	– 94.67	S	S	H	107.45	121.82	
3	S	32.18	14.86	– 100.15	235.24	S	H – 355.45	45.19	– 30.08	
4	H	8.51	– 27.40	– 41.97	S	H	47.74	117.07	19.44	S
5	22.54	– 49.94	– 44.83	S	S	21.83	35.78	– 141.42	– 84.56	S
6	13.73	52.90	S	S	H	50.03	– 192.43	143.50	S	H
7	– 14.09	S	S	H – 44.32	– 50.77	– 234.99	S	S	82.59	
8	31.00	S	12.77	380.53	2.21	– 39.22	S	92.18 –	82.95 –	29.43
9	S	73.98	16.73	– 155.76	43.06	S	S	92.18	– 79.09	– 24.26
10	S	– 6.66	– 132.63	– 249.48	– 50.97	S	– 0.34	83.23	– 86.74	23.97
11	4.22	27.74	– 58.30	179.96	S – 25.16	Closed* –	21.44	39.30	S	
12	42.27	17.02	81.99	S	S	37.74	Closed* – 201.76	11.79	S	
13	18.31	66.58	S	S	1.90	– 51.05	Closed* – 66.72	S	1.69	
14	36.28	S	S	149.85	– 120.00	– 94.71	Closed*	S	S	3.40
15	– 4.23	S	– 21.83	79.04	– 108.91	– 160.47	S	S – 22.74	– 86.80	
16	S	50.68	174.78	65.39	– 63.96	S	S	67.49	118.53	13.13
17	S	– 0.37	– 9.48	– 216.01	66.17	S	– 684.81	– 172.63	– 21.69	39.97
18	– 17.16	– 11.47	36.28	21.89	S – 118.48	– 17.30	– 35.10	113.48	S	
19	– 13.37	– 9.62	5.45	S	S – 19.23	– 144.27	– 230.06	– 14.31	S	
20	25.65	20.72	S	S	20.27	– 101.37	– 382.92	43.63	S	– 79.57
21	– 25.29	S	S	37.59	– 225.43	77.60	– 140.40	S	S	40.04
22	– 3.25	S	79.56	– 36.05	– 74.40	81.85	S	S – 109.41	– 135.75	
23	S	6.28	– 26.77	257.21	– 205.48	S	368.05	– 113.87	40.63	– 70.28
24	S	– 20.71	– 63.35	– 152.42	– 39.26	S	368.05	– 189.02	– 150.53	8.34
25	5.78	3.33	– 58.70	26.78	S – 39.22	56.11	158.69	– 81.55	S	
26	– 4.33	– 8.51	74.17	S	S – 176.83	– 92.58	155.30	– 30.88	S	
27	– 3.25	4.07	S	S	24.06 – 2.96	114.03	– 295.67	S –	58.70	
28	25.29	S	S	80.07	– 27.86	195.70	166.14	S	S	88.86
29	1.44	S	69.25	– 28.32	– 62.05	– 173.14	S	S	67.16	58.84
30	S	9.25	– 46.17	– 237.90	123.47	S	S – 109.52	– 105.18	– 55.97	
Close	**4789.08**	**5882.17**	**7945.26**	**7842.62**	**10336.95**	**10650.92**	**8847.56**	**7591.93**	**9275.06**	**10080.27**
Change	**178.52**	**265.96**	**322.84**	**303.55**	**– 492.33**	**– 564.18**	**– 1102.19**	**– 1071.57**	**– 140.76**	**– 93.65**

Market closed for four days after 9/11 terrorist attack

September is when leaves and stocks tend to fall
On Wall Street it's the worst month of all

End of August Murderous 6 of Last 9 Years,
Average Loss Last 5 Days: Dow –2.9%, S&P –2.7%, NASDAQ –2.4%

MONDAY
D 52.4
S 57.1
N 57.1
28

TUESDAY
D 52.4
S 52.4
N **61.9**
29

When I have to depend upon hope in a trade, I get out of it. — Jesse Livermore

I had an unshakable faith. I had it in my head that if I had to, I'd crawl over broken glass. I'd live in a tent—it was gonna happen. And I think when you have that kind of steely determination...people get out of the way.

Next to Last Day Dow & S&P Up Only Once Last 10 Years

WEDNESDAY
D **28.6**
S **38.1**
N 57.1
30

— Rick Newcombe (Syndicator, *Investor's Business Daily*)

I know nothing grander, better exercise...more positive proof of the past, the triumphant result of faith in human kind, than a well-

Shortest Bear Market in History (45 Days) Ended 8/31/98: S&P –19.3%

THURSDAY
D 47.6
S 52.4
N **71.4**
31

contested national election. — Walt Whitman (American poet, 1819-1892)

The single best predictor of overall excellence is a company's ability to attract, motivate, and retain talented people.

First Trading Day in September Dow Up 8 of Last 10 — Down 11 of 13 1982-1994

FRIDAY
D 47.6
S 52.4
N 52.4
1

— Bruce Pfau (*Fortune*)

Look for an impending crash in the economy when the best-seller lists are filled with books on business strategies and quick-fix

SATURDAY
2

SUNDAY
3

A CORRECTION FOR ALL SEASONS

While there's a rally for every season (page 70), almost always there's a decline or correction, too. Fortunately, corrections tend to be smaller than rallies, and that's what gives the stock market its long-term upward bias. In each season the average bounce outdoes the average setback. On average the net gain between the rally and the correction is smallest in summer and fall.

The summer setback tends to be slightly outdone by the average correction in the fall. Tax selling and portfolio cleaning are the usual explanations – individuals sell to register a tax loss and institutions like to get rid of their losers before preparing year-end statements. The October jinx also plays a major part. Since 1964, there have been 16 fall declines of over 10%, and in nine of them (1966, 1974, 1978, 1979, 1987, 1990, 1997, 2000 and 2002) much damage was done in October, where so many bear markets end. Important October lows were also seen in 1998 and 1999. Most often, it has paid to buy after fourth quarter or late third quarter "waterfall declines" for a rally that may continue into January or even beyond. War in Iraq affected the pattern in 2003. Anticipation of our invasion put the market down in the first quarter. Quick success inspired the bulls which resumed their upward move through the summer.

SEASONAL CORRECTIONS IN DOW JONES INDUSTRIALS

	WINTER SLUMP Nov/Dec High to Q1 Low	SPRING SLUMP Feb/Mar High to Q2 Low	SUMMER SLUMP May/Jun High to Q3 Low	FALL SLUMP Aug/Sep High to Q4 Low
1964	− 0.1%	− 2.4%	− 1.0%	− 2.1%
1965	− 2.5	− 7.3	− 8.3	− 0.9
1966	− 6.0	− 13.2	− 17.7	− 12.7
1967	− 4.2	− 3.9	− 5.5	− 9.9
1968	− 8.8	− 0.3	− 5.5	+ 0.4
1969	− 8.7	− 8.7	− 17.2	− 8.1
1970	− 13.8	− 20.2	− 8.8	− 2.5
1971	− 1.4	− 4.8	− 10.7	− 13.4
1972	− 0.5	− 2.6	− 6.3	− 5.3
1973	− 11.0	− 12.8	− 10.9	− 17.3
1974	− 15.3	− 10.8	− 29.8	− 27.6
1975	− 6.3	− 5.5	− 9.9	− 6.7
1976	− 0.2	− 5.1	− 4.7	− 8.9
1977	− 8.5	− 7.2	− 11.5	− 10.2
1978	− 12.3	− 4.0	− 7.0	− 13.5
1979	− 2.5	− 5.8	− 3.7	− 10.9
1980	− 10.0	− 16.0	− 1.7	− 6.8
1981	− 6.9	− 5.1	− 18.6	− 12.9
1982	− 10.9	− 7.5	− 10.6	− 3.3
1983	− 4.1	− 2.8	− 6.8	− 3.6
1984	− 11.9	− 10.5	− 8.4	− 6.2
1985	− 4.8	− 4.4	− 2.8	− 2.3
1986	− 3.3	− 4.7	− 7.3	− 7.6
1987	− 1.4	− 6.6	− 1.7	− 36.1
1988	− 6.7	− 7.0	− 7.6	− 4.5
1989	− 1.7	− 2.4	− 3.1	− 6.6
1990	− 7.9	− 4.0	− 17.3	− 18.4
1991	− 6.3	− 3.6	− 4.5	− 6.3
1992	+ 0.1	− 3.3	− 5.4	− 7.6
1993	− 2.7	− 3.1	− 3.0	− 2.0
1994	− 4.4	− 9.6	− 4.4	− 7.1
1995	− 0.8	− 0.1	− 0.2	− 2.0
1996	− 3.5	− 4.6	− 7.5	+ 0.2
1997	− 1.8	− 9.8	− 2.2	− 13.3
1998	− 7.0	− 3.1	− 18.2	− 13.1
1999	− 2.7	− 1.7	− 8.0	− 11.5
2000	− 14.8	− 7.4	− 4.1	− 11.8
2001	− 14.5	− 13.6	− 27.4	− 16.2
2002	− 5.1	− 14.2	− 26.7	− 19.5
2003	− 15.8	− 5.3	− 3.1	− 2.1
2004	− 3.9	− 7.7	− 6.3	− 5.7
2005	− 4.5	− 8.5		
Totals	**− 259.4%**	**− 281.2%**	**− 365.4%**	**− 375.8%**
Average	**− 6.2%**	**− 6.7%**	**− 8.9%**	**− 9.2%**

SEPTEMBER

Labor Day (Market Closed)

MONDAY

4

management ideas. — Peter Drucker

When the S&P Index Future premium over "Cash" gets too high, I sell the future and buy the stocks.

Day After Labor Day Dow Up 9 of Last 11 — Crushed in 2002 Off 4.1%

TUESDAY

D 57.1
S 47.6
N **61.9**

5

If the premium disappears, well, buy the future and sell the stocks. — Neil Elliott (Fahnestock)
I've never been poor, only broke. Being poor is a frame of mind. Being broke is only a temporary situation.

WEDNESDAY

D 47.6
S 42.9
N 47.6

6

— Mike Todd (Movie producer, 1903-1958)

THURSDAY

D **33.3**
S **38.1**
N 57.1

7

A small debt produces a debtor; a large one, an enemy. — Publilius Syrus (Syrian-born Roman mime and former slave, 83-43 B.C.)
History is replete with episodes in which the real patriots were the ones who defied their governments.

FRIDAY

D 47.6
S 52.4
N 57.1

8

— Jim Rogers (Financier, *Adventure Capitalist*, b. 1942)

SATURDAY

9

SUNDAY

10

MARKET BEHAVIOR THREE DAYS BEFORE AND THREE DAYS AFTER HOLIDAYS

The *Stock Trader's Almanac* has tracked holiday seasonality annually since the first edition in 1968. Stocks used to rise on the day before holidays and sell off the day after, but nowadays each holiday moves to its own rhythm. Eight holidays are separated into seven groups. Average percent changes for the Dow, S&P 500, NASDAQ and Russell 2000 are shown.

The Dow and S&P consist of blue chips and the largest cap stocks, whereas NASDAQ and the Russell 2000 would be more representative of smaller cap stocks. This is evident on the last day of the year with NASDAQ and the Russell 2000 having a field day, while their larger brethren in the Dow and S&P are showing losses on average.

The best six-day span can be seen for the Russell 2000 on the three days before and three days after Christmas, a gain of about 2.0% on average. Thanks to the Santa Claus Rally, the six days around New Year's Day are up solidly as well. However, trading around the first day of the year has been mixed. Traders have been selling more the first trading day of the year recently, pushing gains and losses into the New Year.

Bullishness before Labor Day and after Memorial Day is affected by strength the first day of September and June. The worst day after a holiday is the day after Easter. Surprisingly, the following day is one of the best second days after a holiday, right up there with the second day after New Year's Day.

Presidents' Day is the least bullish of all the holidays, bearish the day before and three days after. The S&P and NASDAQ have dropped 12 of the last 14 days before Presidents' Day (Dow, 11 of 14; Russell 2000, 9 of 14).

HOLIDAYS: 3 DAYS BEFORE, 3 DAYS AFTER (Average % Change 1980 — July 2005)

	− 3	− 2	− 1		+1	+2	+3
S&P 500	0.12	0.26	− 0.11	**Positive Day After**	− 0.04	0.46	0.12
DJIA	0.06	0.18	− 0.19	**New Year's**	0.17	0.48	0.29
NASDAQ	0.27	0.32	0.29	**Day**	− 0.10	0.83	0.32
Russell 2K	0.32	0.43	0.62	*1/1/06 (Closed 1/2)*	− 0.22	0.41	0.22
S&P 500	0.34	− 0.06	− 0.27	**Negative Before & After**	− 0.14	− 0.07	− 0.09
DJIA	0.37	− 0.03	− 0.19	**Presidents'**	− 0.05	− 0.12	− 0.11
NASDAQ	0.54	0.22	− 0.45	**Day**	− 0.55	− 0.05	− 0.05
Russell 2K	0.39	0.05	− 0.16	*2/20/06*	− 0.42	− 0.12	− 0.04
S&P 500	0.15	− 0.03	0.21	**Positive Before &**	− 0.34	0.41	0.15
DJIA	0.13	− 0.07	0.14	**Negative After**	− 0.20	0.41	0.14
NASDAQ	0.48	0.30	0.34	**Good Friday**	− 0.55	0.39	0.29
Russell 2K	0.25	0.12	0.28	*4/14/06*	− 0.52	0.28	0.10
S&P 500	0.14	− 0.02	0.04	**Positive Day After**	0.35	0.20	0.18
DJIA	0.12	− 0.06	− 0.03	**Memorial**	0.43	0.22	0.12
NASDAQ	0.20	0.20	0.02	**Day**	0.15	− 0.03	0.41
Russell 2K	− 0.04	0.19	0.16	*5/29/06*	0.16	0.11	0.33
S&P 500	0.00	0.09	0.07	**Negative After**	− 0.16	− 0.05	0.11
DJIA	− 0.02	0.07	0.05	**Independence**	− 0.10	− 0.01	0.09
NASDAQ	0.11	0.11	0.05	**Day**	− 0.16	− 0.21	0.32
Russell 2K	0.09	− 0.10	0.02	*7/4/06*	− 0.13	− 0.21	0.12
S&P 500	− 0.07	− 0.34	0.22	**Positive Day Before**	0.01	0.03	− 0.08
DJIA	− 0.07	− 0.40	0.21	**Labor**	0.11	0.10	− 0.18
NASDAQ	0.17	− 0.04	0.23	**Day**	− 0.16	− 0.14	0.13
Russell 2K	0.29	0.02	0.22	*9/4/06*	− 0.07	0.03	0.16
S&P 500	− 0.07	0.01	0.25	**Positive Before & After**	0.24	− 0.15	0.15
DJIA	0.03	0.05	0.30	**Thanksgiving**	0.18	− 0.13	0.21
NASDAQ	− 0.23	− 0.26	0.37	*11/23/06*	0.62	− 0.13	− 0.06
Russell 2K	− 0.15	− 0.17	0.31		0.48	− 0.06	0.02
S&P 500	0.20	0.19	0.23	**Christmas**	0.19	0.09	0.34
DJIA	0.28	0.26	0.30	*12/25/06*	0.23	0.07	0.27
NASDAQ	− 0.16	0.47	0.50		0.13	0.22	0.41
Russell 2K	0.12	0.36	0.40		0.21	0.32	0.54

MONDAY 11

Monday Before September Triple Witching Dow Up 14 of Last 20, Dow Off 685 Points in 2001 (First Trading Day After 9-11)

D 38.1
S 52.4
N 52.4

"In Memory"

Show me a good phone receptionist and I'll show you a good company. — Harvey Mackay (*Pushing the Envelope*, 1999)

Stock prices tend to discount what has been unanimously reported by the mass media.

TUESDAY 12

D 57.1
S 52.4
N 47.6

— Louis Ehrenkrantz (Ehrenkrantz, Lyons & Ross)

WEDNESDAY 13

D 61.9
S 57.1
N 61.9

If you don't keep your employees happy, they won't keep the customers happy. — Red Lobster V.P. (*New York Times* April 23, 1989)
Institutions tend to dump stock in a single transaction and buy, if possible, in smaller lots, gradually accumulating a position.

THURSDAY 14

D 52.4
S 57.1
N 57.1

Therefore, many more big blocks are traded on downticks than on upticks. — Justin Mamis

Every man with a new idea is a crank until the idea succeeds.

FRIDAY 15

September Triple Witching Dow Down 15 of Last 25
September 10th Trading Day NASDAQ Down 18 of Last 22

D 47.6
S 47.6
N 19.1

— Mark Twain (American novelist and satirist, pen name of Samuel Longhorne Clemens, 1835-1910)
The thing always happens that you really believe in. The belief in a thing makes it happen.

SATURDAY 16

SUNDAY 17

MARKET GAINS MORE EIGHT DAYS A MONTH THAN ON ALL 13 REMAINING DAYS COMBINED

For many years the last day plus the first four days were the best days of the month. The market currently exhibits greater bullish bias from the last three trading days of the previous month through the first two days of the current month, and now shows significant bullishness during the middle three trading days nine to eleven, due to 401(k) cash inflows (see pages 136 and 137). This pattern was not as pronounced during the boom years of the 1990s, with market strength all month long. But the last five and a half years have experienced monthly bullishness at the ends, beginnings and middles of months versus losses during the rest of the month. Was 1999's "rest of month" heavy bullishness a bearish omen and 2002's "rest of month" large losses a bullish sign?

SUPER EIGHT DAYS* DOW % CHANGES VS. REST OF MONTH

	Super 8 Days	Rest of Month	Super 8 Days	Rest of Month	Super 8 Days	Rest of Month
	1997		**1998**		**1999**	
Jan	0.80%	0.91%	4.18%	− 2.30%	0.98%	0.08%
Feb	4.19	1.46	5.43	1.55	0.76	1.62
Mar	− 3.83	1.58	3.06	2.53	− 0.68	3.74
Apr	− 4.50	2.66	2.29	− 1.47	2.84	7.09
May	5.49	3.81	2.37	− 1.79	− 0.83	− 1.92
Jun	1.63	2.55	− 4.64	4.47	0.20	0.01
Jul	2.85	2.65	3.55	− 3.43	5.87	− 1.74
Aug	− 2.39	− 1.76	− 4.75	0.17	− 0.35	2.41
Sep	4.51	− 3.57	− 4.92	− 0.59	− 5.83	− 2.32
Oct	2.45	− 6.73	0.68	3.59	− 2.86	2.97
Nov	6.56	− 2.84	6.19	4.57	4.25	2.45
Dec	2.53	− 3.57	− 2.75	2.11	0.29	3.92
Totals	**20.29%**	**− 2.85%**	**10.69%**	**9.41%**	**4.64%**	**18.31%**
Average	**1.69%**	**− 0.24%**	**0.89%**	**0.78%**	**0.39%**	**1.53%**
	2000		**2001**		**2002**	
Jan	− 4.09%	0.47%	2.13%	− 2.36%	− 1.92%	− 0.24%
Feb	0.43	− 9.10	1.41	− 3.36	− 1.41	4.27
Mar	2.76	5.62	− 1.50	− 3.30	4.11	− 2.64
Apr	− 2.79	4.77	− 2.61	9.56	− 2.46	0.08
May	0.71	− 7.86	2.02	1.53	3.62	− 4.07
Jun	5.99	− 4.10	− 2.46	− 2.45	− 2.22	− 6.51
Jul	− 0.65	0.83	2.16	− 2.29	− 5.04	− 4.75
Aug	3.08	3.75	0.24	− 2.48	2.08	4.59
Sep	− 3.27	− 2.34	− 3.62	− 12.05	− 6.58	− 5.00
Oct	− 0.85	− 1.47	4.51	5.36	8.48	− 1.50
Nov	5.81	− 4.06	1.01	2.48	4.74	0.99
Dec	− 2.96	4.44	0.19	1.99	− 0.76	− 4.02
Totals	**4.17%**	**− 9.05%**	**3.48%**	**− 7.37%**	**2.64%**	**− 18.80%**
Average	**0.35%**	**− 0.75%**	**0.29%**	**− 0.61%**	**0.22%**	**− 1.57%**
	2003		**2004**		**2005**	
Jan	1.00%	− 4.86%	3.79%	− 1.02%	− 1.96%	− 1.35%
Feb	2.71	− 4.82	− 1.20	0.83	1.76	− 0.07
Mar	5.22	− 0.90	− 1.64	− 1.69	0.31	− 2.05
Apr	2.87	− 1.91	3.20	− 0.60	− 4.62	1.46
May	3.17	2.46	− 2.92	− 0.51	0.57	2.43
Jun	3.09	− 0.38	1.15	1.36	1.43	− 3.00
Jul	1.18	1.64	− 1.91	− 0.88		
Aug	− 0.74	1.55	0.51	0.40		
Sep	3.58	− 3.47	0.47	− 2.26		
Oct	2.87	1.41	0.85	− 1.82		
Nov	− 0.47	0.48	3.08	3.20		
Dec	2.10	3.70	2.03	1.13		
Totals	**26.58%**	**− 5.10%**	**7.41%**	**− 1.86%**	**− 2.51%**	**− 2.57%**
Average	**2.22%**	**− 0.43%**	**0.62%**	**− 0.16%**	**− 0.42%**	**− 0.43%**

	Super 8 Days*		Rest of Month (13 Days)	
102	Net % Changes	77.39%	Net % Changes	− 19.88%
Month	Average Period	0.76%	Average Period	− 0.195%
Totals	Average Day	0.09%	Average Day	− 0.015%

Super 8 Days = Last 3 + First 2 + Middle 3

SEPTEMBER

MONDAY

D 42.9
S 47.6
N **38.1**

18

— Frank Lloyd Wright (American architect)

Setting a goal is not the main thing. It is deciding how you will go about achieving it and staying with that plan.

TUESDAY

D **28.6**
S 42.9
N 52.4

19

— Tom Landry (Head Coach Dallas Cowboys 1960-1988)

It's not that I am so smart; it's just that I stay with problems longer.

FOMC Meeting

WEDNESDAY

D 52.4
S 57.1
N **71.4**

20

— Albert Einstein (German/American physicist, 1921 Nobel Prize, 1879-1955)

THURSDAY

D **33.3**
S **38.1**
N 47.6

21

Marx's great achievement was to place the system of capitalism on the defensive. — Charles A. Madison (1977)
I've continued to recognize the power individuals have to change virtually anything and everything in their lives in an instant.
I've learned that the resources we need to turn our dreams into reality are within us, merely waiting for the day when we decide to

FRIDAY

D **38.1**
S **38.1**
N 47.6

22

wake up and claim our birthright. — Anthony Robbins (Motivator, advisor, consultant, author, entrepreneur, philanthropist, b. 1960)

Rosh Hashanah

SATURDAY

23

SUNDAY

24

OCTOBER ALMANAC

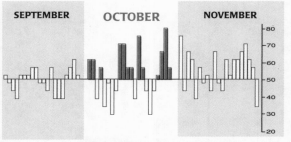

OCTOBER						
S	M	T	W	T	F	S
1	2	3	4	5	6	7
8	9	10	11	12	13	14
15	16	17	18	19	20	21
22	23	24	25	26	27	28
29	30	31				

NOVEMBER						
S	M	T	W	T	F	S
			1	2	3	4
5	6	7	8	9	10	11
12	13	14	15	16	17	18
19	20	21	22	23	24	25
26	27	28	29	30		

Market Probability Chart above is a graphic representation of the S&P 500 Recent Market Probability Calendar on page 121.

◆ Known as the jinx month because of crashes in 1929, 1987, the 554-point drop on October 27, 1997, back-to-back massacres in 1978 and 1979 and Friday the 13th in 1989 ◆ Yet October is a "bear killer" and turned the tide in eleven post-WWII bear markets: 1946, 1957, 1960, 1962, 1966, 1974, 1987, 1990, 1998, 2001 and 2002, eight were Midterm October bottoms ◆ Midterm Election Year Octobers #1 Dow and S&P, #2 NASDAQ ◆ Worst six months of the year ends with October (page 50) ◆ No longer worst month (pages 46 & 54) ◆ Best month last 8 years ◆ October is a great time to buy depressed high-tech stocks (page 116) ◆ Big October gains five years 1999-2003 after atrocious Septembers ◆ Can get into Best Six Months earlier using MACD (page 52).

OCTOBER DAILY POINT CHANGES DOW JONES INDUSTRIALS

Previous Month	1995	1996	1997	1998	1999	2000	2001	2002	2003	2004
Close	4789.08	5882.17	7945.26	7842.62	10336.95	10650.92	8847.56	7591.93	9275.06	10080.27
1	S	22.73	70.24	− 210.09	− 63.95	S	− 10.73	346.86	194.14	112.38
2	− 27.82	29.07	12.03	152.16	S	49.21	113.76	− 183.18	18.60	S
3	− 11.56	− 1.12	11.05	S	S	19.61	173.19	− 38.42	84.51	S
4	− 9.03	60.01	S	S	128.23	64.74	− 62.90	− 188.79	S	23.89
5	22.04	S	S	− 58.45	− 0.64	− 59.56	58.89	S	S	− 38.86
6	6.50	S	61.64	16.74	187.75	− 128.38	S	S	22.67	62.24
7	S	− 13.05	78.09	− 1.29	− 51.29	S	S	− 105.56	59.63	− 114.52
8	S	− 13.04	− 83.25	− 9.78	112.71	S	− 51.83	78.65	− 23.71	− 70.20
9	− 42.99	− 36.15	− 33.64	167.61	S	− 28.11	− 15.50	− 215.22	49.11	S
10	− 5.42	− 8.95	− 16.21	S	S	− 44.03	188.42	247.68	− 5.33	S
11	14.45	47.71	S	S	− 1.58	− 110.61	169.59	316.34	S	26.77
12	29.63	S	S	101.95	− 231.12	− 379.21	− 66.29	S	89.70	− 4.79
13	28.90	S	27.01	63.33	− 184.90	157.60	S	S	89.70	− 74.85
14	S	40.62	24.07	30.64	54.45	S	S	27.11	48.60	− 107.88
15	S	− 5.22	− 38.31	330.58	− 266.90	S	3.46	378.28	− 9.93	38.93
16	− 9.40	16.03	− 119.10	117.40	S	46.62	36.61	− 219.65	− 11.33	S
17	11.56	38.39	− 91.85	S	S	− 149.09	− 151.26	239.01	− 69.93	S
18	− 18.42	35.03	S	S	96.57	− 114.69	− 69.75	47.36	S	22.94
19	24.93	S	S	49.69	88.65	167.96	40.89	S	S	− 58.70
20	− 7.59	S	74.41	39.40	187.43	83.61	S	S	56.15	− 10.69
21	S	− 3.36	139.00	13.38	− 94.67	S	172.92	215.84	− 30.30	− 21.17
22	S	− 29.07	− 25.79	13.91	172.56	S	172.92	− 88.08	− 149.40	− 107.95
23	− 39.38	− 25.34	− 186.88	− 80.85	S	45.13	− 36.95	44.11	14.89	S
24	28.18	− 43.98	− 132.36	S	S	121.35	5.54	− 176.93	− 30.67	S
25	− 29.98	14.54	S	S	− 120.32	− 66.59	117.28	126.65	S	− 7.82
26	− 49.86	S	S	− 20.08	− 47.80	53.64	82.27	S	S	138.49
27	37.93	S	− 554.26	− 66.17	92.76	210.50	S	S	25.70	113.55
28	S	− 34.29	337.17	5.93	227.64	S	S	− 75.95	140.15	2.51
29	S	34.29	8.35	123.06	107.33	S	− 275.67	0.90	26.22	22.93
30	14.82	− 13.79	− 125.00	97.07	S	245.15	− 147.52	58.47	12.08	S
31	− 1.09	36.15	60.41	S	S	135.37	− 46.84	− 30.38	14.51	S
Close	4755.48	6029.38	7442.08	8592.10	10729.86	10971.14	9075.14	8397.03	9801.12	10027.47
Change	− 33.60	147.21	− 503.18	749.48	392.91	320.22	227.58	805.10	526.06	− 52.80

October has killed many a bear
Buy tech stocks and soon wear a grin ear to ear

SEPTEMBER/OCTOBER

Historically September Has Closed Poorly

MONDAY
D 47.6
S 38.1
N 38.1
25

Anyone who has achieved excellence knows that it comes as a result of ceaseless concentration. — Louise Brooks (Writer)

If you can buy all you want of a new issue, you do not want any; if you cannot obtain any, you want all you can buy.

TUESDAY
D 57.1
S 52.4
N 47.6
26

— Rod Fadem (Stifel Nicolaus & Co., *Barron's* 1989)

End of 3rd Quarter Brings Portfolio Window Dressing and Heavy Selling

WEDNESDAY
D 52.4
S 57.1
N 42.9
27

Man's mind, once stretched by a new idea, never regains its original dimensions. — Oliver Wendell Holmes
The dissenter (or "contrary investor") is every human at those moments of his life when he resigns momentarily from the herd and

THURSDAY
D 57.1
S 61.9
N 47.6
28

thinks for himself. — Archibald MacLeish (American poet, writer and political activist, 1892-1982)
I was in search of a one-armed economist so that the guy could never make a statement and then say:

FRIDAY
D 47.6
S 52.4
N 57.1
29

"on the other hand." — Harry S. Truman
I believe in the exceptional man—the entrepreneur who is always out of money,

SATURDAY
30

October Bullish Seasonalities: see pages 80 and 116.

SUNDAY
1

THE BEST INVESTMENT BOOK OF THE YEAR
Reviewed by George A. Schade, CMT

(Reprinted with permission of *SFO magazine, www.sfomag.com*)

Wisdom gained from three decades of studying stock markets and creating timing indicators is what you will find in Gerald Appel's latest book. Appel covers in logical sequence the spectrum of technical market indicators, provides strategies with solid performance, and presents worthy timing "power tools."

To accurately review this book, the reviewer must try to convey the full complement of indicators described. Appel begins with a "no-frills investment strategy" keyed on relative strength selection that investors can use with mutual funds. He describes two indicators to measure market moods that can be kept in less than 15 minutes weekly. The first compares the relative strength of the Nasdaq Composite to the NYSE index. The other is a monetary model that averages the 3- and 5-year Treasury yields.

Appel gives the steps to build all his indicators and provides historical performance numbers. The aim is to identify the most favorable market climates to put on long or short positions. Appel persuades with simplicity, clear articulation, sound logic and tested results. In the tradition of master technicians, he forsakes naming his indicators after himself.

This master technician uses moving averages and rate of change measures to build many of his indicators. Moving averages, of course, can define significant underlying trends, while rate of change measures momentum. The long-, intermediate-, and short-term trends should be identified for a complete picture, and for that purpose the 200-day, 50-day, and 10-day moving averages work well. The 30-month moving average depicts very long-term trends.

Rate of change indicators identify overbought and oversold levels. Appel shows how tracking the 10- and 21-day rate of change in the momentum of new highs, new lows, advances and declines has given excellent buy and sell signals.

Moving averages and rate-of-change measurements create mathematically based indicators that give objective signals that can be tested. Those indicators often have an advantage — due to having historical comparability — over other indicators such as chart patterns that can demand subjective interpretation.

(continued on page 94)

OCTOBER

Yom Kippur
First Trading Day in October Dow Up 6 of Last 9 — Last 3: 4.6%, 2.1%, 1.1%

MONDAY
D 66.7
S 61.9
N 52.4

2

not the bureaucrat who generates cash flow and pays dividends. — Armand Erpf

Early in March (1960), Dr. Arthur F. Burns called on me...Burns' conclusion was that unless some decisive action was taken, and taken soon, we were heading for another economic dip which would hit its low point in October, just before the elections.

TUESDAY
D 47.6
S 61.9
N 57.1

3

— Richard M. Nixon (37th U.S. President, *Six Crises*, 1913-1994)
I keep hearing "Should I buy? Should I buy?" When I start hearing "Should I sell?" that's the bottom.

October Ends "Worst Six Months" for Dow & S&P and
"Worst Four Months" for NASDAQ (Pages 46, 50, 54, 58, 138 & 139)

WEDNESDAY
D 33.3
S 38.1
N 52.4

4

— Nick Moore (Portfolio manager, Jurika & Voyles, *TheStreet.com*, March 12, 2001)

If a battered stock refuses to sink any lower no matter how many negative articles appear in the papers,

THURSDAY
D 61.9
S 57.1
N 61.9

5

that stock is worth a close look. — James L. Fraser (*Contrary Investor*)

Start Looking for MACD Buy Signals (Pages 52 & 58)
Almanac Investor Subscribers Are E-mailed Alerts When They Trigger

FRIDAY
D 38.1
S 33.3
N 42.9

6

To change one's life: Start immediately. Do it flamboyantly. No exceptions. — William James (Philosopher, psychologist, 1842-1910)

There has never been a commercial technology like this (Internet) in the history of the world, whereby the minute you adopt it, it

SATURDAY

7

SUNDAY

8

THE BEST INVESTMENT BOOK OF THE YEAR

(continued from page 92)

Being a proponent of using multiple indicators, Appel does not favor one kind over the other. Even subjective chart patterns, when they reinforce each other, provide synergy that adds weight to a bullish or bearish pattern. Appel emphasizes time and indicator diversity because investment decisions should be based on the consensus of a team of indicators rather than on one or two techniques.

His diversity of indicators extends from visual tools such as the angles of trends to traditional cycles. The slopes and lengths of angles tracing a stock's movement can project a trend's duration and show likely reversal points. He devotes a chapter to political, seasonal and time cycles, which "carry significance but are not necessarily perfectly timed." Rate-of-change measures can identify the nine dominant cycles Appel deems important. A powerful visual tool detailed in the book is the T-formation, which is a formation based on cycles than can project the timeframe of a likely turning point.

There is a chapter on volume extremes, volatility, the Arms Index and the VIX, the indicators that reflect the emotional tone of the stock market. In addition to showing how the Arms Index and VIX can be used to gauge market moods, Appel provides a volatility model based on price change rather than on the more indirect measurements of volatility used in VIX and the Arms Index.

Having invented the Moving Average Convergence-Divergence model, he covers MACD in depth and lists "very important supplementary buy and sell rules." MACD can be improved by using different combinations rather than a single one, as different time spans will distinguish the short-term from the intermediate trend. And he's not reluctant to say when MACD has not given the timeliest signals.

Always searching for new timing tools, Appel ends this book with an explanation of moving average trading channels that can be used in any timeframe. Moving average channels can involve subjective judgments, but these can be well-informed calls if the rules explained here are followed.

Power Tools is a master technician's superb source of well-crafted ideas for timing indicators.

If interested in buying the book, use the "Almanac Investor Reading List" link on our website ***www.stocktradersalmanac.com***.

Columbus Day (Bond Market Closed)

MONDAY
9

D 52.4
S 47.6
N 52.4

forces you to think and act globally. — Robert Hormats (Goldman, Sachs)

With globalization, the big [countries] don't eat the small, the fast eat the slow.

TUESDAY
10

D 28.6
S 28.6
N 42.9

— Thomas L. Friedman (Op-ed columnist, referring to the Arab nations, *New York Times*)

WEDNESDAY
11

D 38.1
S 42.9
N 52.4

Those who cannot remember the past are condemned to repeat it. — George Santayana (American philosopher, poet, 1863-1952)

October Is the Best Month Since 1998

THURSDAY
12

D 71.4
S 71.4
N 76.2

Make it idiot-proof and someone will make a better idiot. — Bumper sticker

FRIDAY
13

D 71.4
S 71.4
N 66.7

An autobiography must be such that one can sue oneself for libel. — Thomas Hoving (Museum director)

SATURDAY
14

SUNDAY
15

YEAR'S TOP INVESTMENT BOOKS

Technical Analysis: Power Tools for Active Investors, Gerald Appel, Prentice-Hall, $44.95. <u>Best Investment Book of the Year</u>. Simply awesome! (See Page 92.)

Fischer Black and the Revolutionary Idea of Finance, Perry Mehrling, Wiley, $29.95. Does a remarkable job of tracing the intellectual and personal development of this genius. Could make a great movie just like, *A Beautiful Mind*. Found it hard to put down!

Winning, Jack Welch with Suzy Welch, Harper Business, $27.95. Who can resist a book on what makes winning companies by the "CEO of the Century"? Can help investors make better stock selections. Bill Gates and Warren Buffett both endorse the book. Psst! The biggest dirty little secret in business is *lack of candor*.

Hot Commodities: How Anyone Can Invest Profitably in the World's Best Market, Jim Rogers, Random House, $25.95. Rogers always seems to be way ahead of the crowd. His commodity index fund is the best performing index fund in the world. Believes that commodities will continue to be hot in the coming years.

Option Writing Strategies for Extraordinary Returns, David G. Funk, McGraw-Hill, $39.95. Conservative investors who are delighted to make 10% to 15% annually, year after year, should buy this book. Worth every penny if only for this Kyle Rosen quote: "In my experience, selling a put is much safer than buying a stock."

Markets in Motion: A Financial Market History 1900 to 2004 (25th Anniversary Edition), Ned Davis Research, Wiley, $49.95. Need to know what the market did over the last 105 years a decade at a time? Giant 16″ by 20″ charts superimpose CPI, T-Bill rate, M2, price-to-dividend ratio, moving averages, discount rate, and important events. Indispensable!

New Markets, New Strategies, Jason Trennert, McGraw-Hill, $27.95. Contains a compelling analysis of the drivers that will move markets in the coming decade. Also, offers up the Thrifty Fifty — stocks that are poised to outperform the market and why.

Mastering Technical Analysis: Using the Tools of Technical Analysis for Profitable Trading, John C. Brooks, McGraw-Hill, $55.00. Technical analyst for over forty years turns many of the techniques and analytical approaches employed in the markets into common sense. Now with Lowry Reports, the oldest technical service (72 years).

Running Money: Hedge Fund Honchos, Monster Markets and My Hunt for the Big Score, Andy Kessler, Harper Business, $24.95. How some hedge fund managers strategize, raise funds, and operate. An excellent and enlightening read and hard to put down, if you are trying to get to sleep. Great for any investor or trader who is determined to "beat the market!"

Think Big, Act Small: How America's Best Performing Companies Keep the Start-up Spirit Alive, Jason Jennings, Penguin, $24.95. Screened 100,000 companies to find the top one-hundredth of 1 percent of American companies who've increased revenues and earnings over 10 percent annually for ten years, and what they all had in common.

(continued on page 98)

RESERVE YOUR *2007 ALMANAC* AT THE 2006 PRICE!

Special Pre-pub Offer! Save 20%

As a special service to our faithful *Stock Trader's Almanac* readers, we are offering you the opportunity to purchase the *2007 Stock Trader's Almanac*—the **Fortieth Anniversary Edition** at 20% off the regular list price! To order, just call us toll free at 800-356-5016 (in Canada call 800-567-4797) or fax us at 800-597-3299 or order online at www.wiley.com/go/sta2006. Be sure to use **promo code ALMA7** when you are placing your order to receive your special discount.

RESERVE YOUR *2007 STOCK TRADER'S ALMANAC* NOW!

☐ **Please reserve _____ copies of your *2007 Stock Trader's Almanac*.**
Just $27.96 (regularly $34.95) plus shipping, handling, and your state sales tax!
Deeper discounts are available for orders of 5 copies or more—call us at 800-356-5016 for details.
Shipping: US: first item $5.00, each additional $3.00; International: first item $10.50, each additional $7.00. Bulk discounts for 5 or more copies available. Call 800-356-5016.

$_____ payment enclosed (Please be sure to include your state sales tax)

☐ Check made payable to **John Wiley & Sons, Inc.** *(US Funds only, drawn on a US bank)*

☐ Charge Credit Card (check one): ☐ Visa ☐ Mastercard ☐ AmEx

Name	E-mail address
Address	Account #
City	Expiration Date
State Zip	Signature

☐ **BECOME A SUBSCRIBER! I want to stay up-to-date! Please send me future editions of the *Stock Trader's Almanac*.** You will automatically be shipped (along with the bill) future editions of the *Stock Trader's Almanac* at the yearly pre-publication discount. It's so easy and convenient!

PROMO CODE: ALMA7   ISBN: 0-471-78377-3

SEND ME MORE OF THE *2006 STOCK TRADER'S ALMANAC* !

☐ Send _____ additional copies of the *2006 Stock Trader's Almanac*.
$34.95 for single copies plus shipping, handling, and your state sales tax!
Shipping: US: first item $5.00, each additional $3.00; International: first item $10.50, each additional $7.00. Bulk discounts for 5 or more copies available. Call 800-356-5016.

$_____ payment enclosed (Please be sure to include your state sales tax)

☐ Check made payable to **John Wiley & Sons, Inc.** *(US Funds only, drawn on a US bank)*

☐ Charge Credit Card (check one): ☐ Visa ☐ Mastercard ☐ AmEx

Name	E-mail address
Address	Account #
City	Expiration Date
State Zip	Signature

ISBN: 0-471-70956-5

RESERVE YOUR
2007 STOCK TRADER'S ALMANAC NOW
AND SAVE 20%.

Mail the postage paid card below to reserve your copy.

NO POSTAGE
NECESSARY
IF MAILED
IN THE
UNITED STATES

BUSINESS REPLY MAIL
FIRST-CLASS MAIL PERMIT NO. 2277 HOBOKEN NJ

POSTAGE WILL BE PAID BY ADDRESSEE

F REID
JOHN WILEY & SONS INC
111 RIVER ST MS 5-01
HOBOKEN NJ 07030-9442

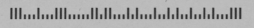

NO POSTAGE
NECESSARY
IF MAILED
IN THE
UNITED STATES

BUSINESS REPLY MAIL
FIRST-CLASS MAIL PERMIT NO. 2277 HOBOKEN NJ

POSTAGE WILL BE PAID BY ADDRESSEE

F REID
JOHN WILEY & SONS INC
111 RIVER ST MS 5-01
HOBOKEN NJ 07030-9442

Monday Before October Expiration Dow Up 21 of 25

MONDAY
D **61.9**
S 57.1
N 57.1
16

The difficult we do immediately; the impossible takes a little longer. — Army Service Forces slogan

I am glad that I paid so little attention to good advice; had I abided by it I might have been saved from my most valuable mistakes.

TUESDAY
D 52.4
S 57.1
N 47.6
17

— Gene Fowler (Journalist, screenwriter, film director, biographer, 1890-1960)
It's not the strongest of the species (think "traders") that survive, nor the most intelligent, but the one most responsive to change.

WEDNESDAY
D 47.6
S **38.1**
N **38.1**
18

— Charles Darwin

Crash of October 19, 1987, Dow Down 22.6% in One Day

THURSDAY
D **71.4**
S **76.2**
N **76.2**
19

Big Business breeds bureaucracy and bureaucrats exactly as big government does. — T.K. Quinn

October Expiration Day Dow Up 5 of Last 7 — Down 267 Points in 1999

FRIDAY
D 52.4
S 57.1
N 57.1
20

An entrepreneur tends to lie some of the time. An entrepreneur in trouble tends to lie most of the time. — Anonymous
...the most successful positions I've taken have been those about which I've been most nervous (and ignored that emotion anyway).
Courage is not about being fearless; courage is about acting appropriately even when you are fearful.

SATURDAY
21

SUNDAY
22

YEAR'S TOP INVESTMENT BOOKS

(continued from page 96)

Precision Trading with Stevenson Price and Time Targets, J.R. Stevenson, Traders Press, $49.00 soft. Unique but simple cycle system for traders to help predict target prices and the time it will take to get there. From a master trader with 50 years of experience.

Trade Like Warren Buffett, James Altucher, Wiley, $49.95. Last year's Best Investment Book author does it again by analyzing Buffett's various investment and arbitrage strategies over the last five decades. A different slant!

McMillan on Options: Second Edition, Lawrence G. McMillan, Wiley, $79.95. "McMillan is an options guru par excellence." This was our endorsement of the First Edition seven years ago. Tells how to use option prices and volume as indicators, shows many seasonal trades, etc. A must for any serious trader or investor.

Encyclopedia of Chart Patterns: Second Edition, Thomas N. Bulkowski, Wiley, $99.95. Premier reference on chart pattern analysis. Nothing like it out there. You can't be a successful professional trader without knowing the contents of this 1000-page volume. New additions and performance probabilities are invaluable!

New Trading Systems and Methods: Fourth Edition, Perry J. Kaufman, Wiley, $125. Futures expert Kaufman updates previous editions in 1175 pages. Essential work for all day traders. Mastering these pages will give any investor an edge.

Money Ain't Free, Will Marshall, iUniverse, $15.95 soft. Former Treasurer of Nalco Chemical shows how to look beyond a company's published numbers. Rather interesting approach that would appeal to Warren Buffett. Values the use of the PEG ratio (price to earnings to growth rate).

Harper Collins	McGraw-Hill	Penguin Group
10 East 53rd Street	Two Penn Plaza	375 Hudson Street
New York NY 10022	New York NY 10121	New York NY 10014
Prentice-Hall	Random House	Traders Press
Upper Saddle River	1745 Broadway	PO Box 6206
New Jersey 07458	New York NY 10019	Greenville SC 29606
John Wiley & Sons	iUniverse (Ste.100)	
111 River Street	2021 Pine Lake Road	
Hoboken NJ 07030	Lincoln NE 68512	

Purchase any of these books, plus past years' selections, from our "Almanac Investor Reading List" at *www.stocktradersalmanac.com*. Various discounts are available.

Late October Time to Buy Depressed Stocks, Especially Techs & Small Caps

MONDAY
D 42.9
S 42.9
N 42.9
23

— Daniel Turov (*Turov on Timing*)

FOMC Meeting

TUESDAY
D 42.9
S 28.6
N 38.1
24

Chance favors the informed mind. — Louis Pasteur (French chemist, founder of microbiology, 1822-1895)

WEDNESDAY
D 38.1
S 42.9
N 28.6
25

Don't be overly concerned about your heirs. Usually, unearned funds do them more harm than good. — Gerald M. Loeb

In a study of 3000 companies, researchers at the University of Pennsylvania found that spending 10% of revenue on capital improvements boosts productivity by 3.9%, but a similar investment in developing human capital increases productivity by 8.5%.

THURSDAY
D 42.9
S 52.4
N 33.3
26

— John A. Byrne (Editor-in-Chief, *Fast Company Magazine*)

We are like tenant farmers chopping down the fence around our house for fuel when we should be using Nature's inexhaustible sources of energy—sun, wind and tide. I'd put my money on the sun and solar energy. What a source of power! I hope we don't have

FRIDAY
D 71.4
S 66.7
N 52.4
27

to wait until oil and coal run out before we tackle that. — Thomas Alva Edison (American inventor, 1093 patents, 1847-1931)

The generally accepted view is that markets are always right—that is, market prices tend to discount future developments accurately even when it is unclear what those developments are. I start with the opposite point of view. I believe that market prices are always wrong in the sense that they present a biased view of the future. — George Soros (1987, Financier, philanthropist,

1929 Crash October 28 & 29, Dow Down 23.0% in Two Days

SATURDAY
28

Daylight Saving Time Ends
November Bullish Seasonalities: see pages 80 and 116.

SUNDAY
29

NOVEMBER ALMANAC

	NOVEMBER					
S	M	T	W	T	F	S
			1	2	3	4
5	6	7	8	9	10	11
12	13	14	15	16	17	18
19	20	21	22	23	24	25
26	27	28	29	30		

	DECEMBER					
S	M	T	W	T	F	S
					1	2
3	4	5	6	7	8	9
10	11	12	13	14	15	16
17	18	19	20	21	22	23
24	25	26	27	28	29	30
31						

Market Probability Chart above is a graphic representation of the S&P 500 Recent Market Probability Calendar on page 121.

◆ #2 S&P month and #3 on Dow since 1950, #3 on NASDAQ since 1971 (pages 46 & 54) ◆ Also start of the "Best Six Months" of the year (page 50) and NASDAQ's Best Three and Eight Months ◆ Simple timing indicator almost triples "Best Six Months" strategy (page 52), doubles NASDAQ's Best Eight (page 58) ◆ Midterm Election Novembers team with October for helluva one-two punch, 8.5% two-month NASDAQ gain ◆ Day before and after Thanksgiving Day combined, only 9 losses in 53 years (page 106) ◆ 2003 broke 10-year Dow winning streak week before Thanksgiving, down last 2.

NOVEMBER DAILY POINT CHANGES DOW JONES INDUSTRIALS

Previous Month	1995	1996	1997	1998	1999	2000	2001	2002	2003	2004
Close	4755.48	6029.38	7442.08	8592.10	10729.86	10971.14	9075.14	8397.03	9801.12	10027.47
1	11.20	− 7.45	S	S	− 81.35	− 71.67	188.76	120.61	S	26.92
2	41.91	S	S	114.05	− 66.67	− 18.96	59.64	S	S	− 18.66
3	16.98	S	232.31	N/C	27.22	− 62.56	S	S	57.34	101.32
4	S	19.75	14.74	76.99	30.58	S	S	53.96	− 19.63	177.71
5	S	39.50	3.44	132.33	64.84	S	117.49	106.67	− 18.00	72.78
6	− 11.56	96.53	− 9.33	59.99	S	159.26	150.09	92.74	36.14	S
7	− 16.98	28.33	− 101.92	S	S	− 25.03	− 36.75	− 184.77	− 47.18	S
8	55.64	13.78	S	S	14.37	− 45.12	33.15	− 49.11	S	3.77
9	11.56	S	S	− 77.50	− 101.53	− 72.81	20.48	S	S	− 4.94
10	6.14	S	− 28.73	− 33.98	− 19.58	− 231.30	S	S	− 53.26	− 0.89
11	S	35.78	6.14	− 40.16	− 2.44	S	S	− 178.18	− 18.74	84.36
12	S	10.44	− 157.41	5.92	174.02	S	− 53.63	27.05	111.04	69.17
13	2.53	8.20	86.44	89.85	S	− 85.70	196.58	12.49	− 10.89	S
14	− 1.09	38.76	84.72	S	S	163.81	72.66	143.64	− 69.26	S
15	50.94	35.03	S	S	− 8.57	26.54	48.78	36.96	S	11.23
16	46.61	S	S	91.66	171.58	− 51.57	5.40	S	S	− 62.59
17	20.59	S	125.74	− 24.97	− 49.24	− 26.16	S	S	− 57.85	61.92
18	S	− 1.12	− 47.40	54.83	152.61	S	S	− 92.52	− 86.67	22.98
19	S	50.69	73.92	14.94	− 31.81	S	109.47	− 11.79	66.30	− 115.64
20	− 6.86	32.42	101.87	103.50	S	− 167.22	− 75.08	148.23	− 71.04	S
21	40.46	− 11.55	54.46	S	S	31.85	− 66.70	222.14	9.11	S
22	18.06	53.29	S	S	85.63	− 95.18	H	− 40.31	S	32.51
23	H	S	S	214.72	− 93.89	H	125.03*	S	S	3.18
24	7.23*	S	− 113.15	− 73.12	12.54	70.91*	S	S	119.26	27.71
25	S	76.03	41.03	13.13	H	S	S	44.56	16.15	H
26	S	− 19.38	− 14.17	H	− 19.26*	S	23.04	− 172.98	15.63	1.92*
27	22.04	− 29.07	H	18.80*	S	75.84	− 110.15	255.26	H	S
28	7.22	H	28.35*	S	S	− 38.49	− 160.74	H	2.89*	S
29	27.46	22.36*	S	S	− 40.99	121.53	117.56	− 35.59*	S	− 46.33
30	− 31.07	S	S	− 216.53	− 70.11	− 214.62	22.14	S	S	− 47.88
Close	5074.49	6521.70	7823.13	9116.55	10877.81	10414.49	9851.56	8896.09	9782.46	10428.02
Change	319.01	492.32	381.05	524.45	147.95	− 556.65	776.42	499.06	− 18.66	400.55

*Shortened trading day

*Astute investors always smile and remember
When stocks seasonally start soaring, and salute November*

OCTOBER/NOVEMBER

MONDAY
D 81.0
S 81.0
N 71.4
30

political activist, author and philosopher, b. 1930)

Halloween 🎃

TUESDAY
D 42.9
S 57.1
N 66.7
31

Choose a job you love, and you will never have to work a day in your life.— Confucius
In the course of evolution and a higher civilization we might be able to get along comfortably without Congress,

First Trading Day in November Has Been Fantastic, Dow Up 22 of Last 27

WEDNESDAY
D 76.2
S 76.2
N 81.0
1

but without Wall Street, never. — Henry Clews (1900)
Never doubt that a small group of thoughtful, committed citizens can change the world: indeed it's the only thing that ever has.

THURSDAY
D 38.1
S 42.9
N 47.6
2

— Margaret Mead (American anthropologist)
Brilliant men are often strikingly ineffectual; they fail to realize that the brilliant insight is not by itself achievement.

FRIDAY
D 66.7
S 66.7
N 85.7
3

They never have learned that insights become effectiveness only through hard systematic work. — Peter Drucker
I have seen it repeatedly throughout the world: politicians get a country in trouble but swear everything is okay in the face of

SATURDAY
4

SUNDAY
5

MIDTERM ELECTION TIME UNUSUALLY BULLISH

Presidential election years tend to produce high drama and frenetic campaigns. Midterm years with only local or state candidates running are less stressful. Could this be the reason for the bullishness that seems to occur in the five days before and three days after midterm congressional elections? We don't think so. So many bear markets seem to occur in midterm years, very often bottoming in October. Also, major military involvements began or were in their early stages in midterm years, such as: World War II, Korea, Vietnam, Kuwait and Iraq. Solidly bullish midterm years as 1954, 1958, and 1986 were exceptions. With so many negative occurrences in midterm years, perhaps the opportunity for investors to make a change for the better by casting their votes translates into an inner bullish feeling before and after midterm elections.

An impressive 2.9% has been the average gain during the eight trading days surrounding midterm election days since 1934. This is equivalent to roughly 40 Dow points per day at present levels. There was only one losing period in 1994 when the Republicans took control of both the House and the Senate for the first time in 40 years. Two other midterm switches occurred in 1946 when control of Congress passed to the Republicans for just two years, and in 1954, when Democrats took back control after two years.

There were nine occasions when the percentage of House seats lost by the President's party was in double digits. The average market gain during the eight-day trading period was 2.3%. In contrast, the average gain in the eight occasions when there were no losses, or losses were in single digits, was 3.4%.

BULLS WIN BATTLE BETWEEN ELEPHANTS AND DONKEYS

Midterm Year	Dow Jones Industrials			President's Party	President in Power
	5 Trading Days Before E. Day	3 Trading Days After E. Day	% Change	% Seats Lost	
1934	93.05	99.02	6.4%	2.9%	Dem
1938	152.21	158.41	4.1	− 21.3	Dem
1942	113.11	116.12	2.7	− 16.9	Dem
1946	164.20	170.79	4.0	− 22.6	Dem*
1950	225.69	229.29	1.6	− 11.0	Dem
1954	356.32	366.00	2.7	− 8.1	Rep*
1958	536.88	554.26	3.2	− 23.9	Rep
1962	588.98	616.13	4.6	− 1.5	Dem
1966	809.63	819.09	1.2	− 15.9	Dem
1970	754.45	771.97	2.3	− 6.3	Rep
1974	659.34	667.16	1.2	− 25.0	Rep
1978	792.45	807.09	1.8	− 5.1	Dem
1982	1006.07	1051.78	4.5	− 13.5	Rep
1986	1845.47	1886.53	2.2	− 2.7	Rep
1990	2448.02	2488.61	1.7	− 4.6	Rep
1994	3863.37	3801.47	− 1.6	− 20.9	Dem*
1998	8366.04	8975.46	7.3	1.9	Dem
2002	8368.94	8537.13	2.0	3.6	Rep
		Total	51.9%		
		Average	2.9%		

*Control switches to other Party

NOVEMBER

November Begins "Best Six Months" for Dow & S&P and
"Best Eight Months" for NASDAQ (Pages 46, 50, 52, 54, 58, 138 & 139)

MONDAY
D **61.9**
S **61.9**
N 57.1

6

overwhelming evidence to the contrary. — Jim Rogers (Financier, *Adventure Capitalist*, b. 1942)

Election Day
Midterm Election Time Unusually Bullish (Page 102)

TUESDAY
D **38.1**
S **38.1**
N 52.4

7

It is impossible to please all the world and one's father. — Jean de La Fontaine (French poet, 1621-1695)
Never lend money to someone who must borrow money to pay interest [on other money owed].

WEDNESDAY
D **61.9**
S 57.1
N 57.1

8

— A Swiss banker's First Rule, quoted by Lester Thurow

Let us have the courage to stop borrowing to meet the continuing deficits. Stop the deficits.

THURSDAY
D **38.1**
S 47.6
N 57.1

9

— Franklin D. Roosevelt (32nd U.S. President, 1932, 1882-1945)
If the winds of fortune are temporarily blowing against you, remember that you can harness them
and make them carry you toward your definite purpose, through the use of your imagination.

FRIDAY
D 57.1
S 52.4
N 57.1

10

— Napoleon Hill (Author, *Think and Grow Rich*, 1883-1970)
Try to surround yourself with people who can give you a little happiness, because you can only pass through this life once, Jack.

Veterans' Day

SATURDAY

11

SUNDAY

12

MOST OF THE SO-CALLED "JANUARY EFFECT" TAKES PLACE IN THE LAST HALF OF DECEMBER

Over the years we reported annually on the fascinating January Effect, showing that small-cap stocks handily outperformed large-cap stocks during January 40 out of 43 years between 1953 and 1995. Readers saw that "Cats and Dogs" on average quadrupled the returns of blue chips in this period. Then, the January Effect disappeared over the next four years.

Looking at the graph on page 110, comparing the Russell 1000 index of large capitalization stocks to the Russell 2000 smaller capitalization stocks shows small cap stocks beginning to outperform the blue chips in mid-December. Narrowing the comparison down to half-month segments was an inspiration and proved to be quite revealing, as you can see in the table below.

18-YEAR AVERAGE RATES OF RETURN (DEC 1987 – FEB 2005)

From 12/15	Russell 1000 Change	Russell 1000 Annualized	Russell 2000 Change	Russell 2000 Annualized
12/15-12/31	2.1%	69.5%	3.5%	145.1%
12/15-01/15	2.3	30.8	4.3	65.0
12/15-01/31	3.2	28.2	5.0	48.2
12/15-02/15	4.1	27.4	6.7	47.8
12/15-02/28	3.6	19.4	7.0	40.0
From 12/31				
12/31-01/15	0.2	2.4	0.7	8.6
12/31-01/31	1.1	8.9	1.4	12.1
12/31-02/15	2.0	12.8	3.1	19.8
12/31-02/28	1.5	7.8	3.3	17.4

26-YEAR AVERAGE RATES OF RETURN (DEC 1979 – FEB 2005)

From 12/15	Russell 1000 Change	Russell 1000 Annualized	Russell 2000 Change	Russell 2000 Annualized
12/15-12/31	1.7%	56.4%	2.9%	112.8%
12/15-01/15	2.4	32.8	4.6	71.6
12/15-01/31	3.3	29.7	5.4	52.3
12/15-02/15	4.1	27.2	7.0	49.8
12/15-02/28	3.8	20.6	7.2	41.6
From 12/31				
12/31-01/15	0.6	8.1	1.6	21.0
12/31-01/31	1.6	13.2	2.4	20.6
12/31-02/15	2.4	15.0	3.9	25.8
12/31-02/28	2.1	10.8	4.1	22.3

Small-cap strength in the last half of December became even more magnified after the 1987 market crash. Note the dramatic shift in gains in the last half of December during the 18-year period starting in 1987, versus the 26 years from 1979 to 2005. With all the beaten-down small stocks being dumped for tax loss purposes, it generally pays to get a head start on the January Effect in mid-December. The leading small-cap sector was hit hardest in the January 2005 correction.

Monday Before November Expiration Dow Down 5 of Last 6 After Up 5 in a Row

MONDAY

D 47.6
S 42.9
N 47.6

13

You don't come back for an encore. — Elvis Presley (1935-1977)

🐂 **TUESDAY**

D **66.7**
S **66.7**
N **61.9**

14

The less a man knows about the past and the present, the more insecure must be his judgment of the future. — Sigmund Freud

Successful innovation is not a feat of intellect, but of will.

Week Before Thanksgiving S&P Up 11 of Last 13, 2003 Broke 11-Year Run

WEDNESDAY

D 52.4
S 47.6
N **38.1**

15

— Joseph A. Schumpeter (Austrian-American economist, *Theory of Economic Development*, 1883-1950)

THURSDAY

D **38.1**
S 42.9
N **23.8**

16

History is a collection of agreed upon lies. — Voltaire (French philosopher)
I don't know where speculation got such a bad name, since I know of no forward leap which was not fathered by speculation.

November Expiration Day Dow Down 4 of Last 6 After Up 4 in a Row

🐻 🐂 **FRIDAY**

D **61.9**
S **61.9**
N 57.1

17

— John Steinbeck
When a company reports higher earnings for its first quarter (over its previous year's first quarter), chances are almost five to one

SATURDAY

18

SUNDAY

19

TRADING THE THANKSGIVING MARKET

For 35 years the combination of the Wednesday before Thanksgiving and the Friday after had a great track record, except for two occasions. Attributing this phenomenon to the warm "holiday spirit" was a no-brainer. But publishing it in the 1987 Almanac was the "kiss of death." Wednesday, Friday and Monday were all crushed, down 6.6% over the three days in 1987. Since 1988 Wednesday-Friday lost six of seventeen times with a total Dow point-gain of 442.22 versus a Wednesday-Monday total Dow point-gain of 653.26 with only four losses. The best strategy seems to be going long into weakness Tuesday or Wednesday and staying in through the following Monday or exiting into strength.

DOW JONES INDUSTRIALS BEFORE AND AFTER THANKSGIVING

	Tuesday Before	Wednesday Before		Friday After	Total Gain Dow Points	Dow Close	Next Monday
1952	− 0.18	1.54		1.22	2.76	283.66	0.04
1953	1.71	0.65		2.45	3.10	280.23	1.14
1954	3.27	1.89		3.16	5.05	387.79	0.72
1955	4.61	0.71		0.26	0.97	482.88	− 1.92
1956	− 4.49	− 2.16		4.65	2.49	472.56	− 2.27
1957	− 9.04	10.69		3.84	14.53	449.87	− 2.96
1958	− 4.37	8.63		8.31	16.94	557.46	2.61
1959	2.94	1.41		1.42	2.83	652.52	6.66
1960	− 3.44	1.37		4.00	5.37	606.47	− 1.04
1961	− 0.77	1.10		2.18	3.28	732.60	− 0.61
1962	6.73	4.31	T	7.62	11.93	644.87	− 2.81
1963	32.03	− 2.52		9.52	7.00	750.52	1.39
1964	− 1.68	− 5.21	H	− 0.28	− 5.49	882.12	− 6.69
1965	2.56	N/C		− 0.78	− 0.78	948.16	− 1.23
1966	− 3.18	1.84	A	6.52	8.36	803.34	− 2.18
1967	13.17	3.07		3.58	6.65	877.60	4.51
1968	8.14	− 3.17	N	8.76	5.59	985.08	− 1.74
1969	− 5.61	3.23		1.78	5.01	812.30	− 7.26
1970	5.21	1.98	K	6.64	8.62	781.35	12.74
1971	− 5.18	0.66		17.96	18.62	816.59	13.14
1972	8.21	7.29	S	4.67	11.96	1025.21	− 7.45
1973	− 17.76	10.08		− 0.98	9.10	854.00	− 29.05
1974	5.32	2.03	G	− 0.63	1.40	618.66	− 15.64
1975	9.76	3.15		2.12	5.27	860.67	− 4.33
1976	− 6.57	1.66	I	5.66	7.32	956.62	− 6.57
1977	6.41	0.78		1.12	1.90	844.42	− 4.85
1978	− 1.56	2.95	V	3.12	6.07	810.12	3.72
1979	− 6.05	− 1.80		4.35	2.55	811.77	16.98
1980	3.93	7.00	I	3.66	10.66	993.34	− 23.89
1981	18.45	7.90		7.80	15.70	885.94	3.04
1982	− 9.01	9.01	N	7.36	16.37	1007.36	− 4.51
1983	7.01	− 0.20		1.83	1.63	1277.44	− 7.62
1984	9.83	6.40	G	18.78	25.18	1220.30	− 7.95
1985	0.12	18.92		− 3.56	15.36	1472.13	− 14.22
1986	6.05	4.64		− 2.53	2.11	1914.23	− 1.55
1987	40.45	− 16.58		− 36.47	− 53.05	1910.48	− 76.93
1988	11.73	14.58		− 17.60	− 3.02	2074.68	6.76
1989	7.25	17.49		18.77	36.26	2675.55	19.42
1990	− 35.15	9.16	D	− 12.13	− 2.97	2527.23	5.94
1991	14.08	− 16.10		− 5.36	− 21.46	2894.68	40.70
1992	25.66	17.56	A	15.94	33.50	3282.20	22.96
1993	3.92	13.41		− 3.63	9.78	3683.95	− 6.15
1994	− 91.52	− 3.36	Y	33.64	30.28	3708.27	31.29
1995	40.46	18.06		7.23*	25.29	5048.84	22.04
1996	− 19.38	− 29.07		22.36*	− 6.71	6521.70	N/C
1997	41.03	− 14.17		28.35*	14.18	7823.13	189.98
1998	− 73.12	13.13		18.80*	31.93	9333.08	− 216.53
1999	− 93.89	12.54		− 19.26*	− 6.72	10988.91	− 40.99
2000	31.85	− 95.18		70.91*	− 24.27	10470.23	75.84
2001	− 75.08	− 66.70		125.03*	58.33	9959.71	23.04
2002	− 172.98	255.26		− 35.59*	219.67	8896.09	− 33.52
2003	16.15	15.63		2.89*	18.52	9899.05	116.59
2004	3.18	27.71		1.92*	29.63	10475.90	− 46.33

*Shortened trading day

NOVEMBER

Trading Thanksgiving Market: Long into Weakness Prior, Exit into Strength After (Page 106)

MONDAY
D 52.4
S 52.4
N 57.1
20

it will also have increased earnings in its second quarter. — Niederhoffer, Cross & Zeckhauser

Everyone blames the foreigners when the economy goes south. Always. It is human nature to blame others, and it is the same all

TUESDAY
D 71.4
S 61.9
N 47.6
21

over the world. — Jim Rogers (Financier, *Adventure Capitalist*, b. 1942)
Pretend that every single person you meet has a sign around his or her neck that says, "Make me feel important." Not only will you

WEDNESDAY
D 71.4
S 61.9
N 66.7
22

succeed in sales, you will succeed in life. — Mary Kay Ash (Mary Kay Cosmetics)

The pursuit of gain is the only way in which people can serve the needs of others whom they do not know.

Thanksgiving (Market Closed)

THURSDAY
23

— Friedrich von Hayek (*Counterrevolution of Science*)
Awareness of competition and ability to react to it is a fundamental competence every business must have if it is to be long lived.

(Shortened Trading Day)

FRIDAY
D 71.4
S 66.7
N 61.9
24

— Paul Allen (Microsoft founder)
When someone told me "We're going with you guys because no one ever got fired for buying Cisco (products)."

SATURDAY
25

December Bullish Seasonalities: see pages 80 and 116.

SUNDAY
26

DECEMBER ALMANAC

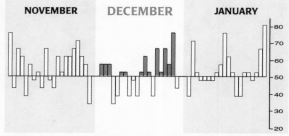

DECEMBER							JANUARY						
S	M	T	W	T	F	S	S	M	T	W	T	F	S
					1	2				1	2	3	4	5	6
3	4	5	6	7	8	9	7	8	9	10	11	12	13
10	11	12	13	14	15	16	14	15	16	17	18	19	20
17	18	19	20	21	22	23	21	22	23	24	25	26	27
24	25	26	27	28	29	30	28	29	30	31			
31													

Market Probability Chart above is a graphic representation of the S&P 500 Recent Market Probability Calendar on page 121.

◆ #1 S&P month average gain 1.7%, #2 Dow 1.8% since 1950 (page 46), #2 NASDAQ 2.1% since 1971 ◆ 2002 worst December since 1931 Dow & S&P, down over 6% Dow and S&P, –9.7% on NASDAQ (pages 141, 145 & 151) ◆ "Free lunch" served on Wall Street at month end (page 112) ◆ Small caps start to outperform larger caps near middle of month (pages 104 & 110) ◆ "Santa Claus Rally" visible in graph above and on page 114 ◆ In 1998 was part of best fourth quarter since 1928 ◆ Only four down Decembers last 14 Midterm Election Years.

DECEMBER DAILY POINT CHANGES DOW JONES INDUSTRIALS

Previous Month	1995	1996	1997	1998	1999	2000	2001	2002	2003	2004
Close	5074.49	6521.70	7823.13	9116.55	10877.81	10414.49	9851.56	8896.09	9782.46	10428.02
1	12.64	S	189.98	16.99	120.58	– 40.95	S	S	116.59	162.20
2	S	N/C	5.72	– 69.00	40.67	S	S	– 33.52	– 45.41	– 5.10
3	S	– 79.01	13.18	– 184.86	247.12	S	– 87.60	– 119.64	19.78	7.09
4	52.39	– 19.75	18.15	136.46	S	186.56	129.88	– 5.08	57.40	S
5	37.93	14.16	98.97	S	S	338.62	220.45	– 114.57	– 68.14	S
6	21.68	– 55.16	S	S	– 61.17	– 234.34	– 15.15	22.49	S	– 45.15
7	– 39.74	S	S	54.33	– 118.36	– 47.02	– 49.68	S	S	– 106.48
8	2.53	S	– 38.29	– 42.49	– 38.53	95.55	S	S	102.59	53.65
9	S	82.00	– 61.18	– 18.79	66.67	S	S	– 172.36	– 41.85	58.59
10	S	9.31	– 70.87	– 167.61	89.91	S	– 128.01	100.85	– 1.56	– 9.60
11	27.46	– 70.73	– 129.80	– 19.82	S	12.89	– 33.08	14.88	86.30	S
12	– 9.40	– 98.81	– 10.69	S	S	42.47	6.44	– 50.74	34.00	S
13	41.55	1.16	S	S	– 32.11	26.17	– 128.36	– 104.69	S	95.10
14	– 34.32	S	S	– 126.16	– 32.42	– 119.45	44.70	S	S	38.13
15	– 5.42	S	84.29	127.70	65.15	– 240.03	S	S	– 19.34	15.00
16	S	– 36.52	53.72	– 32.70	19.57	S	S	193.69	106.74	14.19
17	S	39.98	– 18.90	85.22	12.54	S	80.82	– 92.01	15.70	– 55.72
18	– 101.52	38.44	– 110.91	27.81	S	210.46	106.42	– 88.04	102.82	S
19	34.68	126.87	– 90.21	S	S	– 61.05	72.10	– 82.55	30.14	S
20	– 50.57	10.76	S	S	– 113.16	– 265.44	– 85.31	146.52	S	11.68
21	37.21	S	S	85.22	56.27	168.36	50.16	S	S	97.83
22	1.44	S	63.02	55.61	3.06	148.27	S	S	59.78	56.46
23	S	4.62	– 127.54	157.57	202.16	S	S	– 18.03	3.26	11.23
24	S	33.83*	– 31.64*	15.96*	H	S	N/C*	– 45.18*	– 36.07*	H
25	H	H	H	H	S	H	H	H	H	S
26	12.29	23.83	19.18*	S	S	56.88	52.80	– 15.50	19.48*	S
27	– 4.34	14.23	S	S	– 14.68	110.72	43.17	– 128.83	S	– 50.99
28	– 10.12	S	S	8.76	85.63	65.60	5.68	S	S	78.41
29	21.32	S	113.10	94.23	7.95	– 81.91	S	S	125.33	– 25.35
30	S	– 11.54	123.56	– 46.34	– 31.80	S	S	29.07	– 24.96	– 28.89
31	S	– 101.10	– 7.72	– 93.21	44.26	S	– 115.49	8.78	28.88	17.29
Close	5117.12	6448.27	7908.25	9181.43	11497.12	10786.85	10021.50	8341.63	10453.92	10783.01
Change	42.63	– 73.43	85.12	64.88	619.31	372.36	169.94	– 554.46	671.46	354.99

* Shortened trading day

If Santa Claus should fail to call
Bears may come to Broad and Wall

NOVEMBER/DECEMBER

MONDAY 27
D 71.4
S 71.4
N 57.1

That's what they used to say in IBM's golden age. — Mark Dickey (Formerly of Cisco, now at Smart Pipes, *Fortune*).

TUESDAY 28
D 57.1
S 61.9
N 61.9

In investing, the return you want should depend on whether you want to eat well or sleep well. — J. Kenfield Morley

WEDNESDAY 29
D 47.6
S 57.1
N 71.4

I have a simple philosophy. Fill what's empty. Empty what's full. And scratch where it itches. — Alice Roosevelt Longworth

THURSDAY 30
D 47.6
S 33.3
N 57.1

Central Bankers are brought up pulling the legs off ants. — Paul Volker (Quoted by William Grieder, *Secrets of the Temple*)
I've learned that only through focus can you do world-class things, no matter how capable you are.

FRIDAY 1
After Being Down 3 Straight First Trading Days 2000-2002, Dow Has Posted Back-to-Back 100+ Point Gains
D 52.4
S 57.1
N 71.4

— William H. Gates (Microsoft founder, *Fortune*, July 8, 2002)
What lies behind us and what lies before us are tiny matters, compared to what lies within us.

SATURDAY 2

SUNDAY 3

JANUARY EFFECT NOW STARTS IN MID-DECEMBER

Small-cap stocks tend to outperform big caps in January. Known as the "January Effect," the tendency is clearly revealed by the graph below. The 27 years of daily data for the Russell 2000 index of smaller companies are divided by the Russell 1000 index of largest companies. Then the 27 years are compressed into a single year to show an idealized year-ly pattern. When the graph is descending, big blue chips are outperforming smaller compa-nies; when the graph is rising, smaller companies are moving up faster than their larger brethren.

In a typical year the smaller fry stay on the sidelines while the big boys are on the field. Then, around late October, small stocks begin to wake up and in mid-December, they take off. So many year-end dividends, payouts and bonuses could be a factor. Other major moves are quite evident just before Labor Day — possibly because individual investors are back from vacations — and off the low points in late October and November. After a pause in mid-January, small caps take the lead through the end of February.

RUSSELL 2000/RUSSELL 1000 ONE-YEAR SEASONAL PATTERN

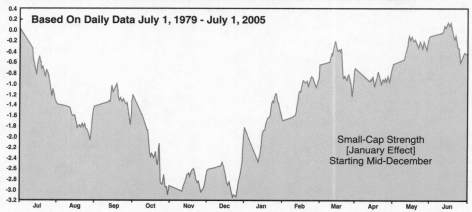

Based On Daily Data July 1, 1979 - July 1, 2005

Small-Cap Strength
[January Effect]
Starting Mid-December

The bottom graph shows the actual ratio of the Russell 2000 divided by the Russell 1000 from 1979. Smaller companies had the upper hand for five years into 1983 as the last major bear trend wound to a close and the nascent bull market logged its first year. After falling behind for about eight years, they came back after the Persian Gulf War bottom in 1990, mov-ing up until 1994 when big caps ruled the latter stages of the millennial bull. For six years the picture was bleak for small fry as the blue chips and tech stocks moved to stratospheric PE ratios. Small caps spiked in late 1999 and early 2000 and have been rising since 2001 with bursts after the bear market ended in October 2002 and the successful test in March 2003. As this first stage of the recovery matures, stocks with lower market capitalizations may pause — but watch for them to outperform first when the next bull phase is imminent.

RUSSELL 2000/RUSSELL 1000 (1979 - JUNE 2005)

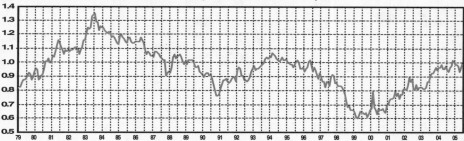

DECEMBER

MONDAY 4
D 61.9
S 57.1
N 66.7

— Ralph Waldo Emerson (American author, poet and philosopher, *Self-Reliance*, 1803-1882)

Analysts are supposed to be critics of corporations. They often end up being public relations spokesmen for them.

TUESDAY 5
D 52.4
S 57.1
N 66.7

— Ralph Wanger (Chief Investment Officer, Acorn Fund)

WEDNESDAY 6
D 42.9
S 33.3
N 57.1

The true mystery of the world is the visible, not the invisible. — Oscar Wilde (Irish-born writer and wit)

The very purpose of existence is to reconcile the glowing opinion we hold of ourselves with the appalling things that other people

Small Cap Strength Starts in Mid-December (Pages 104 & 110)

THURSDAY 7
D 33.3
S 38.1
N 33.3

think about us. — Quentin Crisp (Author, performer, 1908-1999)

FRIDAY 8
D 57.1
S 52.4
N 42.9

When they stop joking with you is when they don't give a damn about you. — Sammy Davis Jr. (American entertainer, 1925-1990)

SATURDAY 9

SUNDAY 10

WALL STREET'S ONLY "FREE LUNCH" SERVED AT YEAR-END

Investors tend to get rid of their losers near year-end for tax purposes, often hammering these stocks down to bargain levels. Over the years the *Almanac* has shown that NYSE stocks selling at their lows on December 15 will usually outperform the market by February 15 in the following year. Preferred stocks, closed-end funds, splits and new issues are eliminated. When there are a huge number of new lows, stocks down the most are selected, even though there are usually good reasons why some stocks have been battered.

BARGAIN STOCKS VS. THE MARKET**

Short Span** Late Dec - Jan/Feb	New Lows Late Dec	% Change Jan/Feb	% Change NYSE Composite	Bargain Stocks Advantage
1974-75	112	48.9%	22.1%	26.8%
1975-76	21	34.9	14.9	20.0
1976-77	2	1.3	− 3.3	4.6
1977-78	15	2.8	− 4.5	7.3
1978-79	43	11.8	3.9	7.9
1979-80	5	9.3	6.1	3.2
1980-81	14	7.1	− 2.0	9.1
1981-82	21	− 2.6	− 7.4	4.8
1982-83	4	33.0	9.7	23.3
1983-84	13	− 3.2	− 3.8	0.6
1984-85	32	19.0	12.1	6.9
1985-86	4	− 22.5	3.9	− 26.4
1986-87	22	9.3	12.5	− 3.2
1987-88	23	13.2	6.8	6.4
1988-89	14	30.0	6.4	23.6
1989-90	25	− 3.1	− 4.8	1.7
1990-91	18	18.8	12.6	6.2
1991-92	23	51.1	7.7	43.4
1992-93	9	8.7	0.6	8.1
1993-94	10	− 1.4	2.0	− 3.4
1994-95	25	14.6	5.7	8.9
1995-96	5	− 11.3	4.5	−15.8
1996-97	16	13.9	11.2	2.7
1997-98	29	9.9	5.7	4.2
1998-99	40	− 2.8	4.3	− 7.1
1999-00	26*	8.9	− 5.4	14.3
2000-01	51[1]	44.4	0.1	44.3
2001-02	12[2]	31.4	− 2.3	33.7
2002-03	33[3]	28.7	3.9	24.8
2003-04	15[4]	16.7	2.3	14.4
2004-05	36[5]	6.8	− 2.8	9.6
31-Year Totals**		**427.8%**	**122.7%**	**304.9%**
Average**		**13.8%**	**4.0%**	**9.8%**

** Dec 15 - Feb 15 (1974-1999) * Chosen 12/29/99 [1] Chosen 12/27/00 [2] 12/26/01-1/16/02, incl NAS stocks
[3] 12/26/02-1/14/03, incl NAS & AMEX stocks [4] 12/26/03-1/13/04, incl NAS, AMEX & OTCBB stocks
[5] 12/28/04-1/11/05, incl NAS, AMEX & OTCBB stocks

However, as tax selling in recent years seems to be continuing down to the last few days of the year, we've altered the strategy the last six years to make our selections from stocks making new lows on the fourth-to-last trading day of the year. We tweaked the strategy further the last four years as few NYSE stocks were left after our screens, adding selections from NASDAQ, AMEX and the OTC Bulletin Board, and e-mailing them to our *Almanac Investor* newsletter subscribers. Over the past few years these stocks tend to start giving back their gains in January. We have advised subscribers to sell in mid-January. Subscribers will receive the list of stocks selected December 27, 2005, via e-mail.

This "Free Lunch" strategy is only an extremely short-term strategy reserved for the nimblest traders. It has performed better after market corrections and when there are more New Lows at year-end. The object is to buy bargain stocks near their 52-week lows and sell any quick, generous gains, as these issues can often be real dogs.

Examination of December trades by NYSE members through the years shows they tend to buy on balance during this month, contrary to other months. See more in our February 2004 and 2005 *Almanac Investor Newsletters* at *stocktradersalmanac.com*.

Monday Before December Triple Witching Dow Up 4 of Last 5 — 2002 Up 2.3%

MONDAY
D 57.1
S 52.4
N 42.9
11

If you don't know who you are, the stock market is an expensive place to find out. — George Goodman (1959)

A national debt, if it is not excessive, will be to us a national blessing.

FOMC Meeting

TUESDAY
D 52.4
S 38.1
N 33.3
12

— Alexander Hamilton (U.S. Treasury Secretary 1789-1795, The Federalist 1788, in April 30, 1781, letter to Robert Morris)
If all the economists in the world were laid end to end, they still wouldn't reach a conclusion.

Triple-Witching Week Dow Up 19 of Last 21

WEDNESDAY
D 42.9
S 47.6
N 57.1
13

— George Bernard Shaw (Irish dramatist, 1856-1950)

THURSDAY
D 42.9
S 38.1
N 38.1
14

Small volume is usually accompanied by a fall in price; large volume by a rise in price. — Charles C. Ying (Computer study)
New indicator: CFO Magazine gave Excellence awards to WorldCom's Scott Sullivan (1998), Enron's Andrew Fastow (1999), and to Tyco's Mark Swartz (2000). All were subsequently indicted.

December Triple Witching Dow Up 18 of 25

FRIDAY
D 57.1
S 52.4
N 52.4
15

— Roger Lowenstein (Financial journalist and author, Origins of the Crash, b. 1954)
People become attached to their burdens, sometimes more than the burdens are attached to them.

Chanukah

SATURDAY
16

SUNDAY
17

IF SANTA CLAUS SHOULD FAIL TO CALL BEARS MAY COME TO BROAD & WALL

Santa Claus tends to come to Wall Street nearly every year, bringing a short, sweet, respectable rally within the last five days of the year and the first two in January. This has been good for an average 1.6% gain since 1969 (1.5% since 1950). Santa's failure to show tends to precede bear markets, or times stocks could be purchased later in the year at much lower prices. Such occasions provide opportunities for long-term players to at least write options on their stocks. We discovered this phenomenon in 1972.

DAILY % CHANGE IN S&P 500 AT YEAR-END

	Trading Days Before Year-End						First Days in January			Rally % Change
	6	5	4	3	2	1	1	2	3	
1969	− 0.4	1.1	0.8	− 0.7	0.4	0.5	1.0	0.5	− 0.7	3.6
1970	0.1	0.6	0.5	1.1	0.2	− 0.1	− 1.1	0.7	0.6	1.9
1971	− 0.4	0.2	1.0	0.3	− 0.4	0.3	− 0.4	0.4	1.0	1.3
1972	− 0.3	− 0.7	0.6	0.4	0.5	1.0	0.9	0.4	− 0.1	3.1
1973	− 1.1	− 0.7	3.1	2.1	− 0.2	0.01	0.1	2.2	− 0.9	6.7
1974	− 1.4	1.4	0.8	− 0.4	0.03	2.1	2.4	0.7	0.5	7.2
1975	0.7	0.8	0.9	− 0.1	− 0.4	0.5	0.8	1.8	1.0	4.3
1976	0.1	1.2	0.7	− 0.4	0.5	0.5	− 0.4	− 1.2	− 0.9	0.8
1977	0.8	0.9	N/C	0.1	0.2	0.2	− 1.3	− 0.3	− 0.8	− 0.3
1978	0.03	1.7	1.3	− 0.9	− 0.4	− 0.2	0.6	1.1	0.8	3.3
1979	− 0.6	0.1	0.1	0.2	− 0.1	0.1	− 2.0	− 0.5	1.2	− 2.2
1980	− 0.4	0.4	0.5	− 1.1	0.2	0.3	0.4	1.2	0.1	2.0
1981	− 0.5	0.2	− 0.2	− 0.5	0.5	0.2	0.2	− 2.2	− 0.7	− 1.8
1982	0.6	1.8	− 1.0	0.3	− 0.7	0.2	− 1.6	2.2	0.4	1.2
1983	− 0.2	− 0.03	0.9	0.3	− 0.2	0.05	− 0.5	1.7	1.2	2.1
1984	− 0.5	0.8	− 0.2	− 0.4	0.3	0.6	− 1.1	− 0.5	− 0.5	− 0.6
1985	− 1.1	− 0.7	0.2	0.9	0.5	0.3	− 0.8	0.6	− 0.1	1.1
1986	− 1.0	0.2	0.1	− 0.9	− 0.5	− 0.5	1.8	2.3	0.2	2.4
1987	1.3	− 0.5	− 2.6	− 0.4	1.3	− 0.3	3.6	1.1	0.1	2.2
1988	− 0.2	0.3	− 0.4	0.1	0.8	− 0.6	− 0.9	1.5	0.2	0.9
1989	0.6	0.8	− 0.2	0.6	0.5	0.8	1.8	− 0.3	− 0.9	4.1
1990	0.5	− 0.6	0.3	− 0.8	0.1	0.5	− 1.1	− 1.4	− 0.3	− 3.0
1991	2.5	0.6	1.4	0.4	2.1	0.5	0.04	0.5	− 0.3	5.7
1992	− 0.3	0.2	− 0.1	− 0.3	0.2	− 0.7	− 0.1	− 0.2	0.04	− 1.1
1993	0.01	0.7	0.1	− 0.1	− 0.4	− 0.5	− 0.2	0.3	0.1	− 0.1
1994	0.01	0.2	0.4	− 0.3	0.1	− 0.4	− 0.03	0.3	− 0.1	0.2
1995	0.8	0.2	0.4	0.04	− 0.1	0.3	0.8	0.1	− 0.6	1.8
1996	− 0.3	0.5	0.6	0.1	− 0.4	− 1.7	− 0.5	1.5	− 0.1	0.1
1997	− 1.5	− 0.7	0.4	1.8	1.8	− 0.04	0.5	0.2	− 1.1	4.0
1998	2.1	− 0.2	− 0.1	1.3	− 0.8	− 0.2	− 0.1	1.4	2.2	1.3
1999	1.6	− 0.1	0.04	0.4	0.1	0.3	− 1.0	− 3.8	0.2	− 4.0
2000	0.8	2.4	0.7	1.0	0.4	− 1.0	− 2.8	5.0	− 1.1	5.7
2001	0.4	− 0.02	0.4	0.7	0.3	− 1.1	0.6	0.9	0.6	1.8
2002	0.2	− 0.5	− 0.3	− 1.6	0.5	0.05	3.3	− 0.05	2.2	1.2
2003	0.3	− 0.2	0.2	1.2	0.01	0.2	− 0.3	1.2	0.1	2.4
2004	0.1	− 0.4	0.7	− 0.01	0.01	− 0.1	− 0.8	− 1.2	− 0.4	− 1.8
Avg	0.09	0.33	0.34	0.12	0.19	0.06	0.05	0.50	0.09	1.6

The couplet above was certainly on the mark in 2000, as the period suffered a horrendous 4.0% loss. On January 14, 2000, the Dow started its 33-month 37.8% slide to the October 2002 midterm election year bottom. NASDAQ cracked eight weeks later, falling 37.3% in 10 weeks, eventually dropping 77.9% by October 2002. This is reminiscent of the Dow during the Depression, when the Dow initially fell 47.9% in just over two months from 381.17 September 3, 1929, only to end down 89.2% at its 20th century low of 41.22 on July 8, 1932. Perhaps October 9, 2002, will prove to be the low for the 21st century. Saddam Hussein cancelled Christmas by invading Kuwait in 1990. Energy prices and Middle East terror woes may have grounded Santa in 2004. Corrections and gyrations ensued in early 2005, keeping the averages mixed with single-digit gains at best at press-time. Less bullishness on last day is due to last-minute portfolio restructuring. Pushing gains and losses into the next tax year often affects year's first trading day.

Week After Triple Witching Dow Up 11 of Last 14

MONDAY
D **66.7**
S **61.9**
N 52.4
18

— George Bernard Shaw (Irish dramatist, 1856-1950)

The job of central banks: To take away the punch bowl just as the party is getting going.

TUESDAY
D 47.6
S 52.4
N 52.4
19

— William McChesney Martin (Federal Reserve Chairman 1951-1970, 1906-1998)
There is no tool to change human nature...people are prone to recurring bouts of optimism and pessimism that manifest themselves from time to time in the buildup or cessation of speculative excesses.

WEDNESDAY
D 47.6
S **38.1**
N 52.4
20

— Alan Greenspan (Fed Chairman, July 18, 2001 monetary policy report to the Congress)

Inflation is the one form of taxation that can be imposed without legislation.

Watch for the Santa Claus Rally (Page 114)

THURSDAY
D **61.9**
S **66.7**
N **76.2**
21

— Milton Friedman (American economist, 1976 Nobel Prize, b. 1912)
Statements by high officials are practically always misleading when they are designed to bolster a falling market.

Last Trading Day Before Christmas Has Been Weak 4 in a Row

FRIDAY
D 57.1
S 52.4
N **61.9**
22

— Gerald M. Loeb

SATURDAY
23

SUNDAY
24

SECTOR SEASONALITY: SELECTED PERCENTAGE PLAYS

Sector seasonality was featured in the first *1968 Almanac*. A Merrill Lynch study showed that buying seven sectors around September or October and selling in the first few months of 1954-1964 tripled the gains of holding them for ten years. Over the past few years we have honed this strategy significantly and now devote a large portion of our time and resources to investing during seasonably favorable periods for different sectors with Exchange Traded Funds (ETFs).

This year, in addition to updating the seasonalities, we have specified beginning third (B), middle third (M) or last third (E) of the month. Below is a sampling of the major seasonalities.

As the ETF universe expands at breakneck speed, more seasonal investment options become available to Almanac Investors. Check our archives at *stocktradersalmanac.com* for updates and revisions to the strategy. We provide entry and exit points to *Almanac Investor* newsletter subscribers. Our new book *Almanac Investor* details sector seasonality and ETFs at length.

SECTOR INDEX SEASONALITY TABLE

Ticker	Sector Index	Start		Finish		Average % Return † 10-Year	5-Year
XNG	Natural Gas	February	E	June	B	19.6	10.4
RXH	Healthcare Prov	March	E	June	M	15.1	14.4
XCI	Computer Tech	April	M	July	M	16.2	6.8
RXP	Healthcare Prod	April	M	July	B	10.4	4.2
MSH	High-Tech	April	M	July	M	16.5	7.8
IIX	Internet	April	M	July	B	17.4	10.3
BTK	Biotech	July	E	March	B	44.9	8.0
XAU	Gold & Silver	July	E	September	E	18.6	18.6
UTY	Utilities	July	E	January	B	12.9	16.8
CMR	Consumer	September	E	June	B	16.4	12.5
RXP	Healthcare Prod ‡	September	B	February	M	14.9	11.0
RXH	Healthcare Prov ‡	September	E	January	B	12.6	12.9
DRG	Pharmaceutical	September	B	February	M	16.0	6.1
XTC	Telecom	September	E	January	M	22.5	21.2
BKX	Banking	October	B	June	B	21.2	16.0
XBD	Broker/Dealer	October	B	April	M	44.5	16.1
XCI	Computer Tech	October	B	February	B	24.3	13.2
CYC	Cyclical	October	B	May	M	21.0	21.8
MSH	High-Tech	October	B	January	M	28.5	22.8
IIX	Internet	October	B	January	B	39.5	25.6
S5MATR *	Materials	October	M	May	M	17.2	20.0
RMS**	Real Estate	October	E	July	B	18.8	23.3
SOX	Semiconductor	October	E	December	B	22.1	20.7
DJT	Transports	October	B	May	B	20.4	16.8
XOI	Oil	December	M	June	M	16.2	19.0

† Average % return based on full seasonality completion through July 2005   ‡ Only nine years of data
* S5MATR Available @ bloomberg.com   ** RMS changed to RMZ June 2005

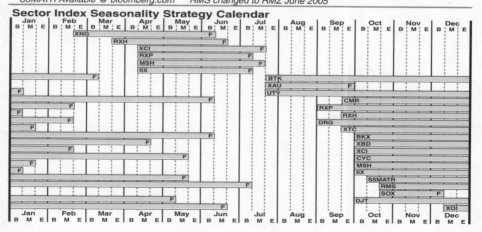

Sector Index Seasonality Strategy Calendar

Christmas Day (Market Closed)

MONDAY
25

The power to tax involves the power to destroy. — John Marshall (U.S. Supreme Court, 1819)

First Trading Day After Christmas Dow Up 9 in a Row 1990-1998, Down 3 of Last 6

TUESDAY
26
D 76.2
S 66.7
N 66.7

A leader has the ability to create infectious enthusiasm. — Ted Turner (Billionaire, *New Yorker Magazine*, April 23, 2001)

A good trader has to have three things: a chronic inability to accept things at face value, to feel continuously unsettled,

FREE LUNCH Menu of New Lows E-mailed to Almanac Investor *Subscribers*

WEDNESDAY
27
D 57.1
S 57.1
N 57.1

and to have humility. — Michael Steinhardt

THURSDAY
28
D 57.1
S 76.2
N 71.4

I do not rule Russia; ten thousand clerks do. — Nicholas I (1795-1855)

The fear of capitalism has compelled socialism to widen freedom, and the fear of socialism has compelled

Last Day of the Year Dow Down 6 of Last 9,
NASDAQ Down 5 Straight After Being Up 29 in a Row!

FRIDAY
29
D 42.9
S 42.9
N 76.2

capitalism to increase equality. — Will and Ariel Durant
When a country lives on borrowed time, borrowed money and borrowed energy, it is just begging the markets to discipline it in their own way at their own time. Usually the markets do it in an orderly way—except when they don't.
— Thomas L. Friedman (Op-ed columnist, *New York Times*, February 24, 2005)

SATURDAY
30

January Bullish Seasonalities: see pages 80 and 116.

SUNDAY
31

2007 STRATEGY CALENDAR

(Option expiration dates encircled)

	MONDAY	TUESDAY	WEDNESDAY	THURSDAY	FRIDAY	SATURDAY	SUNDAY
JANUARY	1 JANUARY New Year's Day	2	3	4	5	6	7
	8	9	10	11	12	13	14
	15 Martin Luther King Day	16	17	18	(19)	20	21
	22	23	24	25	26	27	28
FEBRUARY	29	30	31	1 FEBRUARY	2	3	4
	5	6	7	8	9	10	11
	12	13	14 ♥	15	(16)	17	18
	19 Presidents' Day	20	21 Ash Wednesday	22	23	24	25
MARCH	26	27	28	1 MARCH	2	3	4
	5	6	7	8	9	10	11 Daylight Saving Time Begins
	12	13	14	15	(16)	17 St. Patrick's Day ♣	18
	19	20	21	22	23	24	25
APRIL	26	27	28	29	30	31	1 APRIL
	2	3 Passover	4	5	6 Good Friday	7	8 Easter
	9	10	11	12	13	14	15
	16	17	18	19	(20)	21	22
	23	24	25	26	27	28	29
MAY	30	1 MAY	2	3	4	5	6
	7	8	9	10	11	12	13 Mother's Day
	14	15	16	17	(18)	19	20
	21	22	23	24	25	26	27
JUNE	28 Memorial Day	29	30	31	1 JUNE	2	3
	4	5	6	7	8	9	10
	11	12	13	14	(15)	16	17 Father's Day
	18	19	20	21	22	23	24
	25	26	27	28	29	30	1 JULY

Market closed on shaded weekdays; closes early when half-shaded.

118

2007 STRATEGY CALENDAR
(Option expiration dates encircled)

MONDAY	TUESDAY	WEDNESDAY	THURSDAY	FRIDAY	SATURDAY	SUNDAY	
2	3	4 Independence Day	5	6	7	8	JULY
9	10	11	12	13	14	15	JULY
16	17	18	19	(20)	21	22	JULY
23	24	25	26	27	28	29	JULY
30	31	1 AUGUST	2	3	4	5	AUGUST
6	7	8	9	10	11	12	AUGUST
13	14	15	16	(17)	18	19	AUGUST
20	21	22	23	24	25	26	AUGUST
27	28	29	30	31	1 SEPTEMBER	2	SEPTEMBER
3 Labor Day	4	5	6	7	8	9	SEPTEMBER
10	11	12	13 Rosh Hashanah	14	15	16	SEPTEMBER
17	18	19	20	(21)	22 Yom Kippur	23	SEPTEMBER
24	25	26	27	28	29	30	SEPTEMBER
1 OCTOBER	2	3	4	5	6	7	OCTOBER
8 Columbus Day	9	10	11	12	13	14	OCTOBER
15	16	17	18	(19)	20	21	OCTOBER
22	23	24	25	26	27	28	OCTOBER
29	30	31	1 NOVEMBER	2	3	4 Daylight Saving Time Ends	NOVEMBER
5	6 Election Day	7	8	9	10	11 Veterans' Day	NOVEMBER
12	13	14	15	(16)	17	18	NOVEMBER
19	20	21	22 Thanksgiving	23	24	25	NOVEMBER
26	27	28	29	30	1 DECEMBER	2	DECEMBER
3	4	5 Chanukah	6	7	8	9	DECEMBER
10	11	12	13	14	15	16	DECEMBER
17	18	19	20	(21)	22	23	DECEMBER
24	25 Christmas	26	27	28	29	30	DECEMBER
31	1 JANUARY New Year's Day	2	3	4	5	6	

S&P 500 MARKET PROBABILITY CALENDAR 2006

THE % CHANCE OF THE MARKET RISING ON ANY TRADING DAY OF THE YEAR*

(Based on the number of times the S&P 500 rose on a particular trading day during January 1954-December 2004)

Date	Jan	Feb	Mar	Apr	May	Jun	Jul	Aug	Sep	Oct	Nov	Dec
1	S	56.9	60.8	S	54.9	54.9	S	47.1	62.8	S	64.7	49.0
2	H	56.9	62.8	S	70.6	60.8	S	43.1	S	49.0	54.9	S
3	47.1	51.0	62.8	62.8	58.8	S	66.7	47.1	S	70.6	70.6	S
4	74.5	S	S	56.9	43.1	S	H	52.9	H	52.9	S	51.0
5	52.9	S	S	52.9	41.2	56.9	58.8	S	56.9	62.8	S	60.8
6	49.0	47.1	47.1	54.9	S	56.9	51.0	S	58.8	49.0	52.9	56.9
7	S	49.0	47.1	54.9	S	51.0	60.8	58.8	43.1	S	43.1	41.2
8	S	41.2	58.8	S	49.0	41.2	S	45.1	49.0	S	60.8	49.0
9	45.1	41.2	58.8	S	51.0	41.2	S	54.9	S	49.0	62.8	S
10	49.0	62.8	47.1	60.8	52.9	S	60.8	47.1	S	37.3	56.9	S
11	51.0	S	S	64.7	47.1	S	54.9	47.1	49.0	45.1	S	54.9
12	52.9	S	S	51.0	52.9	62.8	51.0	S	52.9	52.9	S	47.1
13	60.8	47.1	60.8	49.0	S	60.8	47.1	S	62.8	51.0	45.1	47.1
14	S	43.1	45.1	H	S	54.9	72.6	68.6	51.0	S	52.9	43.1
15	S	52.9	62.8	S	54.9	54.9	S	62.8	51.0	S	49.0	47.1
16	H	33.3	62.8	S	49.0	47.1	S	54.9	S	51.0	47.1	S
17	64.7	51.0	54.9	62.8	56.9	S	54.9	51.0	S	54.9	54.9	S
18	54.9	S	S	62.8	41.2	S	41.2	52.9	51.0	37.3	S	56.9
19	52.9	S	S	56.9	45.1	54.9	41.2	S	47.1	68.6	S	47.1
20	47.1	H	51.0	51.0	S	39.2	47.1	S	52.9	49.0	54.9	45.1
21	S	43.1	47.1	54.9	S	51.0	43.1	45.1	52.9	S	58.8	47.1
22	S	41.2	45.1	S	54.9	54.9	S	58.8	37.3	S	64.7	58.8
23	45.1	37.3	43.1	S	43.1	43.1	S	47.1	S	35.3	H	S
24	60.8	56.9	51.0	45.1	54.9	S	43.1	51.0	S	39.2	60.8	S
25	52.9	S	S	58.8	45.1	S	56.9	49.0	49.0	33.3	S	H
26	51.0	S	S	47.1	45.1	39.2	54.9	S	51.0	58.8	S	72.6
27	43.1	51.0	41.2	43.1	S	37.3	51.0	S	54.9	60.8	68.6	54.9
28	S	62.8	49.0	60.8	S	49.0	62.8	45.1	49.0	S	58.8	66.7
29	S		56.9	S	H	60.8	S	52.9	45.1	S	54.9	68.6
30	66.7		35.3	S	52.9	52.9	S	47.1	S	58.8	49.0	S
31	66.7		41.2		60.8		68.6	66.7		54.9		S

* See new trends developing on pages 60, 88 and 136

RECENT S&P 500 MARKET PROBABILITY CALENDAR 2006

THE % CHANCE OF THE MARKET RISING ON ANY TRADING DAY OF THE YEAR*

(Based on the number of times the S&P 500 rose on a particular trading day during January 1984-December 2004**)

Date	Jan	Feb	Mar	Apr	May	Jun	Jul	Aug	Sep	Oct	Nov	Dec
1	S	52.4	47.6	S	61.9	61.9	S	47.6	52.4	S	76.2	57.1
2	H	57.1	57.1	S	71.4	71.4	S	42.9	S	61.9	42.9	S
3	38.1	61.9	61.9	57.1	52.4	S	76.2	42.9	S	61.9	66.7	S
4	71.4	S	S	57.1	23.8	S	H	52.4	H	38.1	S	57.1
5	52.4	S	S	47.6	23.8	52.4	52.4	S	47.6	57.1	S	57.1
6	47.6	38.1	47.6	57.1	S	52.4	33.3	S	42.9	33.3	61.9	33.3
7	S	47.6	52.4	42.9	S	47.6	61.9	57.1	38.1	S	38.1	38.1
8	S	47.6	61.9	S	52.4	33.3	S	52.4	52.4	S	57.1	52.4
9	47.6	42.9	42.9	S	61.9	42.9	S	42.9	S	47.6	47.6	S
10	47.6	71.4	42.9	57.1	57.1	S	61.9	47.6	S	28.6	52.4	S
11	47.6	S	S	57.1	66.7	S	38.1	38.1	52.4	42.9	S	52.4
12	52.4	S	S	42.9	61.9	52.4	61.9	S	52.4	71.4	S	38.1
13	57.1	57.1	61.9	47.6	S	52.4	71.4	S	57.1	71.4	42.9	47.6
14	S	42.9	47.6	H	S	66.7	81.0	71.4	57.1	S	66.7	38.1
15	S	71.4	66.7	S	57.1	57.1	S	57.1	47.6	S	47.6	52.4
16	H	28.6	71.4	S	42.9	57.1	S	71.4	S	57.1	42.9	S
17	76.2	33.3	57.1	61.9	66.7	S	47.6	57.1	S	57.1	61.9	S
18	61.9	S	S	66.7	57.1	S	47.6	61.9	47.6	38.1	S	61.9
19	52.4	S	S	61.9	57.1	61.9	38.1	S	42.9	76.2	S	52.4
20	38.1	H	52.4	42.9	S	42.9	52.4	S	57.1	57.1	52.4	38.1
21	S	38.1	38.1	61.9	S	47.6	28.6	42.9	38.1	S	61.9	66.7
22	S	52.4	47.6	S	52.4	71.4	S	57.1	38.1	S	61.9	52.4
23	38.1	38.1	38.1	S	33.3	33.3	S	52.4	S	42.9	H	S
24	52.4	52.4	52.4	33.3	76.2	S	38.1	66.7	S	28.6	66.7	S
25	52.4	S	S	61.9	52.4	S	76.2	52.4	38.1	42.9	S	H
26	47.6	S	S	57.1	52.4	38.1	57.1	S	52.4	52.4	S	66.7
27	52.4	57.1	52.4	52.4	S	28.6	52.4	S	57.1	66.7	71.4	57.1
28	S	66.7	47.6	61.9	S	52.4	71.4	57.1	61.9	S	61.9	76.2
29	S		61.9	S	H	71.4	S	52.4	52.4	S	57.1	42.9
30	66.7		28.6	S	57.1	47.6	S	38.1	S	81.0	33.3	S
31	81.0		47.6		57.1		76.2	52.4		57.1		S

See new trends developing on pages 60, 88 and 136 ** Based on most recent 21-year period

DOW JONES INDUSTRIALS MARKET PROBABILITY CALENDAR 2006
THE % CHANCE OF THE MARKET RISING ON ANY TRADING DAY OF THE YEAR*

(Based on the number of times the DJIA rose on a particular trading day during January 1954-December 2004)

Date	Jan	Feb	Mar	Apr	May	Jun	Jul	Aug	Sep	Oct	Nov	Dec
1	S	54.9	66.7	S	54.9	56.9	S	45.1	60.8	S	64.7	47.1
2	H	54.9	68.6	S	62.8	52.9	S	45.1	S	49.0	49.0	S
3	54.9	39.2	60.8	56.9	52.9	S	60.8	47.1	S	62.8	68.6	S
4	74.5	S	S	56.9	49.0	S	H	52.9	H	51.0	S	54.9
5	49.0	S	S	52.9	43.1	56.9	62.8	S	58.8	60.8	S	62.8
6	54.9	52.9	49.0	60.8	S	58.8	58.8	S	58.8	47.1	56.9	58.8
7	S	45.1	45.1	52.9	S	52.9	56.9	56.9	43.1	S	43.1	45.1
8	S	41.2	54.9	S	47.1	41.2	S	45.1	45.1	S	62.8	43.1
9	49.0	45.1	58.8	S	51.0	35.3	S	49.0	S	51.0	52.9	S
10	47.1	62.8	51.0	58.8	49.0	S	60.8	51.0	S	39.2	58.8	S
11	47.1	S	S	64.7	49.0	S	54.9	45.1	39.2	39.2	S	54.9
12	47.1	S	S	62.8	54.9	60.8	52.9	S	52.9	54.9	S	58.8
13	58.8	41.2	54.9	54.9	S	56.9	37.3	S	58.8	56.9	45.1	41.2
14	S	51.0	49.0	H	S	54.9	64.7	66.7	47.1	S	51.0	51.0
15	S	54.9	58.8	S	52.9	49.0	S	58.8	51.0	S	56.9	47.1
16	H	35.3	62.8	S	45.1	49.0	S	52.9	S	52.9	47.1	S
17	56.9	47.1	56.9	72.6	54.9	S	47.1	43.1	S	51.0	52.9	S
18	60.8	S	S	64.7	45.1	S	43.1	52.9	49.0	41.2	S	58.8
19	41.2	S	S	54.9	49.0	49.0	45.1	S	39.2	62.8	S	52.9
20	37.3	H	51.0	52.9	S	41.2	47.1	S	47.1	49.0	51.0	54.9
21	S	51.0	45.1	51.0	S	52.9	45.1	45.1	47.1	S	60.8	49.0
22	S	35.3	39.2	S	47.1	51.0	S	58.8	41.2	S	68.6	60.8
23	41.2	45.1	49.0	S	33.3	43.1	S	49.0	S	37.3	H	S
24	47.1	60.8	35.3	49.0	54.9	S	47.1	51.0	S	47.1	60.8	S
25	58.8	S	S	58.8	41.2	S	58.8	51.0	51.0	27.5	S	H
26	56.9	S	S	51.0	43.1	41.2	54.9	S	52.9	51.0	S	72.6
27	47.1	47.1	49.0	45.1	S	47.1	47.1	S	47.1	56.9	64.7	51.0
28	S	54.9	47.1	54.9	S	43.1	60.8	45.1	49.0	S	56.9	56.9
29	S		56.9	S	H	56.9	S	52.9	41.2	S	51.0	56.9
30	64.7		41.2	S	52.9	54.9	S	41.2	S	60.8	51.0	S
31	60.8		41.2		62.8		56.9	62.8		54.9		S

See new trends developing on pages 60, 88 and 136

THE % CHANCE OF THE MARKET RISING ON ANY TRADING DAY OF THE YEAR*

(Based on the number of times the DJIA rose on a particular trading day during January 1984-December 2004**)

Date	Jan	Feb	Mar	Apr	May	Jun	Jul	Aug	Sep	Oct	Nov	Dec
1	S	52.4	57.1	S	61.9	71.4	S	42.9	47.6	S	76.2	52.4
2	H	52.4	66.7	S	66.7	57.1	S	52.4	S	66.7	38.1	S
3	57.1	42.9	61.9	61.9	42.9	S	71.4	42.9	S	47.6	66.7	S
4	71.4	S	S	57.1	38.1	S	H	52.4	H	33.3	S	61.9
5	47.6	S	S	42.9	28.6	57.1	57.1	S	57.1	61.9	S	52.4
6	57.1	38.1	47.6	71.4	S	61.9	33.3	S	47.6	38.1	61.9	42.9
7	S	52.4	52.4	38.1	S	47.6	57.1	52.4	33.3	S	38.1	33.3
8	S	38.1	52.4	S	57.1	42.9	S	47.6	47.6	S	61.9	57.1
9	42.9	47.6	52.4	S	66.7	33.3	S	47.6	S	52.4	38.1	S
10	47.6	61.9	47.6	57.1	61.9	S	57.1	52.4	S	28.6	57.1	S
11	47.6	S	S	61.9	66.7	S	42.9	42.9	38.1	38.1	S	57.1
12	57.1	S	S	57.1	57.1	57.1	71.4	S	57.1	71.4	S	52.4
13	52.4	52.4	47.6	57.1	S	42.9	61.9	S	61.9	71.4	47.6	42.9
14	S	52.4	57.1	H	S	66.7	71.4	66.7	52.4	S	66.7	42.9
15	S	71.4	57.1	S	52.4	47.6	S	52.4	47.6	S	52.4	57.1
16	H	33.3	71.4	S	47.6	57.1	S	66.7	S	61.9	38.1	S
17	61.9	33.3	52.4	76.2	57.1	S	47.6	47.6	S	52.4	61.9	S
18	61.9	S	S	76.2	57.1	S	52.4	57.1	42.9	47.6	S	66.7
19	38.1	S	S	57.1	66.7	52.4	38.1	S	28.6	71.4	S	47.6
20	38.1	H	61.9	38.1	S	38.1	47.6	S	52.4	52.4	52.4	47.6
21	S	47.6	42.9	57.1	S	47.6	38.1	42.9	33.3	S	71.4	61.9
22	S	52.4	33.3	S	47.6	61.9	S	61.9	38.1	S	71.4	57.1
23	33.3	42.9	42.9	S	33.3	42.9	S	47.6	S	42.9	H	S
24	38.1	52.4	28.6	33.3	71.4	S	42.9	61.9	S	42.9	71.4	S
25	71.4	S	S	61.9	42.9	S	71.4	47.6	47.6	38.1	S	H
26	61.9	S	S	57.1	52.4	42.9	57.1	S	57.1	42.9	S	76.2
27	57.1	47.6	57.1	52.4	S	42.9	47.6	S	52.4	71.4	71.4	57.1
28	S	52.4	42.9	52.4	S	47.6	61.9	52.4	57.1	S	57.1	57.1
29	S		66.7	S	H	61.9	S	52.4	47.6	S	47.6	42.9
30	61.9		42.9	S	66.7	42.9	S	28.6	S	81.0	47.6	S
31	66.7		38.1		57.1		66.7	47.6		42.9		S

*See new trends developing on pages 60, 88 and 136 ** Based on most recent 21-year period*

NASDAQ COMPOSITE MARKET PROBABILITY CALENDAR 2006

THE % CHANCE OF THE MARKET RISING ON ANY TRADING DAY OF THE YEAR*

(Based on the number of times the NASDAQ rose on a particular trading day during January 1972-December 2004)

Date	Jan	Feb	Mar	Apr	May	Jun	Jul	Aug	Sep	Oct	Nov	Dec
1	S	63.6	63.6	S	60.6	57.6	S	51.5	54.6	S	72.7	63.6
2	H	69.7	57.6	S	72.7	75.8	S	39.4	S	48.5	51.5	S
3	51.5	60.6	72.7	39.4	66.7	S	51.5	48.5	S	63.6	75.8	S
4	78.8	S	S	60.6	54.6	S	H	63.6	H	54.6	S	60.6
5	60.6	S	S	60.6	54.6	60.6	48.5	S	66.7	63.6	S	63.6
6	66.7	66.7	54.6	51.5	S	60.6	39.4	S	57.6	60.6	54.6	60.6
7	S	54.6	54.6	51.5	S	57.6	51.5	60.6	57.6	S	45.5	42.4
8	S	48.5	57.6	S	57.6	48.5	S	39.4	54.6	S	54.6	51.5
9	51.5	51.5	57.6	S	57.6	45.5	S	54.6	S	60.6	63.6	S
10	57.6	66.7	51.5	63.6	39.4	S	60.6	51.5	S	48.5	63.6	S
11	54.6	S	S	66.7	57.6	S	63.6	54.6	45.5	48.5	S	42.4
12	57.6	S	S	57.6	57.6	60.6	57.6	S	45.5	75.8	S	39.4
13	69.7	51.5	69.7	51.5	S	60.6	72.7	S	60.6	63.6	51.5	45.5
14	S	57.6	48.5	H	S	63.6	75.8	63.6	57.6	S	57.6	39.4
15	S	60.6	54.6	S	60.6	54.6	S	57.6	33.3	S	42.4	45.5
16	H	48.5	66.7	S	57.6	45.5	S	51.5	S	51.5	39.4	S
17	69.7	57.6	54.6	63.6	54.6	S	66.7	57.6	S	51.5	57.6	S
18	69.7	S	S	51.5	42.4	S	45.5	51.5	42.4	36.4	S	54.6
19	66.7	S	S	60.6	45.5	51.5	48.5	S	54.6	75.8	S	51.5
20	45.5	H	60.6	60.6	S	48.5	54.6	S	66.7	63.6	54.6	51.5
21	S	39.4	39.4	54.6	S	60.6	45.5	36.4	54.6	S	54.6	69.7
22	S	48.5	39.4	S	51.5	51.5	S	66.7	48.5	S	69.7	66.7
23	48.5	54.6	60.6	S	48.5	51.5	S	57.6	S	39.4	H	S
24	54.6	57.6	57.6	45.5	60.6	S	51.5	48.5	S	39.4	60.6	S
25	42.4	S	S	48.5	51.5	S	57.6	51.5	48.5	33.3	S	H
26	63.6	S	S	66.7	57.6	48.5	51.5	S	45.5	42.4	S	72.7
27	57.6	54.6	39.4	57.6	S	42.4	48.5	S	45.5	57.6	57.6	51.5
28	S	57.6	48.5	75.8	S	57.6	51.5	54.6	48.5	S	66.7	72.7
29	S		54.6	S	H	69.7	S	54.6	51.5	S	66.7	84.9
30	60.6		48.5	S	51.5	75.8	S	60.6	S	57.6	66.7	S
31	66.7		66.7		72.7		60.6	75.8		66.7		S

*See new trends developing on page 137 — Based on NASDAQ composite, prior to February 5, 1971, based on National Quotation Bureau indices

RECENT NASDAQ COMPOSITE MARKET PROBABILITY CALENDAR 2006

THE % CHANCE OF THE MARKET RISING ON ANY TRADING DAY OF THE YEAR*

(Based on the number of times the NASDAQ rose on a particular trading day during January 1984-December 2004**)

Date	Jan	Feb	Mar	Apr	May	Jun	Jul	Aug	Sep	Oct	Nov	Dec
1	S	71.4	66.7	S	66.7	61.9	S	52.4	52.4	S	81.0	71.4
2	H	71.4	47.6	S	71.4	81.0	S	38.1	S	52.4	47.6	S
3	57.1	61.9	76.2	42.9	71.4	S	61.9	42.9	S	57.1	85.7	S
4	85.7	S	S	47.6	42.9	S	H	61.9	H	52.4	S	66.7
5	61.9	S	S	61.9	42.9	57.1	52.4	S	61.9	61.9	S	66.7
6	61.9	61.9	52.4	47.6	S	61.9	38.1	S	47.6	42.9	57.1	57.1
7	S	57.1	57.1	38.1	S	52.4	52.4	52.4	57.1	S	52.4	33.3
8	S	52.4	52.4	S	66.7	42.9	S	47.6	57.1	S	57.1	42.9
9	47.6	47.6	52.4	S	57.1	47.6	S	47.6	S	52.4	57.1	S
10	57.1	57.1	52.4	61.9	42.9	S	66.7	52.4	S	42.9	57.1	S
11	57.1	S	S	61.9	61.9	S	57.1	47.6	52.4	52.4	S	42.9
12	57.1	S	S	52.4	52.4	52.4	61.9	S	47.6	76.2	S	33.3
13	66.7	47.6	61.9	52.4	S	52.4	76.2	S	61.9	66.7	47.6	57.1
14	S	61.9	42.9	H	S	57.1	81.0	76.2	57.1	S	61.9	38.1
15	S	66.7	52.4	S	61.9	57.1	S	61.9	19.1	S	38.1	52.4
16	H	33.3	76.2	S	52.4	47.6	S	61.9	S	57.1	23.8	S
17	61.9	47.6	57.1	66.7	66.7	S	57.1	57.1	S	47.6	57.1	S
18	71.4	S	S	47.6	47.6	S	47.6	47.6	38.1	38.1	S	52.4
19	76.2	S	S	61.9	61.9	47.6	38.1	S	52.4	76.2	S	52.4
20	38.1	H	61.9	47.6	S	47.6	47.6	S	71.4	57.1	57.1	52.4
21	S	42.9	38.1	52.4	S	57.1	33.3	42.9	47.6	S	47.6	76.2
22	S	52.4	33.3	S	47.6	57.1	S	76.2	47.6	S	66.7	61.9
23	47.6	57.1	52.4	S	42.9	42.9	S	61.9	S	42.9	H	S
24	57.1	52.4	52.4	47.6	61.9	S	38.1	52.4	S	38.1	61.9	S
25	42.9	S	S	52.4	47.6	S	66.7	47.6	38.1	28.6	S	H
26	71.4	S	S	61.9	61.9	47.6	61.9	S	47.6	33.3	S	66.7
27	61.9	52.4	38.1	61.9	S	33.3	52.4	S	42.9	52.4	57.1	57.1
28	S	61.9	47.6	76.2	S	57.1	57.1	57.1	47.6	S	61.9	71.4
29	S		52.4	S	H	71.4	S	61.9	57.1	S	71.4	76.2
30	57.1		42.9	S	61.9	81.0	S	57.1	S	71.4	57.1	S
31	71.4		66.7		76.2		71.4	71.4		66.7		S

* See new trends developing on page 137   ** Based on most recent 21-year period

DECENNIAL CYCLE: A MARKET PHENOMENON

By arranging each year's market gain or loss so the first and succeeding years of each decade fall into the same column, certain interesting patterns emerge — strong fifth and eighth years; weak first, seventh and zero years.

This fascinating phenomenon was first presented by Edgar Lawrence Smith in *Common Stocks and Business Cycles* (William-Frederick Press, 1959). Anthony Gaubis co-pioneered the decennial pattern with Smith.

When Smith first cut graphs of market prices into ten-year segments and placed them above one another, he observed that each decade tended to have three bull market cycles and that the longest and strongest bull markets seem to favor the middle years of a decade.

Don't place too much emphasis on the decennial cycle nowadays, other than the extraordinary fifth and zero years, as the stock market is more influenced by the quadrennial presidential election cycle, shown on page 127. Also, the last half-century, which has been the most prosperous in U.S. history, has distributed the returns among most years of the decade. Interestingly, NASDAQ suffered its worst bear market ever in a zero year, giving us the rare experience of witnessing a bubble burst.

2005 looks likely to keep fifth years' twelve-and-zero winning streak, but with the gyrations experienced to date, we don't expect 2005 to be a huge gainer year-over-year. After another test of the 2004 lows in 2005, recovery highs are likely to be revisited in late 2005/early 2006. Midterm 2006 promises another correction and perhaps the next bear market. Midterm election years have historically been host to a plethora of major bottoms (see pages 127 and 128).

THE TEN-YEAR STOCK MARKET CYCLE
Annual % Change In Dow Jones Industrial Average
Year Of Decade

DECADES	1st	2nd	3rd	4th	5th	6th	7th	8th	9th	10th
1881-1890	3.0%	− 2.9%	− 8.5%	−18.8%	20.1%	12.4%	− 8.4%	4.8%	5.5%	−14.1%
1891-1900	17.6	− 6.6	−24.6	− 0.6	2.3	− 1.7	21.3	22.5	9.2	7.0
1901-1910	− 8.7	− 0.4	−23.6	41.7	38.2	− 1.9	−37.7	46.6	15.0	−17.9
1911-1920	0.4	7.6	−10.3	− 5.4	81.7	− 4.2	−21.7	10.5	30.5	−32.9
1921-1930	12.7	21.7	− 3.3	26.2	30.0	0.3	28.8	48.2	−17.2	−33.8
1931-1940	−52.7	−23.1	66.7	4.1	38.5	24.8	−32.8	28.1	− 2.9	−12.7
1941-1950	−15.4	7.6	13.8	12.1	26.6	− 8.1	2.2	− 2.1	12.9	17.6
1951-1960	14.4	8.4	− 3.8	44.0	20.8	2.3	−12.8	34.0	16.4	− 9.3
1961-1970	18.7	−10.8	17.0	14.6	10.9	−18.9	15.2	4.3	−15.2	4.8
1971-1980	6.1	14.6	−16.6	−27.6	38.3	17.9	−17.3	− 3.1	4.2	14.9
1981-1990	− 9.2	19.6	20.3	− 3.7	27.7	22.6	2.3	11.8	27.0	− 4.3
1991-2000	20.3	4.2	13.7	2.1	33.5	26.0	22.6	16.1	25.2	− 6.2
2001-2010	− 7.1	−16.8	25.3	3.1						
Total % Change	0.1%	23.1%	66.1%	91.8%	368.6%	71.5%	−38.3%	221.7%	110.6%	− 86.9%
Avg % Change	0.01%	1.8%	5.1%	7.1%	30.7%	6.0%	− 3.2%	18.5%	9.2%	−7.2%
Up Years	8	7	6	8	12	7	6	10	9	4
Down Years	5	6	7	5	0	5	6	2	3	8

Based on annual close; Cowles indices 1881-1885; 12 Mixed Stocks, 10 Rails, 2 Inds 1886-1889;
20 Mixed Stocks, 18 Rails, 2 Inds 1890-1896; Railroad average 1897 (First industrial average published May 26, 1896)

PRESIDENTIAL ELECTION/STOCK MARKET CYCLE
THE 172-YEAR SAGA CONTINUES

It is no mere coincidence that the last two years (pre-election year and election year) of the 43 administrations since 1833 produced a total net market gain of 745.9%, dwarfing the 227.6% gain of the first two years of these administrations.

Presidential elections every four years have a profound impact on the economy and the stock market. Wars, recessions and bear markets tend to start or occur in the first half of the term; prosperous times and bull markets, in the latter half. After nine straight annual Dow gains during the millennial bull, the 4-year election cycle appears to be back on track. 2001-2004 are a textbook example.

STOCK MARKET ACTION SINCE 1833
Annual % Change In Dow Jones Industrial Average[1]

4-Year Cycle Beginning	Elected President	Post-Election Year	Mid-Term Year	Pre-Election Year	Election Year
1833	Jackson (D)	− 0.9	13.0	3.1	− 11.7
1837	Van Buren (D)	− 11.5	1.6	− 12.3	5.5
1841*	W.H. Harrison (W)**	− 13.3	− 18.1	45.0	15.5
1845*	Polk (D)	8.1	− 14.5	1.2	− 3.6
1849*	Taylor (W)	N/C	18.7	− 3.2	19.6
1853*	Pierce (D)	− 12.7	− 30.2	1.5	4.4
1857	Buchanan (D)	− 31.0	14.3	− 10.7	14.0
1861*	Lincoln (R)	− 1.8	55.4	38.0	6.4
1865	Lincoln (R)**	− 8.5	3.6	1.6	10.8
1869	Grant (R)	1.7	5.6	7.3	6.8
1873	Grant (R)	− 12.7	2.8	− 4.1	− 17.9
1877	Hayes (R)	− 9.4	6.1	43.0	18.7
1881	Garfield (R)**	3.0	− 2.9	− 8.5	− 18.8
1885*	Cleveland (D)	20.1	12.4	− 8.4	4.8
1889*	B. Harrison (R)	5.5	− 14.1	17.6	− 6.6
1893*	Cleveland (D)	− 24.6	− 0.6	2.3	− 1.7
1897*	McKinley (R)	21.3	22.5	9.2	7.0
1901	McKinley (R)**	− 8.7	− 0.4	− 23.6	41.7
1905	T. Roosevelt (R)	38.2	− 1.9	− 37.7	46.6
1909	Taft (R)	15.0	− 17.9	0.4	7.6
1913*	Wilson (D)	− 10.3	− 5.4	81.7	− 4.2
1917	Wilson (D)	− 21.7	10.5	30.5	− 32.9
1921*	Harding (R)**	12.7	21.7	− 3.3	26.2
1925	Coolidge (R)	30.0	0.3	28.8	48.2
1929	Hoover (R)	− 17.2	− 33.8	− 52.7	− 23.1
1933*	F. Roosevelt (D)	66.7	4.1	38.5	24.8
1937	F. Roosevelt (D)	− 32.8	28.1	− 2.9	− 12.7
1941	F. Roosevelt (D)	− 15.4	7.6	13.8	12.1
1945	F. Roosevelt (D)**	26.6	− 8.1	2.2	− 2.1
1949	Truman (D)	12.9	17.6	14.4	8.4
1953*	Eisenhower (R)	− 3.8	44.0	20.8	2.3
1957	Eisenhower (R)	− 12.8	34.0	16.4	− 9.3
1961*	Kennedy (D)**	18.7	− 10.8	17.0	14.6
1965	Johnson (D)	10.9	− 18.9	15.2	4.3
1969*	Nixon (R)	− 15.2	4.8	6.1	14.6
1973	Nixon (R)***	− 16.6	− 27.6	38.3	17.9
1977*	Carter (D)	− 17.3	− 3.1	4.2	14.9
1981*	Reagan (R)	− 9.2	19.6	20.3	− 3.7
1985	Reagan (R)	27.7	22.6	2.3	11.8
1989	G. H. W. Bush (R)	27.0	− 4.3	20.3	4.2
1993*	Clinton (D)	13.7	2.1	33.5	26.0
1997	Clinton (D)	22.6	16.1	25.2	− 6.2
2001*	G. W. Bush (R)	− 7.1	− 16.8	25.3	3.1
Total % Gain		**67.9 %**	**159.7%**	**457.6%**	**288.3%**
Average % Gain		**1.6 %**	**3.7%**	**10.6%**	**6.7%**
# Up		19	25	32	29
# Down		23	18	11	14

*Party in power ousted   **Death in office   ***Resigned   **D**—Democrat, **W**—Whig, **R**—Republican

[1] Based on annual close; Prior to 1886 based on Cowles and other indices; 12 Mixed Stocks, 10 Rails, 2 Inds 1886-1889; 20 Mixed Stocks, 18 Rails, 2 Inds 1890-1896; Railroad average 1897 (First industrial average published May 26, 1896)

BULL AND BEAR MARKETS SINCE 1900

— Beginning —		— Ending —		Bull		Bear	
Date	DJIA	Date	DJIA	% Gain	Days	% Change	Days
9/24/00	38.80	6/17/01	57.33	47.8%	266	− 46.1%	875
11/9/03	30.88	1/19/06	75.45	144.3	802	− 48.5	665
11/15/07	38.83	11/19/09	73.64	89.6	735	− 27.4	675
9/25/11	53.43	9/30/12	68.97	29.1	371	− 24.1	668
7/30/14	52.32	11/21/16	110.15	110.5	845	− 40.1	393
12/19/17	65.95	11/3/19	119.62	81.4	684	− 46.6	660
8/24/21	63.90	3/20/23	105.38	64.9	573	− 18.6	221
10/27/23	85.76	9/3/29	381.17	344.5	2138	− 47.9	71
11/13/29	198.69	4/17/30	294.07	48.0	155	− 86.0	813
7/8/32	41.22	9/7/32	79.93	93.9	61	− 37.2	173
2/27/33	50.16	2/5/34	110.74	120.8	343	− 22.8	171
7/26/34	85.51	3/10/37	194.40	127.3	958	− 49.1	386
3/31/38	98.95	11/12/38	158.41	60.1	226	− 23.3	147
4/8/39	121.44	9/12/39	155.92	28.4	157	− 40.4	959
4/28/42	92.92	5/29/46	212.50	128.7	1492	− 23.2	353
5/17/47	163.21	6/15/48	193.16	18.4	395	− 16.3	363
6/13/49	161.60	1/5/53	293.79	81.8	1302	− 13.0	252
9/14/53	255.49	4/6/56	521.05	103.9	935	− 19.4	564
10/22/57	419.79	1/5/60	685.47	63.3	805	− 17.4	294
10/25/60	566.05	12/13/61	734.91	29.8	414	− 27.1	195
6/26/62	535.76	2/9/66	995.15	85.7	1324	− 25.2	240
10/7/66	744.32	12/3/68	985.21	32.4	788	− 35.9	539
5/26/70	631.16	4/28/71	950.82	50.6	337	− 16.1	209
11/23/71	797.97	1/11/73	1051.70	31.8	415	− 45.1	694
12/6/74	577.60	9/21/76	1014.79	75.7	655	− 26.9	525
2/28/78	742.12	9/8/78	907.74	22.3	192	− 16.4	591
4/21/80	759.13	4/27/81	1024.05	34.9	371	− 24.1	472
8/12/82	776.92	11/29/83	1287.20	65.7	474	− 15.6	238
7/24/84	1086.57	8/25/87	2722.42	150.6	1127	− 36.1	55
10/19/87	1738.74	7/17/90	2999.75	72.5	1002	− 21.2	86
10/11/90	2365.10	7/17/98	9337.97	294.8	2836	− 19.3	45
8/31/98	7539.07	1/14/00	11722.98	55.5	501	− 29.7	616
9/21/01	8235.81	3/19/02	10635.25	29.1	179	− 31.5	204
10/9/02	7286.27	3/4/05	10940.55	50.2*	877*	*At Press-time	
			Average	**84.4%**	**728**	**− 30.8%**	**406**

Based on Dow Jones Industrial Average   1900-2000 Data: Ned Davis Research
The NYSE was closed from 7/31/1914 to 12/11/1914 due to World War I.
DJIA figures were then adjusted back to reflect the composition change from 12 to 20 stocks in September 1916.

Bear markets begin at the end of one bull market and end at the start of the next bull market (7/17/90 to 10/11/90 as an example). The high at Dow 3978.36 on 1/31/94, was followed by a 9.7 percent correction. A 10.3 percent correction occurred between the 5/22/96 closing high of 5778 and the intraday low on 7/16/96. The longest bull market on record ended on 7/17/98, and the shortest bear market on record ended on 8/31/98, when the new bull market began. The greatest bull super cycle in history that began 8/12/82 ended in 2000 after the Dow gained 1409% and NASDAQ climbed 3072%. The Dow gained only 497% in the eight-year super bull from 1921 to the top in 1929. NASDAQ suffered its worst loss ever, down 77.9%, nearly as much as the 89.2% drop in the Dow from 1929 to the bottom in 1932. The Dow has rallied 50.2% since the 10/9/02 bear market low; S&P 500, 60.3% and NASDAQ 99.1%! From their late 2004/early 2005 highs the Dow corrected 8.5%; S&P, 7.2% and NASDAQ 12.6%. The Dow has not been able to surpass its March 2005 high but the S&P and NASDAQ have cleared those levels, albeit by less than 2% at press-time.

DIRECTORY OF TRADING PATTERNS & DATABANK

CONTENTS

A TYPICAL DAY IN THE MARKET

Half-hourly data became available for the Dow Jones Industrial Average starting in January 1987. The NYSE switched 10:00am openings to 9:30am in October 1985. Below is the comparison between half-hourly performance 1987-July 1, 2005 and hourly November 1963-June 1985. Stronger openings and closings in a more bullish climate are evident. Morning and afternoon weaknesses appear an hour earlier.

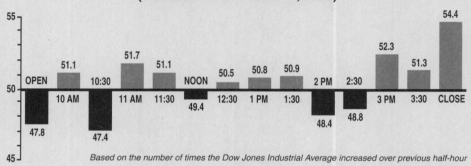

MARKET % PERFORMANCE EACH HALF-HOUR OF THE DAY (JANUARY 1987 – JULY 1, 2005)

Based on the number of times the Dow Jones Industrial Average increased over previous half-hour

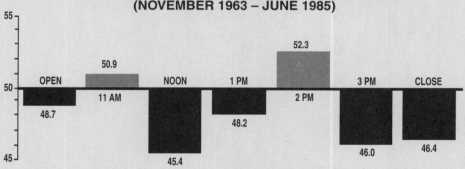

MARKET % PERFORMANCE EACH HOUR OF THE DAY (NOVEMBER 1963 – JUNE 1985)

Based on the number of times the Dow Jones Industrial Average increased over previous hour

On the opposite page, half-hourly movements since January 1987 are separated by day of the week. From 1953 to 1989 Monday was the worst day of the week, especially during long bear markets, but times changed. Monday reversed positions and became the best day of the week and on the plus side twelve years in a row from 1990 to 2000. During the last five years (2001-July 2005) Monday and Friday are net losers, Friday the worst; and the middle three days are net gainers, Wednesday the best. In 2004 and 2005 so far, Monday-Wednesday were net gainers with Thursday and Friday netting losses. On all days stocks do tend to firm up near the close with weakness early morning and from 2 to 2:30 frequently.

THROUGH THE WEEK ON A HALF-HOURLY BASIS

From the chart showing the percentage of times the Dow Jones Industrial Average rose over the preceding half-hour (January 1987–July 1, 2005*) the typical week unfolds.

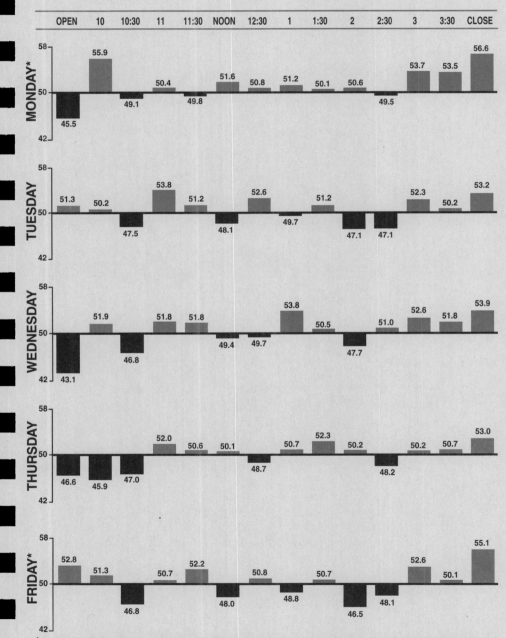

*Research indicates that where Tuesday is the first trading day of the week, it follows the Monday pattern. Therefore, all such Tuesdays were combined with the Mondays here. Thursdays that are the final trading day of a given week behave like Fridays, and were similarly grouped with Fridays.

MONDAY NOW MOST PROFITABLE DAY OF WEEK

Between 1952 and 1989 Monday was the worst trading day of the week. The first trading day of the week (including Tuesday, when Monday is a holiday) rose only 44.3% of the time, while the other trading days closed higher 54.8% of the time. (NYSE Saturday trading discontinued June 1952.)

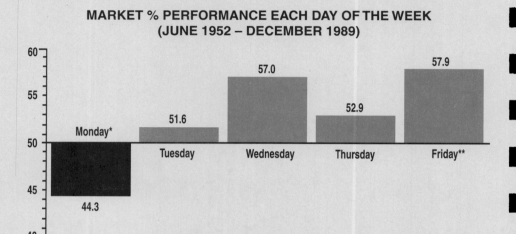

**MARKET % PERFORMANCE EACH DAY OF THE WEEK
(JUNE 1952 – DECEMBER 1989)**

A dramatic reversal occurred in 1990 — Monday became the most powerful day of the week. However, during the bear market years of 2001 and 2002 combined Monday once again was the worst day of the week and Friday became a day to avoid, as traders were not inclined to stay long over the weekend during uncertain market times. See pages 60 and 134.

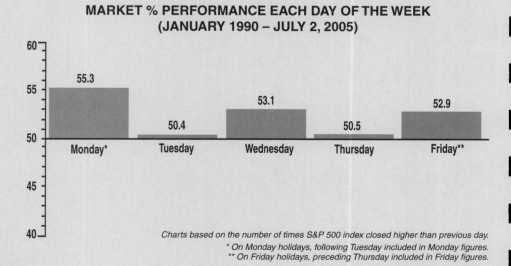

**MARKET % PERFORMANCE EACH DAY OF THE WEEK
(JANUARY 1990 – JULY 2, 2005)**

Charts based on the number of times S&P 500 index closed higher than previous day.
* On Monday holidays, following Tuesday included in Monday figures.
** On Friday holidays, preceding Thursday included in Friday figures.

NASDAQ STRONGEST LAST 3 DAYS OF WEEK

Despite 20 years less data, daily trading patterns on NASDAQ through 1989 appear to be fairly similar to the S&P across on page 132 except for more bullishness on Thursdays. During the mostly flat markets of the 1970s and early 1980s, it would appear that apprehensive investors decided to throw in the towel over weekends and sell on Mondays and Tuesdays.

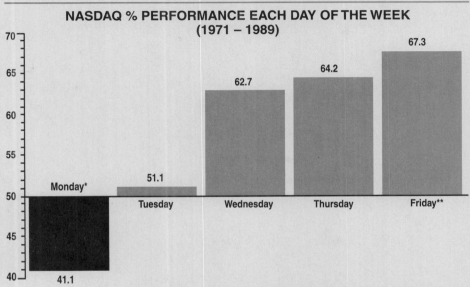

Notice the vast difference in the daily trading pattern between NASDAQ and S&P from January 1, 1990, to recent times. The reason for so much more bullishness is that NASDAQ moved up 1010%, over three times as much during the 1990-2000 period. The gain for the S&P was 332% and for the Dow Jones industrials, 326%. NASDAQ's weekly patterns are beginning to move in step with the rest of the market. Notice on page 135 Monday's weakness during the 2000 to 2002 bear market.

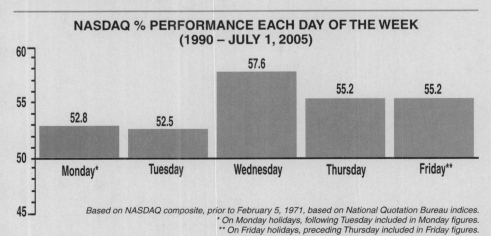

Based on NASDAQ composite, prior to February 5, 1971, based on National Quotation Bureau indices.
* On Monday holidays, following Tuesday included in Monday figures.
** On Friday holidays, preceding Thursday included in Friday figures.

S&P DAILY PERFORMANCE EACH YEAR SINCE 1952

To determine if market trend alters performance of different days of the week, we separated twenty bear years of 1953, '56, '57, '60, '62, '66, '69, '70, '73, '74, '77, '78, '81, '84, '87, '90, '94, 2000, 2001 and 2002 from 34 bull market years. While Tuesday and Thursday did not vary much between bull and bear years, Mondays and Fridays were sharply affected. There was a swing of 10.3 percentage points in Monday's and 10.9 in Friday's performance. Mondays have been much stronger since 1990.

PERCENTAGE OF TIMES MARKET CLOSED HIGHER THAN PREVIOUS DAY
(1953 – JULY 1, 2005)

	Monday*	Tuesday	Wednesday	Thursday	Friday**
1952	48.4%	55.6%	58.1%	51.9%	66.7%
1953	32.7	50.0	54.9	57.5	56.6
1954	50.0	57.5	63.5	59.2	73.1
1955	50.0	45.7	63.5	60.0	78.9
1956	36.5	39.6	46.9	50.0	59.6
1957	25.0	54.0	66.7	48.9	44.2
1958	59.6	52.0	59.6	68.1	72.6
1959	42.3	53.1	55.8	48.9	69.8
1960	34.6	50.0	44.2	54.0	59.6
1961	52.9	54.4	64.7	56.0	67.3
1962	28.3	52.1	54.0	51.0	50.0
1963	46.2	63.3	51.0	57.5	69.2
1964	40.4	48.0	61.5	58.7	77.4
1965	44.2	57.5	55.8	51.0	71.2
1966	36.5	47.8	53.9	42.0	57.7
1967	38.5	50.0	60.8	64.0	69.2
1968†	49.1	57.5	64.3	42.6	54.9
1969	30.8	45.8	50.0	67.4	50.0
1970	38.5	46.0	63.5	48.9	52.8
1971	44.2	64.6	57.7	55.1	51.9
1972	38.5	60.9	57.7	51.0	67.3
1973	32.1	51.1	52.9	44.9	44.2
1974	32.7	57.1	51.0	36.7	30.8
1975	53.9	38.8	61.5	56.3	55.8
1976	55.8	55.3	55.8	40.8	58.5
1977	40.4	40.4	46.2	53.1	53.9
1978	51.9	43.5	59.6	54.0	48.1
1979	54.7	53.2	58.8	66.0	44.2
1980	55.8	54.2	71.7	35.4	59.6
1981	44.2	38.8	55.8	53.2	47.2
1982	46.2	39.6	44.2	44.9	50.0
1983	55.8	46.8	61.5	52.0	55.8
1984	39.6	63.8	31.4	46.0	44.2
1985	44.2	61.2	54.9	56.3	53.9
1986	51.9	44.9	67.3	58.3	55.8
1987	51.9	57.1	63.5	61.7	49.1
1988	51.9	61.7	51.9	48.0	59.6
1989	51.9	47.8	69.2	58.0	69.2
1990	67.9	53.2	52.9	40.0	51.9
1991	44.2	46.9	52.9	49.0	51.9
1992	51.9	49.0	53.9	56.3	45.3
1993	65.4	41.7	55.8	44.9	48.1
1994	55.8	46.8	52.9	48.0	59.6
1995	63.5	56.5	63.5	62.0	63.5
1996	54.7	44.9	51.0	57.1	63.5
1997	67.3	67.4	42.3	41.7	57.7
1998	57.7	62.5	57.7	38.3	60.4
1999	46.2	29.8	67.3	53.1	57.7
2000	51.9	43.5	40.4	56.0	46.2
2001	45.3	51.1	44.0	59.2	43.1
2002	40.4	37.5	56.9	38.8	48.1
2003	59.6	62.5	42.3	58.3	50.0
2004	51.9	61.7	59.6	52.1	52.8
2005 ‡	65.4	52.2	57.7	56.0	38.5
Average	**47.2%**	**51.2%**	**55.8%**	**52.2%**	**56.6%**
34 Bull Years	**51.2%**	**52.9%**	**58.1%**	**53.1%**	**60.7%**
20 Bear Years	**40.9%**	**48.5%**	**52.1%**	**50.6%**	**49.8%**

Based on S&P 500

† Most Wednesdays closed last 7 months of 1968.   ‡ Six months only, not included in averages.
* On Monday holidays, following Tuesday included in Monday figures.
** On Friday holidays, preceding Thursday included in Friday figures.

NASDAQ DAILY PERFORMANCE EACH YEAR SINCE 1971

After dropping a hefty 77.9% from its 2000 high (versus -37.8% on the Dow and -49.1% on the S&P 500), NASDAQ tech stocks still outpace the blue chips and big caps — but not by nearly as much as they did. From January 1, 1971, through June 30, 2005, NASDAQ moved up an impressive 2196%. The Dow (up 1125%) and the S&P (up 1193%) gained just over half as much.

Monday's performance on NASDAQ was lackluster during the three-year bear market of 2000-2002. As NASDAQ rebounded sharply in 2003, up 50% for the year, strength returned to Monday as well as on Tuesday and Thursday. Wednesday and Friday were weak in 2003 with Friday losing the most ground though Wednesday was down more frequently. Tuesday was best in 2004 with Thursday and Friday net losers. So far in 2005 only Monday has netted a gain.

PERCENTAGE OF TIMES NASDAQ CLOSED HIGHER THAN PREVIOUS DAY (1971 – JULY 1, 2005)

	Monday*	Tuesday	Wednesday	Thursday	Friday**
1971	51.9%	52.1%	59.6%	65.3%	71.2%
1972	30.8	60.9	63.5	57.1	78.9
1973	34.0	48.9	52.9	53.1	48.1
1974	30.8	44.9	52.9	51.0	42.3
1975	44.2	42.9	63.5	64.6	63.5
1976	50.0	63.8	67.3	59.2	58.5
1977	51.9	40.4	53.9	63.3	73.1
1978	48.1	47.8	73.1	72.0	84.6
1979	45.3	53.2	64.7	86.0	82.7
1980	46.2	64.6	84.9	52.1	73.1
1981	42.3	32.7	67.3	76.6	69.8
1982	34.6	47.9	59.6	51.0	63.5
1983	42.3	44.7	67.3	68.0	73.1
1984	22.6	53.2	35.3	52.0	51.9
1985	36.5	59.2	62.8	68.8	66.0
1986	38.5	55.1	65.4	72.9	75.0
1987	42.3	49.0	65.4	68.1	66.0
1988	50.0	55.3	61.5	66.0	63.5
1989	38.5	54.4	71.2	72.0	75.0
1990	54.7	42.6	60.8	46.0	55.8
1991	51.9	59.2	66.7	65.3	51.9
1992	44.2	53.1	59.6	60.4	45.3
1993	55.8	56.3	69.2	57.1	67.3
1994	51.9	46.8	54.9	52.0	55.8
1995	50.0	52.2	63.5	64.0	63.5
1996	50.9	57.1	64.7	61.2	63.5
1997	65.4	59.2	53.9	52.1	55.8
1998	59.6	58.3	65.4	44.7	58.5
1999	61.5	40.4	63.5	57.1	65.4
2000	40.4	41.3	42.3	60.0	57.7
2001	41.5	57.8	52.0	55.1	47.1
2002	44.2	37.5	56.9	46.9	46.2
2003	57.7	60.4	40.4	60.4	46.2
2004	57.7	59.6	53.9	50.0	50.9
2005†	61.5	60.9	50.0	44.0	50.0
Average	**46.1%**	**51.5%**	**60.6%**	**60.3%**	**62.1%**
24 Bull Years	**48.5%**	**54.1%**	**63.3%**	**62.1%**	**65.4%**
10 Bear Years	**40.5%**	**45.5%**	**54.1%**	**56.1%**	**54.1%**

Based on NASDAQ composite; prior to February 5, 1971 based on National Quotation Bureau indices.
† Six months only, not included in averages.
* On Monday holidays, following Tuesday included in Monday figures.
** On Friday holidays, preceding Thursday included in Friday figures.

MONTHLY CASH INFLOWS INTO S&P STOCKS

For many years, the last trading day of the month, plus the first four of the following month, were the best market days of the month. This pattern is quite clear in the first chart showing these five consecutive trading days towering above the other 16 trading days of the average month in the 1953-1981 period. The rationale was that individuals and institutions tended to operate similarly, causing a massive flow of cash into stocks near beginnings of months.

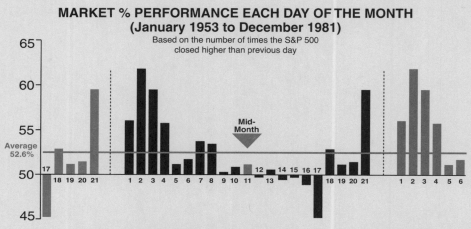

MARKET % PERFORMANCE EACH DAY OF THE MONTH
(January 1953 to December 1981)

Based on the number of times the S&P 500
closed higher than previous day

Clearly "front-running" traders took advantage of this phenomenon, drastically altering the previous pattern. The second chart from 1982 onward shows the trading shift caused by these "anticipators" to the last three trading days of the month plus the first two. Another astonishing development shows the ninth, tenth, and eleventh trading days rising strongly as well. Perhaps the enormous growth of 401(k) retirement plans (participants' salaries are usually paid twice monthly) is responsible for this new mid-month bulge. First trading days of the month have produced the greatest gains in recent years (see page 62).

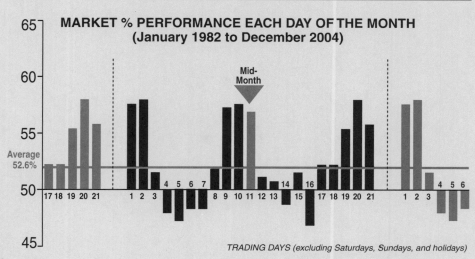

MARKET % PERFORMANCE EACH DAY OF THE MONTH
(January 1982 to December 2004)

TRADING DAYS (excluding Saturdays, Sundays, and holidays)

MONTHLY CASH INFLOWS INTO NASDAQ STOCKS

NASDAQ stocks moved up 58.1% of the time through 1981 compared to 52.6% for the S&P across the page. Ends and beginnings of the month are fairly similar, specifically the last plus the first four trading days. But notice how investors piled into NASDAQ stocks until mid-month. NASDAQ rose 118.6% from January 1, 1971, to December 31, 1981, compared to 33.0% for the S&P.

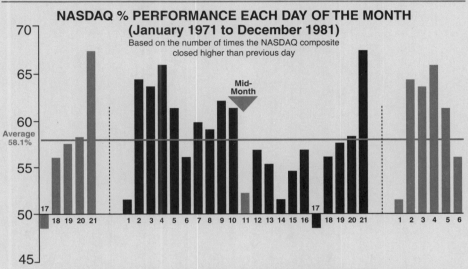

NASDAQ % PERFORMANCE EACH DAY OF THE MONTH
(January 1971 to December 1981)
Based on the number of times the NASDAQ composite closed higher than previous day

After the air was let out of the market 2000-2002, S&P's 889.9% gain over the last 23 years is more evenly matched with NASDAQ's 1010.8% gain. Last three, first four and middle ninth and tenth days rose the most. Where the S&P has six days of the month that go down more often than up, NASDAQ has none. NASDAQ exhibits the most strength on the last trading day of the month.

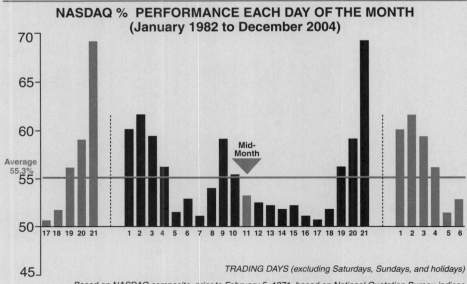

NASDAQ % PERFORMANCE EACH DAY OF THE MONTH
(January 1982 to December 2004)

TRADING DAYS (excluding Saturdays, Sundays, and holidays)

Based on NASDAQ composite, prior to February 5, 1971, based on National Quotation Bureau indices

NOVEMBER, DECEMBER, AND JANUARY YEAR'S BEST THREE-MONTH SPAN

The most important observation to be made from a chart showing the average monthly percent change in market prices since 1950 is that institutions (mutual funds, pension funds, banks, etc.) determine the trading patterns in today's market.

The "investment calendar" reflects the annual, semi-annual and quarterly operations of institutions during January, April and July. October, besides being the last campaign month before elections, is also the time when most bear markets seem to end, as in 1946, 1957, 1960, 1966, 1974, 1987, 1990, 1998 and 2002. (August and September tend to combine to make the worst consecutive two-month period.)

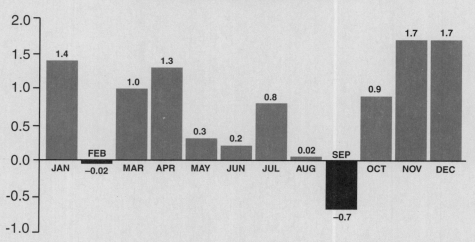

S&P 500 MONTHLY % PERFORMANCE
JANUARY 1950 – JUNE 2005

Average month-to-month % change in S&P 500
(Based on monthly closing prices)

Unusual year-end strength comes from corporate and private pension funds, producing a 4.8% gain on average between November 1 and January 31. September's dismal performance makes it the worst month of the year. In the last twenty-one years it has only been up six times—four in a row 1995-1998. October is the top month since 1990.

In midterm election years since 1950, the best three months are October +3.3% (10-4), November +2.9% (11-3), and December +1.7% (10-4). January drops to tenth place with a –0.9% average loss, preceded by April, May and August, and followed by September and June in the loss column.

See page 46 for monthly performance tables for the S&P 500 and the Dow Jones industrials. See pages 50 and 52 for unique six-month switching strategies.

On page 72 you can see how the first month of the first three quarters far outperforms the second and the third months since 1950 and note the improvement in May's and October's performance since 1991.

NOVEMBER THROUGH JUNE
NASDAQ'S EIGHT-MONTH RUN

The two-and-a-half-year plunge of 77.9% in NASDAQ stocks between March 10, 2000, and October 9, 2002, brought several horrendous monthly losses (the two greatest were November 2000, –22.9% and February 2001, –22.4) which trimmed average monthly performance over the 34½-year period. Ample Octobers in six of the last seven years, plus two huge turnarounds in 2001 (+12.8%) and 2002 (+13.5%) has put bear-killing October in the number one spot since 1998. January's 3.7% average gain is still awesome, and twice S&P's 1.8% January average since 1971.

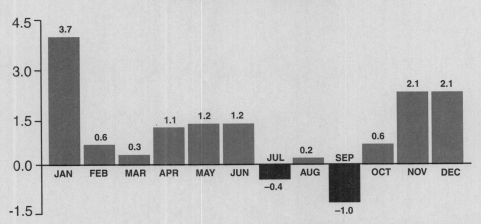

**NASDAQ MONTHLY % PERFORMANCE
JANUARY 1971 – JUNE 2005**

Average month-to-month % change in NASDAQ composite, prior to February 5, 1971, based on National Quotation Bureau indices (Based on monthly closing prices)

Bear in mind when comparing NASDAQ to the S&P across the page that there are 21 fewer years of data here. During this 34½-year (1971-June 2005) period, NASDAQ gained 2195.5%, while the S&P and the Dow rose only 1192.8% and 1124.8%, respectively. On page 54 you can see a statistical monthly comparison between NASDAQ and the Dow.

Year-end strength is even more pronounced in NASDAQ, producing a 7.9% gain on average between November 1 and January 31—1.6 times greater than that of the S&P 500 across the page. September is the worst month of the year for the over-the-counter index as well, posting a deeper average loss of –1.0%. These extremes underscore NASDAQ's higher volatility—and potential for moves of greater magnitude.

In midterm election years since 1971, the best three months are October +5.2% (6-2), November +2.0% (6-2), and March +1.4% (5-3). NASDAQ Januarys also drop to tenth place with a –1.6% average loss, preceded by August and June, and followed by July and September in the loss column. See page 58 for NASDAQ's impressive eight-month switching strategy using MACD timing.

STANDARD & POOR'S 500
MONTHLY PERCENT CHANGES

	JAN	FEB	MAR	APR	MAY	JUN
1950	1.7%	1.0%	0.4%	4.5%	3.9%	— 5.8%
1951	6.1	0.6	— 1.8	4.8	— 4.1	— 2.6
1952	1.6	— 3.6	4.8	— 4.3	2.3	4.6
1953	— 0.7	— 1.8	— 2.4	— 2.6	— 0.3	— 1.6
1954	5.1	0.3	3.0	4.9	3.3	0.1
1955	1.8	0.4	— 0.5	3.8	— 0.1	8.2
1956	— 3.6	3.5	6.9	— 0.2	— 6.6	3.9
1957	— 4.2	— 3.3	2.0	3.7	3.7	— 0.1
1958	4.3	— 2.1	3.1	3.2	1.5	2.6
1959	0.4	— 0.02	0.1	3.9	1.9	— 0.4
1960	— 7.1	0.9	— 1.4	— 1.8	2.7	2.0
1961	6.3	2.7	2.6	0.4	1.9	— 2.9
1962	— 3.8	1.6	— 0.6	— 6.2	— 8.6	— 8.2
1963	4.9	— 2.9	3.5	4.9	1.4	— 2.0
1964	2.7	1.0	1.5	0.6	1.1	1.6
1965	3.3	— 0.1	— 1.5	3.4	— 0.8	— 4.9
1966	0.5	— 1.8	— 2.2	2.1	— 5.4	— 1.6
1967	7.8	0.2	3.9	4.2	— 5.2	1.8
1968	— 4.4	— 3.1	0.9	8.2	1.1	0.9
1969	— 0.8	— 4.7	3.4	2.1	— 0.2	— 5.6
1970	— 7.6	5.3	0.1	— 9.0	— 6.1	— 5.0
1971	4.0	0.9	3.7	3.6	— 4.2	0.1
1972	1.8	2.5	0.6	0.4	1.7	— 2.2
1973	— 1.7	— 3.7	— 0.1	— 4.1	— 1.9	— 0.7
1974	— 1.0	— 0.4	— 2.3	— 3.9	— 3.4	— 1.5
1975	12.3	6.0	2.2	4.7	4.4	4.4
1976	11.8	— 1.1	3.1	— 1.1	— 1.4	4.1
1977	— 5.1	— 2.2	— 1.4	0.02	— 2.4	4.5
1978	— 6.2	— 2.5	2.5	8.5	0.4	— 1.8
1979	4.0	— 3.7	5.5	0.2	— 2.6	3.9
1980	5.8	— 0.4	—10.2	4.1	4.7	2.7
1981	— 4.6	1.3	3.6	— 2.3	— 0.2	— 1.0
1982	— 1.8	— 6.1	— 1.0	4.0	— 3.9	— 2.0
1983	3.3	1.9	3.3	7.5	— 1.2	3.5
1984	— 0.9	— 3.9	1.3	0.5	— 5.9	1.7
1985	7.4	0.9	— 0.3	— 0.5	5.4	1.2
1986	0.2	7.1	5.3	— 1.4	5.0	1.4
1987	13.2	3.7	2.6	— 1.1	0.6	4.8
1988	4.0	4.2	— 3.3	0.9	0.3	4.3
1989	7.1	— 2.9	2.1	5.0	3.5	— 0.8
1990	— 6.9	0.9	2.4	— 2.7	9.2	— 0.9
1991	4.2	6.7	2.2	0.03	3.9	— 4.8
1992	— 2.0	1.0	— 2.2	2.8	0.1	— 1.7
1993	0.7	1.0	1.9	— 2.5	2.3	0.1
1994	3.3	— 3.0	— 4.6	1.2	1.2	— 2.7
1995	2.4	3.6	2.7	2.8	3.6	2.1
1996	3.3	0.7	0.8	1.3	2.3	0.2
1997	6.1	0.6	— 4.3	5.8	5.9	4.3
1998	1.0	7.0	5.0	0.9	— 1.9	3.9
1999	4.1	— 3.2	3.9	3.8	— 2.5	5.4
2000	— 5.1	— 2.0	9.7	— 3.1	— 2.2	2.4
2001	3.5	— 9.2	— 6.4	7.7	0.5	— 2.5
2002	— 1.6	— 2.1	3.7	— 6.1	— 0.9	— 7.2
2003	— 2.7	— 1.7	1.0	8.0	5.1	1.1
2004	1.7	1.2	— 1.6	— 1.7	1.2	1.8
2005	— 2.5	1.9	— 1.9	— 2.0	3.0	— 0.01
TOTALS	77.5%	— 1.0%	55.3%	71.8%	17.2%	13.5%
AVG.	1.4%	— 0.02%	1.0%	1.3%	0.3%	0.2%
# Up	35	30	36	37	32	30
# Down	21	26	20	19	24	26

JUL	AUG	SEP	OCT	NOV	DEC		Year's Change
0.8%	3.3%	5.6%	0.4%	— 0.1%	4.6%	1950	21.8%
6.9	3.9	— 0.1	— 1.4	— 0.3	3.9	1951	16.5
1.8	— 1.5	— 2.0	— 0.1	4.6	3.5	1952	11.8
2.5	— 5.8	0.1	5.1	0.9	0.2	1953	— 6.6
5.7	— 3.4	8.3	— 1.9	8.1	5.1	1954	45.0
6.1	— 0.8	1.1	— 3.0	7.5	— 0.1	1955	26.4
5.2	— 3.8	— 4.5	0.5	— 1.1	3.5	1956	2.6
1.1	— 5.6	— 6.2	— 3.2	1.6	— 4.1	1957	— 14.3
4.3	1.2	4.8	2.5	2.2	5.2	1958	38.1
3.5	— 1.5	— 4.6	1.1	1.3	2.8	1959	8.5
— 2.5	2.6	— 6.0	— 0.2	4.0	4.6	1960	— 3.0
3.3	2.0	— 2.0	2.8	3.9	0.3	1961	23.1
6.4	1.5	— 4.8	0.4	10.2	1.3	1962	— 11.8
— 0.3	4.9	— 1.1	3.2	— 1.1	2.4	1963	18.9
1.8	— 1.6	2.9	0.8	— 0.5	0.4	1964	13.0
1.3	2.3	3.2	2.7	— 0.9	0.9	1965	9.1
— 1.3	— 7.8	— 0.7	4.8	0.3	— 0.1	1966	— 13.1
4.5	— 1.2	3.3	— 2.9	0.1	2.6	1967	20.1
— 1.8	1.1	3.9	0.7	4.8	— 4.2	1968	7.7
— 6.0	4.0	— 2.5	4.4	— 3.5	— 1.9	1969	— 11.4
7.3	4.4	3.3	— 1.1	4.7	5.7	1970	0.1
— 4.1	3.6	— 0.7	— 4.2	— 0.3	8.6	1971	10.8
0.2	3.4	— 0.5	0.9	4.6	1.2	1972	15.6
3.8	— 3.7	4.0	— 0.1	—11.4	1.7	1973	— 17.4
— 7.8	— 9.0	—11.9	16.3	— 5.3	— 2.0	1974	— 29.7
— 6.8	— 2.1	— 3.5	6.2	2.5	— 1.2	1975	31.5
— 0.8	— 0.5	2.3	— 2.2	— 0.8	5.2	1976	19.1
— 1.6	— 2.1	— 0.2	— 4.3	2.7	0.3	1977	— 11.5
5.4	2.6	— 0.7	— 9.2	1.7	1.5	1978	1.1
0.9	5.3	NC	— 6.9	4.3	1.7	1979	12.3
6.5	0.6	2.5	1.6	10.2	— 3.4	1980	25.8
— 0.2	— 6.2	— 5.4	4.9	3.7	— 3.0	1981	— 9.7
— 2.3	11.6	0.8	11.0	3.6	1.5	1982	14.8
— 3.3	1.1	1.0	— 1.5	1.7	— 0.9	1983	17.3
— 1.6	10.6	— 0.3	— 0.01	— 1.5	2.2	1984	1.4
— 0.5	— 1.2	— 3.5	4.3	6.5	4.5	1985	26.3
— 5.9	7.1	— 8.5	5.5	2.1	— 2.8	1986	14.6
4.8	3.5	— 2.4	—21.8	— 8.5	7.3	1987	2.0
— 0.5	— 3.9	4.0	2.6	— 1.9	1.5	1988	12.4
8.8	1.6	— 0.7	— 2.5	1.7	2.1	1989	27.3
— 0.5	— 9.4	— 5.1	— 0.7	6.0	2.5	1990	— 6.6
4.5	2.0	— 1.9	1.2	— 4.4	11.2	1991	26.3
3.9	— 2.4	0.9	0.2	3.0	1.0	1992	4.5
— 0.5	3.4	— 1.0	1.9	— 1.3	1.0	1993	7.1
3.1	3.8	— 2.7	2.1	— 4.0	1.2	1994	— 1.5
3.2	— 0.03	4.0	— 0.5	4.1	1.7	1995	34.1
— 4.6	1.9	5.4	2.6	7.3	— 2.2	1996	20.3
7.8	— 5.7	5.3	— 3.4	4.5	1.6	1997	31.0
— 1.2	—14.6	6.2	8.0	5.9	5.6	1998	26.7
— 3.2	— 0.6	— 2.9	6.3	1.9	5.8	1999	19.5
— 1.6	6.1	— 5.3	— 0.5	— 8.0	0.4	2000	— 10.1
— 1.1	— 6.4	— 8.2	1.8	7.5	0.8	2001	— 13.0
— 7.9	0.5	—11.0	8.6	5.7	— 6.0	2002	— 23.4
1.6	1.8	— 1.2	5.5	0.7	5.1	2003	26.4
— 3.4	0.2	0.9	1.4	3.9	3.2	2004	9.0
45.7%	1.1%	—38.3%	50.8%	95.4%	95.7%		
0.8%	0.02%	— 0.7%	0.9%	1.7%	1.7%		
29	30	22	33	37	42		
26	25	32	22	18	13		

STANDARD & POOR'S 500
MONTHLY CLOSING PRICES

	JAN	FEB	MAR	APR	MAY	JUN
1950	17.05	17.22	17.29	18.07	18.78	17.69
1951	21.66	21.80	21.40	22.43	21.52	20.96
1952	24.14	23.26	24.37	23.32	23.86	24.96
1953	26.38	25.90	25.29	24.62	24.54	24.14
1954	26.08	26.15	26.94	28.26	29.19	29.21
1955	36.63	36.76	36.58	37.96	37.91	41.03
1956	43.82	45.34	48.48	48.38	45.20	46.97
1957	44.72	43.26	44.11	45.74	47.43	47.37
1958	41.70	40.84	42.10	43.44	44.09	45.24
1959	55.42	55.41	55.44	57.59	58.68	58.47
1960	55.61	56.12	55.34	54.37	55.83	56.92
1961	61.78	63.44	65.06	65.31	66.56	64.64
1962	68.84	69.96	69.55	65.24	59.63	54.75
1963	66.20	64.29	66.57	69.80	70.80	69.37
1964	77.04	77.80	78.98	79.46	80.37	81.69
1965	87.56	87.43	86.16	89.11	88.42	84.12
1966	92.88	91.22	89.23	91.06	86.13	84.74
1967	86.61	86.78	90.20	94.01	89.08	90.64
1968	92.24	89.36	90.20	97.59	98.68	99.58
1969	103.01	98.13	101.51	103.69	103.46	97.71
1970	85.02	89.50	89.63	81.52	76.55	72.72
1971	95.88	96.75	100.31	103.95	99.63	99.70
1972	103.94	106.57	107.20	107.67	109.53	107.14
1973	116.03	111.68	111.52	106.97	104.95	104.26
1974	96.57	96.22	93.98	90.31	87.28	86.00
1975	76.98	81.59	83.36	87.30	91.15	95.19
1976	100.86	99.71	102.77	101.64	100.18	104.28
1977	102.03	99.82	98.42	98.44	96.12	100.48
1978	89.25	87.04	89.21	96.83	97.24	95.53
1979	99.93	96.28	101.59	101.76	99.08	102.91
1980	114.16	113.66	102.09	106.29	111.24	114.24
1981	129.55	131.27	136.00	132.81	132.59	131.21
1982	120.40	113.11	111.96	116.44	111.88	109.61
1983	145.30	148.06	152.96	164.42	162.39	168.11
1984	163.41	157.06	159.18	160.05	150.55	153.18
1985	179.63	181.18	180.66	179.83	189.55	191.85
1986	211.78	226.92	238.90	235.52	247.35	250.84
1987	274.08	284.20	291.70	288.36	290.10	304.00
1988	257.07	267.82	258.89	261.33	262.16	273.50
1989	297.47	288.86	294.87	309.64	320.52	317.98
1990	329.08	331.89	339.94	330.80	361.23	358.02
1991	343.93	367.07	375.22	375.35	389.83	371.16
1992	408.79	412.70	403.69	414.95	415.35	408.14
1993	438.78	443.38	451.67	440.19	450.19	450.53
1994	481.61	467.14	445.77	450.91	456.50	444.27
1995	470.42	487.39	500.71	514.71	533.40	544.75
1996	636.02	640.43	645.50	654.17	669.12	670.63
1997	786.16	790.82	757.12	801.34	848.28	885.14
1998	980.28	1049.34	1101.75	1111.75	1090.82	1133.84
1999	1279.64	1238.33	1286.37	1335.18	1301.84	1372.71
2000	1394.46	1366.42	1498.58	1452.43	1420.60	1454.60
2001	1366.01	1239.94	1160.33	1249.46	1255.82	1224.42
2002	1130.20	1106.73	1147.39	1076.92	1067.14	989.82
2003	855.70	841.15	849.18	916.92	963.59	974.50
2004	1131.13	1144.94	1126.21	1107.30	1120.68	1140.84
2005	1181.27	1203.60	1180.59	1156.85	1191.50	1191.33

STANDARD & POOR'S 500
MONTHLY CLOSING PRICES

JUL	AUG	SEP	OCT	NOV	DEC	
17.84	18.42	19.45	19.53	19.51	20.41	**1950**
22.40	23.28	23.26	22.94	22.88	23.77	**1951**
25.40	25.03	24.54	24.52	25.66	26.57	**1952**
24.75	23.32	23.35	24.54	24.76	24.81	**1953**
30.88	29.83	32.31	31.68	34.24	35.98	**1954**
43.52	43.18	43.67	42.34	45.51	45.48	**1955**
49.39	47.51	45.35	45.58	45.08	46.67	**1956**
47.91	45.22	42.42	41.06	41.72	39.99	**1957**
47.19	47.75	50.06	51.33	52.48	55.21	**1958**
60.51	59.60	56.88	57.52	58.28	59.89	**1959**
55.51	56.96	53.52	53.39	55.54	58.11	**1960**
66.76	68.07	66.73	68.62	71.32	71.55	**1961**
58.23	59.12	56.27	56.52	62.26	63.10	**1962**
69.13	72.50	71.70	74.01	73.23	75.02	**1963**
83.18	81.83	84.18	84.86	84.42	84.75	**1964**
85.25	87.17	89.96	92.42	91.61	92.43	**1965**
83.60	77.10	76.56	80.20	80.45	80.33	**1966**
94.75	93.64	96.71	93.90	94.00	96.47	**1967**
97.74	98.86	102.67	103.41	108.37	103.86	**1968**
91.83	95.51	93.12	97.24	93.81	92.06	**1969**
78.05	81.52	84.21	83.25	87.20	92.15	**1970**
95.58	99.03	98.34	94.23	93.99	102.09	**1971**
107.39	111.09	110.55	111.58	116.67	118.05	**1972**
108.22	104.25	108.43	108.29	95.96	97.55	**1973**
79.31	72.15	63.54	73.90	69.97	68.56	**1974**
88.75	86.88	83.87	89.04	91.24	90.19	**1975**
103.44	102.91	105.24	102.90	102.10	107.46	**1976**
98.85	96.77	96.53	92.34	94.83	95.10	**1977**
100.68	103.29	102.54	93.15	94.70	96.11	**1978**
103.81	109.32	109.32	101.82	106.16	107.94	**1979**
121.67	122.38	125.46	127.47	140.52	135.76	**1980**
130.92	122.79	116.18	121.89	126.35	122.55	**1981**
107.09	119.51	120.42	133.71	138.54	140.64	**1982**
162.56	164.40	166.07	163.55	166.40	164.93	**1983**
150.66	166.68	166.10	166.09	163.58	167.24	**1984**
190.92	188.63	182.08	189.82	202.17	211.28	**1985**
236.12	252.93	231.32	243.98	249.22	242.17	**1986**
318.66	329.80	321.83	251.79	230.30	247.08	**1987**
272.02	261.52	271.91	278.97	273.70	277.72	**1988**
346.08	351.45	349.15	340.36	345.99	353.40	**1989**
356.15	322.56	306.05	304.00	322.22	330.22	**1990**
387.81	395.43	387.86	392.46	375.22	417.09	**1991**
424.21	414.03	417.80	418.68	431.35	435.71	**1992**
448.13	463.56	458.93	467.83	461.79	466.45	**1993**
458.26	475.49	462.69	472.35	453.69	459.27	**1994**
562.06	561.88	584.41	581.50	605.37	615.93	**1995**
639.95	651.99	687.31	705.27	757.02	740.74	**1996**
954.29	899.47	947.28	914.62	955.40	970.43	**1997**
1120.67	957.28	1017.01	1098.67	1163.63	1229.23	**1998**
1328.72	1320.41	1282.71	1362.93	1388.91	1469.25	**1999**
1430.83	1517.68	1436.51	1429.40	1314.95	1320.28	**2000**
1211.23	1133.58	1040.94	1059.78	1139.45	1148.08	**2001**
911.62	916.07	815.28	885.76	936.31	879.82	**2002**
990.31	1008.01	995.97	1050.71	1058.20	1111.92	**2003**
1101.72	1104.24	1114.58	1130.20	1173.82	1211.92	**2004**
						2005

DOW JONES INDUSTRIALS
MONTHLY PERCENT CHANGES

	JAN	FEB	MAR	APR	MAY	JUN
1950	0.8%	0.8%	1.3%	4.0%	4.2%	− 6.4%
1951	5.7	1.3	− 1.6	4.5	− 3.7	− 2.8
1952	0.5	− 3.9	3.6	− 4.4	2.1	4.3
1953	− 0.7	− 1.9	− 1.5	− 1.8	− 0.9	− 1.5
1954	4.1	0.7	3.0	5.2	2.6	1.8
1955	1.1	0.7	− 0.5	3.9	− 0.2	6.2
1956	− 3.6	2.7	5.8	0.8	− 7.4	3.1
1957	− 4.1	− 3.0	2.2	4.1	2.1	− 0.3
1958	3.3	− 2.2	1.6	2.0	1.5	3.3
1959	1.8	1.6	− 0.3	3.7	3.2	− 0.03
1960	− 8.4	1.2	− 2.1	− 2.4	4.0	2.4
1961	5.2	2.1	2.2	0.3	2.7	− 1.8
1962	− 4.3	1.1	− 0.2	− 5.9	− 7.8	− 8.5
1963	4.7	− 2.9	3.0	5.2	1.3	− 2.8
1964	2.9	1.9	1.6	− 0.3	1.2	1.3
1965	3.3	0.1	− 1.6	3.7	− 0.5	− 5.4
1966	1.5	− 3.2	− 2.8	1.0	− 5.3	− 1.6
1967	8.2	− 1.2	3.2	3.6	− 5.0	0.9
1968	− 5.5	− 1.7	0.02	8.5	− 1.4	− 0.1
1969	0.2	− 4.3	3.3	1.6	− 1.3	− 6.9
1970	− 7.0	4.5	1.0	− 6.3	− 4.8	− 2.4
1971	3.5	1.2	2.9	4.1	− 3.6	− 1.8
1972	1.3	2.9	1.4	1.4	0.7	− 3.3
1973	− 2.1	− 4.4	− 0.4	− 3.1	− 2.2	− 1.1
1974	0.6	0.6	− 1.6	− 1.2	− 4.1	0.03
1975	14.2	5.0	3.9	6.9	1.3	5.6
1976	14.4	− 0.3	2.8	− 0.3	− 2.2	2.8
1977	− 5.0	− 1.9	− 1.8	0.8	− 3.0	2.0
1978	− 7.4	− 3.6	2.1	10.6	0.4	− 2.6
1979	4.2	− 3.6	6.6	− 0.8	− 3.8	2.4
1980	4.4	− 1.5	− 9.0	4.0	4.1	2.0
1981	− 1.7	2.9	3.0	− 0.6	− 0.6	− 1.5
1982	− 0.4	− 5.4	− 0.2	3.1	− 3.4	− 0.9
1983	2.8	3.4	1.6	8.5	− 2.1	1.8
1984	− 3.0	− 5.4	0.9	0.5	− 5.6	2.5
1985	6.2	− 0.2	− 1.3	− 0.7	4.6	1.5
1986	1.6	8.8	6.4	− 1.9	5.2	0.9
1987	13.8	3.1	3.6	− 0.8	0.2	5.5
1988	1.0	5.8	− 4.0	2.2	− 0.1	5.4
1989	8.0	− 3.6	1.6	5.5	2.5	− 1.6
1990	− 5.9	1.4	3.0	− 1.9	8.3	0.1
1991	3.9	5.3	1.1	− 0.9	4.8	− 4.0
1992	1.7	1.4	− 1.0	3.8	1.1	− 2.3
1993	0.3	1.8	1.9	− 0.2	2.9	− 0.3
1994	6.0	− 3.7	− 5.1	1.3	2.1	− 3.5
1995	0.2	4.3	3.7	3.9	3.3	2.0
1996	5.4	1.7	1.9	− 0.3	1.3	0.2
1997	5.7	0.9	− 4.3	6.5	4.6	4.7
1998	− 0.02	8.1	3.0	3.0	− 1.8	0.6
1999	1.9	− 0.6	5.2	10.2	− 2.1	3.9
2000	− 4.8	− 7.4	7.8	− 1.7	− 2.0	− 0.7
2001	0.9	− 3.6	→ 5.9	8.7	1.6	− 3.8
2002	− 1.0	1.9	2.9	− 4.4	− 0.2	− 6.9
2003	− 3.5	− 2.0	1.3	6.1	4.4	1.5
2004	0.3	0.9	− 2.1	− 1.3	− 0.4	2.4
2005	− 2.7	2.6	− 2.4	− 3.0	2.7	− 1.8
TOTALS	74.8%	11.3%	50.3%	99.1%	5.6%	− 5.2%
AVG.	1.3%	0.2%	0.9%	1.8%	0.1%	− 0.1%
# Up	37	32	35	34	29	28
# Down	19	24	21	22	27	28

JUL	AUG	SEP	OCT	NOV	DEC		Year's Change
0.1%	3.6%	4.4%	— 0.6%	1.2%	3.4%	1950	17.6%
6.3	4.8	0.3	— 3.2	— 0.4	3.0	1951	14.4
1.9	— 1.6	— 1.6	— 0.5	5.4	2.9	1952	8.4
2.7	— 5.1	1.1	4.5	2.0	— 0.2	1953	— 3.8
4.3	— 3.5	7.3	— 2.3	9.8	4.6	1954	44.0
3.2	0.5	— 0.3	— 2.5	6.2	1.1	1955	20.8
5.1	— 3.0	— 5.3	1.0	— 1.5	5.6	1956	2.3
1.0	— 4.8	— 5.8	— 3.3	2.0	— 3.2	1957	—12.8
5.2	1.1	4.6	2.1	2.6	4.7	1958	34.0
4.9	— 1.6	— 4.9	2.4	1.9	3.1	1959	16.4
— 3.7	1.5	— 7.3	0.04	2.9	3.1	1960	— 9.3
3.1	2.1	— 2.6	0.4	2.5	1.3	1961	18.7
6.5	1.9	— 5.0	1.9	10.1	0.4	1962	—10.8
— 1.6	4.9	0.5	3.1	— 0.6	1.7	1963	17.0
1.2	— 0.3	4.4	— 0.3	0.3	— 0.1	1964	14.6
1.6	1.3	4.2	3.2	— 1.5	2.4	1965	10.9
— 2.6	— 7.0	— 1.8	4.2	— 1.9	— 0.7	1966	—18.9
5.1	— 0.3	2.8	— 5.1	— 0.4	3.3	1967	15.2
— 1.6	1.5	4.4	1.8	3.4	— 4.2	1968	4.3
— 6.6	2.6	— 2.8	5.3	— 5.1	— 1.5	1969	—15.2
7.4	4.1	— 0.5	— 0.7	5.1	5.6	1970	4.8
— 3.7	4.6	— 1.2	— 5.4	— 0.9	7.1	1971	6.1
— 0.5	4.2	— 1.1	0.2	6.6	0.2	1972	14.6
3.9	— 4.2	6.7	1.0	—14.0	3.5	1973	—16.6
— 5.6	—10.4	—10.4	9.5	— 7.0	— 0.4	1974	—27.6
— 5.4	0.5	— 5.0	5.3	2.9	— 1.0	1975	38.3
— 1.8	— 1.1	1.7	— 2.6	— 1.8	6.1	1976	17.9
— 2.9	— 3.2	— 1.7	— 3.4	1.4	0.2	1977	—17.3
5.3	1.7	— 1.3	— 8.5	0.8	0.7	1978	— 3.1
0.5	4.9	— 1.0	— 7.2	0.8	2.0	1979	4.2
7.8	— 0.3	—0.02	— 0.9	7.4	— 3.0	1980	14.9
— 2.5	— 7.4	— 3.6	0.3	4.3	— 1.6	1981	— 9.2
— 0.4	11.5	— 0.6	10.7	4.8	0.7	1982	19.6
— 1.9	1.4	1.4	— 0.6	4.1	— 1.4	1983	20.3
— 1.5	9.8	— 1.4	0.1	— 1.5	1.9	1984	— 3.7
0.9	— 1.0	— 0.4	3.4	7.1	5.1	1985	27.7
— 6.2	6.9	— 6.9	6.2	1.9	— 1.0	1986	22.6
6.3	3.5	— 2.5	—23.2	— 8.0	5.7	1987	2.3
— 0.6	— 4.6	4.0	1.7	— 1.6	2.6	1988	11.8
9.0	2.9	— 1.6	— 1.8	2.3	1.7	1989	27.0
0.9	—10.0	— 6.2	— 0.4	4.8	2.9	1990	— 4.3
4.1	0.6	— 0.9	1.7	— 5.7	9.5	1991	20.3
2.3	— 4.0	0.4	— 1.4	2.4	— 0.1	1992	4.2
0.7	3.2	— 2.6	3.5	0.1	1.9	1993	13.7
3.8	4.0	— 1.8	1.7	— 4.3	2.5	1994	2.1
3.3	— 2.1	3.9	— 0.7	6.7	0.8	1995	33.5
— 2.2	1.6	4.7	2.5	8.2	— 1.1	1996	26.0
7.2	— 7.3	4.2	— 6.3	5.1	1.1	1997	22.6
— 0.8	—15.1	4.0	9.6	6.1	0.7	1998	16.1
— 2.9	1.6	— 4.5	3.8	1.4	5.7	1999	25.2
0.7	6.6	— 5.0	3.0	— 5.1	3.6	2000	— 6.2
0.2	— 5.4	—11.1	2.6	8.6	1.7	2001	— 7.1
— 5.5	— 0.8	—12.4	10.6	5.9	— 6.2	2002	—16.8
2.8	2.0	— 1.5	5.7	— 0.2	6.9	2003	25.3
— 2.8	0.3	— 0.9	— 0.5	4.0	3.4	2004	3.1
						2005	
55.9%	— 2.7%	—58.4%	31.5%	91.7%	98.9%		
1.0%	— 0.1%	— 1.1%	0.6%	1.7%	1.8%		
33	31	19	32	37	40		
22	24	36	23	18	15		

DOW JONES INDUSTRIALS MONTHLY POINT CHANGES

	JAN	FEB	MAR	APR	MAY	JUN
1950	1.66	1.65	2.61	8.28	9.09	— 14.31
1951	13.42	3.22	— 4.11	11.19	— 9.48	— 7.01
1952	1.46	— 10.61	9.38	— 11.83	5.31	11.32
1953	— 2.13	— 5.50	— 4.40	— 5.12	— 2.47	— 4.02
1954	11.49	2.15	8.97	15.82	8.16	6.04
1955	4.44	3.04	— 2.17	15.95	— 0.79	26.52
1956	— 17.66	12.91	28.14	4.33	— 38.07	14.73
1957	— 20.31	— 14.54	10.19	19.55	10.57	— 1.64
1958	14.33	— 10.10	6.84	9.10	6.84	15.48
1959	10.31	9.54	— 1.79	22.04	20.04	— 0.19
1960	— 56.74	7.50	— 13.53	— 14.89	23.80	15.12
1961	32.31	13.88	14.55	2.08	18.01	— 12.76
1962	— 31.14	8.05	— 1.10	— 41.62	— 51.97	— 52.08
1963	30.75	— 19.91	19.58	35.18	9.26	— 20.08
1964	22.39	14.80	13.15	— 2.52	9.79	10.94
1965	28.73	0.62	— 14.43	33.26	— 4.27	— 50.01
1966	14.25	— 31.62	— 27.12	8.91	— 49.61	— 13.97
1967	64.20	— 10.52	26.61	31.07	— 44.49	7.70
1968	— 49.64	— 14.97	0.17	71.55	— 13.22	— 1.20
1969	2.30	— 40.84	30.27	14.70	— 12.62	— 64.37
1970	— 56.30	33.53	7.98	— 49.50	— 35.63	— 16.91
1971	29.58	10.33	25.54	37.38	— 33.94	— 16.67
1972	11.97	25.96	12.57	13.47	6.55	— 31.69
1973	— 21.00	— 43.95	— 4.06	— 29.58	— 20.02	— 9.70
1974	4.69	4.98	— 13.85	— 9.93	— 34.58	0.24
1975	87.45	35.36	29.10	53.19	10.95	46.70
1976	122.87	— 2.67	26.84	— 2.60	— 21.62	27.55
1977	— 50.28	— 17.95	— 17.29	7.77	— 28.24	17.64
1978	— 61.25	— 27.80	15.24	79.96	3.29	— 21.66
1979	34.21	— 30.40	53.36	— 7.28	— 32.57	19.65
1980	37.11	— 12.71	— 77.39	31.31	33.79	17.07
1981	— 16.72	27.31	29.29	— 6.12	— 6.00	— 14.87
1982	— 3.90	— 46.71	— 1.62	25.59	— 28.82	— 7.61
1983	29.16	36.92	17.41	96.17	— 26.22	21.98
1984	— 38.06	— 65.95	10.26	5.86	— 65.90	27.55
1985	75.20	— 2.76	— 17.23	— 8.72	57.35	20.05
1986	24.32	138.07	109.55	— 34.63	92.73	16.01
1987	262.09	65.95	80.70	— 18.33	5.21	126.96
1988	19.39	113.40	— 83.56	44.27	— 1.21	110.59
1989	173.75	— 83.93	35.23	125.18	61.35	— 40.09
1990	—162.66	36.71	79.96	— 50.45	219.90	4.03
1991	102.73	145.79	31.68	— 25.99	139.63	—120.75
1992	54.56	44.28	— 32.20	123.65	37.76	— 78.36
1993	8.92	60.78	64.30	— 7.56	99.88	— 11.35
1994	224.27	—146.34	—196.06	45.73	76.68	—133.41
1995	9.42	167.19	146.64	163.58	143.87	90.96
1996	278.18	90.32	101.52	— 18.06	74.10	11.45
1997	364.82	64.65	—294.26	425.51	322.05	341.75
1998	— 1.75	639.22	254.09	263.56	—163.42	52.07
1999	177.40	— 52.25	479.58	1002.88	—229.30	411.06
2000	—556.59	—812.22	793.61	—188.01	—211.58	— 74.44
2001	100.51	—392.08	—616.50	856.19	176.97	—409.54
2002	—101.50	186.13	297.81	—457.72	— 20.97	—681.99
2003	—287.82	—162.73	101.05	487.96	370.17	135.18
2004	34.15	95.85	—226.22	—132.13	— 37.12	247.03
2005	—293.07	276.29	—262.47	—311.25	274.97	—192.51
TOTALS	690.27	317.32	1062.41	2758.38	1103.94	— 249.82
# Up	37	32	35	34	29	28
# Down	19	24	21	22	27	28

146

DOW JONES INDUSTRIALS MONTHLY POINT CHANGES

JUL	AUG	SEP	OCT	NOV	DEC	Year's Close	
0.29	7.47	9.49	− 1.35	2.59	7.81	235.41	1950
15.22	12.39	0.91	− 8.81	− 1.08	7.96	269.23	1951
5.30	− 4.52	− 4.43	− 1.38	14.43	8.24	291.90	1952
7.12	− 14.16	2.82	11.77	5.56	− 0.47	280.90	1953
14.39	− 12.12	24.66	− 8.32	34.63	17.62	404.39	1954
14.47	2.33	− 1.56	− 11.75	28.39	5.14	488.40	1955
25.03	− 15.77	− 26.79	4.60	− 7.07	26.69	499.47	1956
5.23	− 24.17	− 28.05	− 15.26	8.83	− 14.18	435.69	1957
24.81	5.64	23.46	11.13	14.24	26.19	583.65	1958
31.28	− 10.47	− 32.73	14.92	12.58	20.18	679.36	1959
− 23.89	9.26	− 45.85	0.22	16.86	18.67	615.89	1960
21.41	14.57	− 18.73	2.71	17.68	9.54	731.14	1961
36.65	11.25	− 30.20	10.79	59.53	2.80	652.10	1962
− 11.45	33.89	3.47	22.44	− 4.71	12.43	762.95	1963
9.60	− 2.62	36.89	− 2.29	2.35	− 1.30	874.13	1964
13.71	11.36	37.48	30.24	− 14.11	22.55	969.26	1965
− 22.72	− 58.97	14.19	32.85	− 15.48	− 5.90	785.69	1966
43.98	− 2.95	25.37	− 46.92	− 3.93	29.30	905.11	1967
− 14.80	13.01	39.78	16.60	32.69	− 41.33	943.75	1968
− 57.72	21.25	− 23.63	42.90	− 43.69	− 11.94	800.36	1969
50.59	30.46	− 3.90	− 5.07	38.48	44.83	838.92	1970
− 32.71	39.64	− 10.88	− 48.19	− 7.66	58.86	890.20	1971
− 4.29	38.99	− 10.46	2.25	62.69	1.81	1020.02	1972
34.69	− 38.83	59.53	9.48	−134.33	28.61	850.86	1973
− 44.98	− 78.85	− 70.71	57.65	− 46.86	− 2.42	616.24	1974
− 47.48	3.83	− 41.46	42.16	24.63	− 8.26	852.41	1975
− 18.14	10.90	16.45	− 25.26	− 17.71	57.43	1004.65	1976
− 26.23	− 28.58	− 14.38	− 28.76	11.35	1.47	831.17	1977
43.32	14.55	− 11.00	− 73.37	6.58	5.98	805.01	1978
4.44	41.21	− 9.05	− 62.88	6.65	16.39	838.74	1979
67.40	− 2.73	− 0.17	− 7.93	68.85	− 29.35	963.99	1980
− 24.54	− 70.87	− 31.49	2.57	36.43	− 13.98	875.00	1981
− 3.33	92.71	− 5.06	95.47	47.56	7.26	1046.54	1982
− 22.74	16.94	16.97	− 7.93	50.82	− 17.38	1258.64	1983
− 17.12	109.10	− 17.67	0.67	− 18.44	22.63	1211.57	1984
11.99	− 13.44	− 5.38	45.68	97.82	74.54	1546.67	1985
−117.41	123.03	− 130.76	110.23	36.42	− 18.28	1895.95	1986
153.54	90.88	− 66.67	−602.75	−159.98	105.28	1938.83	1987
− 12.98	− 97.08	81.26	35.74	− 34.14	54.06	2168.57	1988
220.60	76.61	− 44.45	− 47.74	61.19	46.93	2753.20	1989
24.51	− 290.84	− 161.88	− 10.15	117.32	74.01	2633.66	1990
118.07	18.78	− 26.83	52.33	−174.42	274.15	3168.83	1991
75.26	− 136.43	14.31	− 45.38	78.88	− 4.05	3301.11	1992
23.39	111.78	− 96.13	125.47	3.36	70.14	3754.09	1993
139.54	148.92	− 70.23	64.93	−168.89	95.21	3834.44	1994
152.37	− 97.91	178.52	− 33.60	319.01	42.63	5117.12	1995
−125.72	87.30	265.96	147.21	492.32	− 73.43	6448.27	1996
549.82	− 600.19	322.84	−503.18	381.05	85.12	7908.25	1997
− 68.73	−1344.22	303.55	749.48	524.45	64.88	9181.43	1998
−315.65	174.13	− 492.33	392.91	147.95	619.31	11497.12	1999
74.09	693.12	− 564.18	320.22	−556.65	372.36	10786.85	2000
20.41	− 573.06	−1102.19	227.58	776.42	169.94	10021.50	2001
−506.67	− 73.09	−1071.57	805.10	499.06	−554.46	8341.63	2002
248.36	182.02	− 140.76	526.06	− 18.66	671.46	10453.92	2003
−295.77	34.21	− 93.65	−52.80	400.55	354.99	10783.01	2004
							2005
465.81	**−1332.14**	**−3055.68**	**2363.29**	**3112.39**	**2838.67**		
33	31	19	32	37	40		
22	24	36	23	18	15		

DOW JONES INDUSTRIALS MONTHLY CLOSING PRICES

	JAN	FEB	MAR	APR	MAY	JUN
1950	201.79	203.44	206.05	214.33	223.42	209.11
1951	248.83	252.05	247.94	259.13	249.65	242.64
1952	270.69	260.08	269.46	257.63	262.94	274.26
1953	289.77	284.27	279.87	274.75	272.28	268.26
1954	292.39	294.54	303.51	319.33	327.49	333.53
1955	408.83	411.87	409.70	425.65	424.86	451.38
1956	470.74	483.65	511.79	516.12	478.05	492.78
1957	479.16	464.62	474.81	494.36	504.93	503.29
1958	450.02	439.92	446.76	455.86	462.70	478.18
1959	593.96	603.50	601.71	623.75	643.79	643.60
1960	622.62	630.12	616.59	601.70	625.50	640.62
1961	648.20	662.08	676.63	678.71	696.72	683.96
1962	700.00	708.05	706.95	665.33	613.36	561.28
1963	682.85	662.94	682.52	717.70	726.96	706.88
1964	785.34	800.14	813.29	810.77	820.56	831.50
1965	902.86	903.48	889.05	922.31	918.04	868.03
1966	983.51	951.89	924.77	933.68	884.07	870.10
1967	849.89	839.37	865.98	897.05	852.56	860.26
1968	855.47	840.50	840.67	912.22	899.00	897.80
1969	946.05	905.21	935.48	950.18	937.56	873.19
1970	744.06	777.59	785.57	736.07	700.44	683.53
1971	868.50	878.83	904.37	941.75	907.81	891.14
1972	902.17	928.13	940.70	954.17	960.72	929.03
1973	999.02	955.07	951.01	921.43	901.41	891.71
1974	855.55	860.53	846.68	836.75	802.17	802.41
1975	703.69	739.05	768.15	821.34	832.29	878.99
1976	975.28	972.61	999.45	996.85	975.23	1002.78
1977	954.37	936.42	919.13	926.90	898.66	916.30
1978	769.92	742.12	757.36	837.32	840.61	818.95
1979	839.22	808.82	862.18	854.90	822.33	841.98
1980	875.85	863.14	785.75	817.06	850.85	867.92
1981	947.27	974.58	1003.87	997.75	991.75	976.88
1982	871.10	824.39	822.77	848.36	819.54	811.93
1983	1075.70	1112.62	1130.03	1226.20	1199.98	1221.96
1984	1220.58	1154.63	1164.89	1170.75	1104.85	1132.40
1985	1286.77	1284.01	1266.78	1258.06	1315.41	1335.46
1986	1570.99	1709.06	1818.61	1783.98	1876.71	1892.72
1987	2158.04	2223.99	2304.69	2286.36	2291.57	2418.53
1988	1958.22	2071.62	1988.06	2032.33	2031.12	2141.71
1989	2342.32	2258.39	2293.62	2418.80	2480.15	2440.06
1990	2590.54	2627.25	2707.21	2656.76	2876.66	2880.69
1991	2736.39	2882.18	2913.86	2887.87	3027.50	2906.75
1992	3223.39	3267.67	3235.47	3359.12	3396.88	3318.52
1993	3310.03	3370.81	3435.11	3427.55	3527.43	3516.08
1994	3978.36	3832.02	3635.96	3681.69	3758.37	3624.96
1995	3843.86	4011.05	4157.69	4321.27	4465.14	4556.10
1996	5395.30	5485.62	5587.14	5569.08	5643.18	5654.63
1997	6813.09	6877.74	6583.48	7008.99	7331.04	7672.79
1998	7906.50	8545.72	8799.81	9063.37	8899.95	8952.02
1999	9358.83	9306.58	9786.16	10789.04	10559.74	10970.80
2000	10940.53	10128.31	10921.92	10733.91	10522.33	10447.89
2001	10887.36	10495.28	9878.78	10734.97	10911.94	10502.40
2002	9920.00	10106.13	10403.94	9946.22	9925.25	9243.26
2003	8053.81	7891.08	7992.13	8480.09	8850.26	8985.44
2004	10488.07	10583.92	10357.70	10225.57	10188.45	10435.48
2005	10489.94	10766.23	10503.76	10192.51	10467.48	10274.97

DOW JONES INDUSTRIALS MONTHLY CLOSING PRICES

JUL	AUG	SEP	OCT	NOV	DEC	
209.40	216.87	226.36	225.01	227.60	235.41	**1950**
257.86	270.25	271.16	262.35	261.27	269.23	**1951**
279.56	275.04	270.61	269.23	283.66	291.90	**1952**
275.38	261.22	264.04	275.81	281.37	280.90	**1953**
347.92	335.80	360.46	352.14	386.77	404.39	**1954**
465.85	468.18	466.62	454.87	483.26	488.40	**1955**
517.81	502.04	475.25	479.85	472.78	499.47	**1956**
508.52	484.35	456.30	441.04	449.87	435.69	**1957**
502.99	508.63	532.09	543.22	557.46	583.65	**1958**
674.88	664.41	631.68	646.60	659.18	679.36	**1959**
616.73	625.99	580.14	580.36	597.22	615.89	**1960**
705.37	719.94	701.21	703.92	721.60	731.14	**1961**
597.93	609.18	578.98	589.77	649.30	652.10	**1962**
695.43	729.32	732.79	755.23	750.52	762.95	**1963**
841.10	838.48	875.37	873.08	875.43	874.13	**1964**
881.74	893.10	930.58	960.82	946.71	969.26	**1965**
847.38	788.41	774.22	807.07	791.59	785.69	**1966**
904.24	901.29	926.66	879.74	875.81	905.11	**1967**
883.00	896.01	935.79	952.39	985.08	943.75	**1968**
815.47	836.72	813.09	855.99	812.30	800.36	**1969**
734.12	764.58	760.68	755.61	794.09	838.92	**1970**
858.43	898.07	887.19	839.00	831.34	890.20	**1971**
924.74	963.73	953.27	955.52	1018.21	1020.02	**1972**
926.40	887.57	947.10	956.58	822.25	850.86	**1973**
757.43	678.58	607.87	665.52	618.66	616.24	**1974**
831.51	835.34	793.88	836.04	860.67	852.41	**1975**
984.64	973.74	990.19	964.93	947.22	1004.65	**1976**
890.07	861.49	847.11	818.35	829.70	831.17	**1977**
862.27	876.82	865.82	792.45	799.03	805.01	**1978**
846.42	887.63	878.58	815.70	822.35	838.74	**1979**
935.32	932.59	932.42	924.49	993.34	963.99	**1980**
952.34	881.47	849.98	852.55	888.98	875.00	**1981**
808.60	901.31	896.25	991.72	1039.28	1046.54	**1982**
1199.22	1216.16	1233.13	1225.20	1276.02	1258.64	**1983**
1115.28	1224.38	1206.71	1207.38	1188.94	1211.57	**1984**
1347.45	1334.01	1328.63	1374.31	1472.13	1546.67	**1985**
1775.31	1898.34	1767.58	1877.81	1914.23	1895.95	**1986**
2572.07	2662.95	2596.28	1993.53	1833.55	1938.83	**1987**
2128.73	2031.65	2112.91	2148.65	2114.51	2168.57	**1988**
2660.66	2737.27	2692.82	2645.08	2706.27	2753.20	**1989**
2905.20	2614.36	2452.48	2442.33	2559.65	2633.66	**1990**
3024.82	3043.60	3016.77	3069.10	2894.68	3168.83	**1991**
3393.78	3257.35	3271.66	3226.28	3305.16	3301.11	**1992**
3539.47	3651.25	3555.12	3680.59	3683.95	3754.09	**1993**
3764.50	3913.42	3843.19	3908.12	3739.23	3834.44	**1994**
4708.47	4610.56	4789.08	4755.48	5074.49	5117.12	**1995**
5528.91	5616.21	5882.17	6029.38	6521.70	6448.27	**1996**
8222.61	7622.42	7945.26	7442.08	7823.13	7908.25	**1997**
8883.29	7539.07	7842.62	8592.62	9116.55	9181.43	**1998**
10655.15	10829.28	10336.95	10729.86	10877.81	11497.12	**1999**
10521.98	11215.10	10650.92	10971.14	10414.49	10786.85	**2000**
10522.81	9949.75	8847.56	9075.14	9851.56	10021.50	**2001**
8736.59	8663.50	7591.93	8397.03	8896.09	8341.63	**2002**
9233.80	9415.82	9275.06	9801.12	9782.46	10453.92	**2003**
10139.71	10173.92	10080.27	10027.47	10428.02	10783.01	**2004**
						2005

NASDAQ COMPOSITE
MONTHLY PERCENT CHANGES

	JAN	FEB	MAR	APR	MAY	JUN
1971	10.2%	2.6%	4.6%	6.0%	− 3.6%	− 0.4%
1972	4.2	5.5	2.2	2.5	0.9	− 1.8
1973	− 4.0	− 6.2	− 2.4	− 8.2	− 4.8	− 1.6
1974	3.0	− 0.6	− 2.2	− 5.9	− 7.7	− 5.3
1975	16.6	4.6	3.6	3.8	5.8	4.7
1976	12.1	3.7	0.4	− 0.6	− 2.3	2.6
1977	− 2.4	− 1.0	− 0.5	1.4	0.1	4.3
1978	− 4.0	0.6	4.7	8.5	4.4	0.05
1979	6.6	− 2.6	7.5	1.6	− 1.8	5.1
1980	7.0	− 2.3	− 17.1	6.9	7.5	4.9
1981	− 2.2	0.1	6.1	3.1	3.1	− 3.5
1982	− 3.8	− 4.8	− 2.1	5.2	− 3.3	− 4.1
1983	6.9	5.0	3.9	8.2	5.3	3.2
1984	− 3.7	− 5.9	− 0.7	− 1.3	− 5.9	2.9
1985	12.7	2.0	− 1.7	0.5	3.6	1.9
1986	3.3	7.1	4.2	2.3	4.4	1.3
1987	12.2	8.4	1.2	− 2.8	− 0.3	2.0
1988	4.3	6.5	2.1	1.2	− 2.3	6.6
1989	5.2	− 0.4	1.8	5.1	4.4	− 2.4
1990	− 8.6	2.4	2.3	− 3.6	9.3	0.7
1991	10.8	9.4	6.5	0.5	4.4	− 6.0
1992	5.8	2.1	− 4.7	− 4.2	1.1	− 3.7
1993	2.9	− 3.7	2.9	− 4.2	5.9	0.5
1994	3.0	− 1.0	− 6.2	− 1.3	0.2	− 4.0
1995	0.4	5.1	3.0	3.3	2.4	8.0
1996	0.7	3.8	0.1	8.1	4.4	− 4.7
1997	6.9	− 5.1	− 6.7	3.2	11.1	3.0
1998	3.1	9.3	3.7	1.8	− 4.8	6.5
1999	14.3	− 8.7	7.6	3.3	− 2.8	8.7
2000	− 3.2	19.2	− 2.6	− 15.6	− 11.9	16.6
2001	12.2	−22.4	− 14.5	15.0	− 0.3	2.4
2002	− 0.8	−10.5	6.6	− 8.5	− 4.3	− 9.4
2003	− 1.1	1.3	0.3	9.2	9.0	1.7
2004	3.1	− 1.8	− 1.8	− 3.7	3.5	3.1
2005	− 5.2	− 0.5	− 2.6	− 3.9	7.6	− 0.5
TOTALS	128.5%	21.2%	9.5%	36.9%	42.3%	43.4%
AVG.	3.7%	0.6%	0.3%	1.1%	1.2%	1.2%
# Up	24	19	21	22	21	22
# Down	11	16	14	13	14	13

Based on NASDAQ composite, prior to February 5, 1971, based on National Quotation Bureau indices

NASDAQ COMPOSITE MONTHLY PERCENT CHANGES

JUL	AUG	SEP	OCT	NOV	DEC		Year's Change
— 2.3%	3.0%	0.6%	— 3.6%	— 1.1%	9.8%	**1971**	27.4%
— 1.8	1.7	— 0.3	0.5	2.1	0.6	**1972**	17.2
7.6	— 3.5	6.0	— 0.9	— 15.1	— 1.4	**1973**	— 31.1
— 7.9	— 10.9	— 10.7	17.2	— 3.5	— 5.0	**1974**	— 35.1
— 4.4	— 5.0	— 5.9	3.6	2.4	— 1.5	**1975**	29.8
1.1	— 1.7	1.7	— 1.0	0.9	7.4	**1976**	26.1
0.9	— 0.5	0.7	— 3.3	5.8	1.8	**1977**	7.3
5.0	6.9	— 1.6	— 16.4	3.2	2.9	**1978**	12.3
2.3	6.4	— 0.3	— 9.6	6.4	4.8	**1979**	28.1
8.9	5.7	3.4	2.7	8.0	— 2.8	**1980**	33.9
— 1.9	— 7.5	— 8.0	8.4	3.1	— 2.7	**1981**	— 3.2
— 2.3	6.2	5.6	13.3	9.3	0.04	**1982**	18.7
— 4.6	— 3.8	1.4	— 7.4	4.1	— 2.5	**1983**	19.9
— 4.2	10.9	— 1.8	— 1.2	— 1.8	2.0	**1984**	— 11.2
1.7	— 1.2	— 5.8	4.4	7.3	3.5	**1985**	31.4
— 8.4	3.1	— 8.4	2.9	— 0.3	— 2.8	**1986**	7.5
2.4	4.6	— 2.3	— 27.2	— 5.6	8.3	**1987**	— 5.4
— 1.9	— 2.8	3.0	— 1.4	— 2.9	2.7	**1988**	15.4
4.3	3.4	0.8	— 3.7	0.1	— 0.3	**1989**	19.3
— 5.2	— 13.0	— 9.6	— 4.3	8.9	4.1	**1990**	— 17.8
5.5	4.7	0.2	3.1	— 3.5	11.9	**1991**	56.8
3.1	— 3.0	3.6	3.8	7.9	3.7	**1992**	15.5
0.1	5.4	2.7	2.2	— 3.2	3.0	**1993**	14.7
2.3	6.0	— 0.2	1.7	— 3.5	0.2	**1994**	— 3.2
7.3	1.9	2.3	— 0.7	2.2	— 0.7	**1995**	39.9
— 8.8	5.6	7.5	— 0.4	5.8	— 0.1	**1996**	22.7
10.5	— 0.4	6.2	— 5.5	0.4	— 1.9	**1997**	21.6
— 1.2	— 19.9	13.0	4.6	10.1	12.5	**1998**	39.6
— 1.8	3.8	0.2	8.0	12.5	22.0	**1999**	85.6
— 5.0	11.7	— 12.7	— 8.3	— 22.9	— 4.9	**2000**	— 39.3
— 6.2	— 10.9	— 17.0	12.8	14.2	1.0	**2001**	— 21.1
— 9.2	— 1.0	— 10.9	13.5	11.2	— 9.7	**2002**	— 31.5
6.9	4.3	— 1.3	8.1	1.5	2.2	**2003**	50.0
— 7.8	— 2.6	3.2	4.1	6.2	3.7	**2004**	8.6
						2005	
— 15.0%	7.6%	— 34.7%	20.0%	70.2%	71.8%		
— 0.4%	0.2%	— 1.0%	0.6%	2.1%	2.1%		
16	18	18	18	23	21		
18	16	16	16	11	13		

151

NASDAQ COMPOSITE
MONTHLY CLOSING PRICES

	JAN	FEB	MAR	APR	MAY	JUN
1971	98.77	101.34	105.97	112.30	108.25	107.80
1972	118.87	125.38	128.14	131.33	132.53	130.08
1973	128.40	120.41	117.46	107.85	102.64	100.98
1974	94.93	94.35	92.27	86.86	80.20	75.96
1975	69.78	73.00	75.66	78.54	83.10	87.02
1976	87.05	90.26	90.62	90.08	88.04	90.32
1977	95.54	94.57	94.13	95.48	95.59	99.73
1978	100.84	101.47	106.20	115.18	120.24	120.30
1979	125.82	122.56	131.76	133.82	131.42	138.13
1980	161.75	158.03	131.00	139.99	150.45	157.78
1981	197.81	198.01	210.18	216.74	223.47	215.75
1982	188.39	179.43	175.65	184.70	178.54	171.30
1983	248.35	260.67	270.80	293.06	308.73	318.70
1984	268.43	252.57	250.78	247.44	232.82	239.65
1985	278.70	284.17	279.20	280.56	290.80	296.20
1986	335.77	359.53	374.72	383.24	400.16	405.51
1987	392.06	424.97	430.05	417.81	416.54	424.67
1988	344.66	366.95	374.64	379.23	370.34	394.66
1989	401.30	399.71	406.73	427.55	446.17	435.29
1990	415.81	425.83	435.54	420.07	458.97	462.29
1991	414.20	453.05	482.30	484.72	506.11	475.92
1992	620.21	633.47	603.77	578.68	585.31	563.60
1993	696.34	670.77	690.13	661.42	700.53	703.95
1994	800.47	792.50	743.46	733.84	735.19	705.96
1995	755.20	793.73	817.21	843.98	864.58	933.45
1996	1059.79	1100.05	1101.40	1190.52	1243.43	1185.02
1997	1379.85	1309.00	1221.70	1260.76	1400.32	1442.07
1998	1619.36	1770.51	1835.68	1868.41	1778.87	1894.74
1999	2505.89	2288.03	2461.40	2542.85	2470.52	2686.12
2000	3940.35	4696.69	4572.83	3860.66	3400.91	3966.11
2001	2772.73	2151.83	1840.26	2116.24	2110.49	2160.54
2002	1934.03	1731.49	1845.35	1688.23	1615.73	1463.21
2003	1320.91	1337.52	1341.17	1464.31	1595.91	1622.80
2004	2066.15	2029.82	1994.22	1920.15	1986.74	2047.79
2005	2062.41	2051.72	1999.23	1921.65	2068.22	2056.96

Based on NASDAQ composite, prior to February 5, 1971, based on National Quotation Bureau indices

JUL	AUG	SEP	OCT	NOV	DEC	
105.27	108.42	109.03	105.10	103.97	114.12	**1971**
127.75	129.95	129.61	130.24	132.96	133.73	**1972**
108.64	104.87	111.20	110.17	93.51	92.19	**1973**
69.99	62.37	55.67	65.23	62.95	59.82	**1974**
83.19	79.01	74.33	76.99	78.80	77.62	**1975**
91.29	89.70	91.26	90.35	91.12	97.88	**1976**
100.65	100.10	100.85	97.52	103.15	105.05	**1977**
126.32	135.01	132.89	111.12	114.69	117.98	**1978**
141.33	150.44	149.98	135.53	144.26	151.14	**1979**
171.81	181.52	187.76	192.78	208.15	202.34	**1980**
211.63	195.75	180.03	195.24	201.37	195.84	**1981**
167.35	177.71	187.65	212.63	232.31	232.41	**1982**
303.96	292.42	296.65	274.55	285.67	278.60	**1983**
229.70	254.64	249.94	247.03	242.53	247.35	**1984**
301.29	297.71	280.33	292.54	313.95	324.93	**1985**
371.37	382.86	350.67	360.77	359.57	349.33	**1986**
434.93	454.97	444.29	323.30	305.16	330.47	**1987**
387.33	376.55	387.71	382.46	371.45	381.38	**1988**
453.84	469.33	472.92	455.63	456.09	454.82	**1989**
438.24	381.21	344.51	329.84	359.06	373.84	**1990**
502.04	525.68	526.88	542.98	523.90	586.34	**1991**
580.83	563.12	583.27	605.17	652.73	676.95	**1992**
704.70	742.84	762.78	779.26	754.39	776.80	**1993**
722.16	765.62	764.29	777.49	750.32	751.96	**1994**
1001.21	1020.11	1043.54	1036.06	1059.20	1052.13	**1995**
1080.59	1141.50	1226.92	1221.51	1292.61	1291.03	**1996**
1593.81	1587.32	1685.69	1593.61	1600.55	1570.35	**1997**
1872.39	1499.25	1693.84	1771.39	1949.54	2192.69	**1998**
2638.49	2739.35	2746.16	2966.43	3336.16	4069.31	**1999**
3766.99	4206.35	3672.82	3369.63	2597.93	2470.52	**2000**
2027.13	1805.43	1498.80	1690.20	1930.58	1950.40	**2001**
1328.26	1314.85	1172.06	1329.75	1478.78	1335.51	**2002**
1735.02	1810.45	1786.94	1932.21	1960.26	2003.37	**2003**
1887.36	1838.10	1896.84	1974.99	2096.81	2175.44	**2004**
						2005

BEST & WORST DOW DAYS SINCE 1901 BY POINTS AND PERCENT

BEST TWENTY DAYS SINCE 1901 BY POINTS

Day	DJIA Close	Points Change	% Change
3/16/2000	10630.60	499.19	4.9
7/24/2002	8191.29	488.95	6.3
7/29/2002	8711.88	447.49	5.4
4/5/2001	9918.05	402.63	4.2
4/18/2001	10615.83	399.10	3.9
9/8/1998	8020.78	380.53	5.0
10/15/2002	8255.68	378.28	4.8
9/24/2001	8603.86	368.05	4.5
10/1/2002	7938.79	346.86	4.6
5/16/2001	11215.92	342.95	3.2
12/5/2000	10898.72	338.62	3.2
10/28/1997	7498.32	337.17	4.7
10/15/1998	8299.36	330.58	4.1
7/5/2002	9379.50	324.53	3.6
3/15/2000	10131.41	320.17	3.3
10/11/2002	7850.29	316.34	4.2
5/8/2002	10141.83	305.28	3.1
4/3/2000	11221.93	300.01	2.7
1/3/2001	10945.75	299.60	2.8
9/1/1998	7827.43	288.36	3.8

WORST TWENTY DAYS SINCE 1901 BY POINTS

Day	DJIA Close	Points Change	% Change
9/17/2001	8920.70	− 684.81	− 7.1
4/14/2000	10305.77	− 617.78	− 5.7
10/27/1997	7161.15	− 554.26	− 7.2
8/31/1998	7539.07	− 512.61	− 6.4
10/19/1987	1738.74	− 508.00	− 22.6
3/12/2001	10208.25	− 436.37	− 4.1
7/19/2002	8019.26	− 390.23	− 4.6
9/20/2001	8376.21	− 382.92	− 4.4
10/12/2000	10034.58	− 379.21	− 3.6
3/7/2000	9796.03	− 374.47	− 3.7
1/4/2000	10997.93	− 359.58	− 3.2
8/27/1998	8165.99	− 357.36	− 4.2
9/3/2002	8308.05	− 355.45	− 4.1
3/14/2001	9973.46	− 317.34	− 3.1
3/24/2003	8214.68	− 307.29	− 3.6
8/4/1998	8487.31	− 299.43	− 3.4
9/27/2002	7701.45	− 295.67	− 3.7
2/18/2000	10219.52	− 295.05	− 2.8
4/3/2001	9485.71	− 292.22	− 3.0
1/28/2000	10738.87	− 289.15	− 2.6

BEST TWENTY DAYS SINCE 1950 BY %

Day	DJIA Close	Points Change	% Change
10/21/1987	2027.85	186.84	10.1
7/24/2002	8191.29	488.95	6.3
10/20/1987	1841.01	102.27	5.9
7/29/2002	8711.88	447.49	5.4
5/27/1970	663.20	32.04	5.1
9/8/1998	8020.78	380.53	5.0
10/29/1987	1938.33	91.51	5.0
3/16/2000	10630.60	499.19	4.9
8/17/1982	831.24	38.81	4.9
10/15/2002	8255.68	378.28	4.8
10/9/1974	631.02	28.39	4.7
10/28/1997	7498.32	337.17	4.7
5/29/1962	603.96	27.03	4.7
10/1/2002	7938.79	346.86	4.6
1/17/1991	2623.51	114.60	4.6
11/26/1963	743.52	32.03	4.5
9/24/2001	8603.86	368.05	4.5
11/1/1978	827.79	35.34	4.5
11/3/1982	1065.49	43.41	4.2

WORST TWENTY DAYS SINCE 1950 BY %

Day	DJIA Close	Points Change	% Change
10/19/1987	1738.74	− 508.00	− 22.6
10/26/1987	1793.93	− 156.83	− 8.0
10/27/1997	7161.15	− 554.26	− 7.2
9/17/2001	8920.70	− 684.81	− 7.1
10/13/1989	2569.26	− 190.58	− 6.9
1/8/1988	1911.31	− 140.58	− 6.9
9/26/1955	455.56	− 31.89	− 6.5
8/31/1998	7539.07	− 512.61	− 6.4
5/28/1962	576.93	− 34.95	− 5.7
4/14/2000	10305.77	− 617.78	− 5.7
4/14/1988	2005.64	− 101.46	− 4.8
6/26/1950	213.91	− 10.44	− 4.7
7/19/2002	8019.26	− 390.23	− 4.6
9/11/1986	1792.89	− 86.61	− 4.6
10/16/1987	2246.74	− 108.35	− 4.6
9/20/2001	8376.21	− 382.92	− 4.4
8/27/1998	8165.99	− 357.36	− 4.2
9/3/2002	8308.05	− 355.45	− 4.1
3/12/2001	10208.25	− 436.37	− 4.1
11/30/1987	1833.55	− 76.93	− 4.0

BEST FIFTEEN DAYS 1901-1949 BY %

Day	DJIA Close	Points Change	% Change
3/15/1933	62.10	8.26	15.3
10/6/1931	99.34	12.86	14.9
10/30/1929	258.47	28.40	12.3
9/21/1932	75.16	7.67	11.4
8/3/1932	58.22	5.06	9.5
2/11/1932	78.60	6.80	9.5
11/14/1929	217.28	18.59	9.4
12/18/1931	80.69	6.90	9.4
2/13/1932	85.82	7.22	9.2
5/6/1932	59.01	4.91	9.1
4/19/1933	68.31	5.66	9.0
10/8/1931	105.79	8.47	8.7
6/10/1932	48.94	3.62	8.0
9/5/1939	148.12	10.03	7.3
6/3/1931	130.37	8.67	7.1

WORST FIFTEEN DAYS 1901-1949 BY %

Day	DJIA Close	Points Change	% Change
10/28/1929	260.64	− 38.33	− 12.8
10/29/1929	230.07	− 30.57	− 11.7
11/6/1929	232.13	− 25.55	− 9.9
8/12/1932	63.11	− 5.79	− 8.4
3/14/1907	55.84	− 5.05	− 8.3
7/21/1933	88.71	− 7.55	− 7.8
10/18/1937	125.73	− 10.57	− 7.8
2/1/1917	88.52	− 6.91	− 7.2
10/5/1932	66.07	− 5.09	− 7.2
9/24/1931	107.79	− 8.20	− 7.1
7/20/1933	96.26	− 7.32	− 7.1
7/30/1914	52.32	− 3.88	− 6.9
11/11/1929	220.39	− 16.14	− 6.8
5/14/1940	128.27	− 9.36	− 6.8
10/5/1931	86.48	− 6.29	− 6.8

BEST & WORST NASDAQ DAYS
SINCE 1971 BY POINTS AND PERCENT

BEST TWENTY DAYS SINCE 1971 BY POINTS

Day	NASDAQ Close	Points Change	% Change
1/3/2001	2616.69	324.83	14.2
12/5/2000	2889.80	274.05	10.5
4/18/2000	3793.57	254.41	7.2
5/30/2000	3459.48	254.37	7.9
10/19/2000	3418.60	247.04	7.8
10/13/2000	3316.77	242.09	7.9
6/2/2000	3813.38	230.88	6.4
4/25/2000	3711.23	228.75	6.6
4/17/2000	3539.16	217.87	6.6
6/1/2000	3582.50	181.59	5.3
4/7/2000	4446.45	178.89	4.2
10/31/2000	3369.63	178.23	5.6
12/22/2000	2517.02	176.90	7.6
11/14/2000	3138.27	171.55	5.8
2/23/2000	4550.33	168.21	3.8
1/10/2000	4049.67	167.05	4.3
12/8/2000	2917.43	164.77	6.0
3/3/2000	4914.79	160.28	3.4
4/18/2001	2079.44	156.22	8.1
1/7/2000	3882.62	155.49	4.2

WORST TWENTY DAYS SINCE 1971 BY POINTS

Day	NASDAQ Close	Points Change	% Change
4/14/2000	3321.29	− 355.49	− 9.7
4/3/2000	4223.68	− 349.15	− 7.6
4/12/2000	3769.63	− 286.27	− 7.1
4/10/2000	4188.20	− 258.25	− 5.8
1/4/2000	3901.69	− 229.46	− 5.6
3/14/2000	4706.63	− 200.61	− 4.1
5/10/2000	3384.73	− 200.28	− 5.6
5/23/2000	3164.55	− 199.66	− 5.9
10/25/2000	3229.57	− 190.22	− 5.6
3/29/2000	4644.67	− 189.22	− 3.9
3/20/2000	4610.00	− 188.13	− 3.9
3/30/2000	4457.89	− 186.78	− 4.0
11/8/2000	3231.70	− 184.09	− 5.4
7/28/2000	3663.00	− 179.23	− 4.7
12/20/2000	2332.78	− 178.93	− 7.1
1/2/2001	2291.86	− 178.66	− 7.2
5/2/2000	3785.45	− 172.63	− 4.4
11/10/2000	3028.99	− 171.36	− 5.4
4/24/2000	3482.48	− 161.40	− 4.4
1/5/2001	2407.65	− 159.18	− 6.2

BEST TWENTY DAYS SINCE 1971 BY %

Day	NASDAQ Close	Points Change	% Change
1/3/2001	2616.69	324.83	14.2
12/5/2000	2889.80	274.05	10.5
4/5/2001	1785.00	146.20	8.9
4/18/2001	2079.44	156.22	8.1
5/30/2000	3459.48	254.37	7.9
10/13/2000	3316.77	242.09	7.9
10/19/2000	3418.60	247.04	7.8
5/8/2002	1696.29	122.47	7.8
12/22/2000	2517.02	176.90	7.6
10/21/1987	351.86	24.07	7.3
4/18/2000	3793.57	254.41	7.2
4/25/2000	3711.23	228.75	6.6
4/17/2000	3539.16	217.87	6.6
6/2/2000	3813.38	230.88	6.4
4/10/2001	1852.03	106.32	6.1
9/8/1998	1660.86	94.34	6.0
12/8/2000	2917.43	164.77	6.0
10/3/2001	1580.81	88.48	5.9
7/29/2002	1335.25	73.13	5.8
11/14/2000	3138.27	171.55	5.8

WORST TWENTY DAYS SINCE 1971 BY %

Day	NASDAQ Close	Points Change	% Change
10/19/1987	360.21	− 46.12	−11.4
4/14/2000	3321.29	− 355.49	− 9.7
10/20/1987	327.79	− 32.42	− 9.0
10/26/1987	298.90	− 29.55	− 9.0
8/31/1998	1499.25	− 140.43	− 8.6
4/3/2000	4223.68	− 349.15	− 7.6
1/2/2001	2291.86	− 178.66	− 7.2
12/20/2000	2332.78	− 178.93	− 7.1
4/12/2000	3769.63	− 286.27	− 7.1
10/27/1997	1535.09	− 115.83	− 7.0
9/17/2001	1579.55	− 115.83	− 6.8
3/12/2001	1923.38	− 129.40	− 6.3
1/5/2001	2407.65	− 159.18	− 6.2
4/3/2001	1673.00	− 109.97	− 6.2
3/27/1980	124.09	− 8.13	− 6.1
3/28/2001	1854.13	− 118.13	− 6.0
5/23/2000	3164.55	− 199.66	− 5.9
4/10/2000	4188.20	− 258.25	− 5.8
5/10/2000	3384.73	− 200.28	− 5.6
4/19/1999	2345.61	− 138.43	− 5.6

Based on NASDAQ composite, prior to February 5, 1971, based on National Quotation Bureau indices

BEST & WORST <u>DOW</u> WEEKS
SINCE 1901 BY POINTS AND PERCENT

BEST TWENTY WEEKS SINCE 1901 BY POINTS

Week Ending	DJIA Close	Points Change	% Change
3/17/2000	10595.23	666.41	6.7
3/21/2003	8521.97	662.26	8.4
9/28/2001	8847.56	611.75	7.4
7/2/1999	11139.24	586.68	5.6
4/20/2000	10844.05	538.28	5.2
3/24/2000	11112.72	517.49	4.9
10/16/1998	8416.76	517.24	6.5
3/3/2000	10367.20	505.08	5.1
6/2/2000	10794.76	495.52	4.8
5/18/2001	11301.74	480.43	4.4
10/18/2002	8322.40	472.11	6.0
1/8/1999	9643.32	461.89	5.0
4/20/2001	10579.85	452.91	4.5
10/22/1999	10470.25	450.54	4.5
8/9/2002	8745.45	432.32	5.2
3/5/1999	9736.08	429.50	4.6
5/17/2002	10353.08	413.16	4.2
3/1/2002	10368.86	400.71	4.0
11/6/1998	8975.46	383.36	4.5
10/8/1999	10649.76	376.76	3.7

WORST TWENTY WEEKS SINCE 1901 BY POINTS

Week Ending	DJIA Close	Points Change	% Change
9/21/2001	8235.81	−1369.70	− 14.3
3/16/2001	9823.41	− 821.21	− 7.7
4/14/2000	10305.77	− 805.71	− 7.3
7/12/2002	8684.53	− 694.97	− 7.4
7/19/2002	8019.26	− 665.27	− 7.7
10/15/1999	10019.71	− 630.05	− 5.9
2/11/2000	10425.21	− 538.59	− 4.9
9/24/1999	10279.33	− 524.30	− 4.9
1/28/2000	10738.87	− 512.84	− 4.6
8/28/1998	8051.68	− 481.97	− 5.6
8/31/2001	9949.75	− 473.42	− 4.5
1/21/2000	11251.71	− 471.27	− 4.0
1/24/2003	8131.01	− 455.73	− 5.3
3/10/2000	9928.82	− 438.38	− 4.2
9/4/1998	7640.25	− 411.43	− 5.1
10/13/2000	10192.18	− 404.36	− 3.8
7/24/1998	8937.36	− 400.61	− 4.3
1/9/1998	7580.42	− 384.62	− 4.8
3/28/2003	8145.77	− 376.20	− 4.4
2/23/2001	10441.90	− 357.92	− 3.3

BEST TWENTY WEEKS SINCE 1950 BY %

Week Ending	DJIA Close	Points Change	% Change
10/11/1974	658.17	73.61	12.6
8/20/1982	869.29	81.24	10.3
10/8/1982	986.85	79.11	8.7
3/21/2003	8521.97	662.26	8.4
8/3/1984	1202.08	87.46	7.8
9/28/2001	8847.56	611.75	7.4
9/20/1974	670.76	43.57	6.9
3/17/2000	10595.23	666.41	6.7
10/16/1998	8416.76	517.24	6.5
6/7/1974	853.72	51.55	6.4
11/2/1962	604.58	35.56	6.2
1/9/1976	911.13	52.42	6.1
11/5/1982	1051.78	60.06	6.1
10/18/2002	8322.40	472.11	6.0
6/3/1988	2071.30	114.86	5.9
1/18/1991	2646.78	145.29	5.8
12/18/1987	1975.30	108.26	5.8
11/14/1980	986.35	53.93	5.8
5/29/1970	700.44	38.27	5.8
12/11/1987	1867.04	100.30	5.7

WORST TWENTY WEEKS SINCE 1950 BY %

Week Ending	DJIA Close	Points Change	% Change
9/21/2001	8235.81	−1369.70	− 14.3
10/23/1987	1950.76	− 295.98	− 13.2
10/16/1987	2246.74	− 235.47	− 9.5
10/13/1989	2569.26	− 216.26	− 7.8
3/16/2001	9823.41	− 821.21	− 7.7
7/19/2002	8019.26	− 665.27	− 7.7
12/4/1987	1766.74	− 143.74	− 7.5
9/13/1974	627.19	− 50.69	− 7.5
9/12/1986	1758.72	− 141.03	− 7.4
7/12/2002	8684.53	− 694.97	− 7.4
9/27/1974	621.95	− 48.81	− 7.3
4/14/2000	10305.77	− 805.71	− 7.3
6/30/1950	209.11	− 15.24	− 6.8
6/22/1962	539.19	− 38.99	− 6.7
12/6/1974	577.60	− 41.06	− 6.6
10/20/1978	838.01	− 59.08	− 6.6
10/12/1979	838.99	− 58.62	− 6.5
8/23/1974	686.80	− 44.74	− 6.1
10/9/1987	2482.21	− 158.78	− 6.0
10/4/1974	584.56	− 37.39	− 6.0

BEST TEN WEEKS 1901-1949 BY %

Week Ending	DJIA Close	Points Change	% Change
8/6/32	66.56	12.30	22.7
6/25/38	131.94	18.71	16.5
2/13/32	85.82	11.37	15.3
4/22/33	72.24	9.36	14.9
10/10/31	105.61	12.84	13.8
7/30/32	54.26	6.42	13.4
6/27/31	156.93	17.97	12.9
9/24/32	74.83	8.39	12.6
8/27/32	75.61	8.43	12.5
3/18/33	60.56	6.72	12.5

WORST TEN WEEKS 1901-1949 BY %

Week Ending	DJIA Close	Points Change	% Change
7/22/33	88.42	− 17.68	− 16.7
5/18/40	122.43	− 22.42	− 15.5
10/8/32	61.17	− 10.92	− 15.1
10/3/31	92.77	− 14.59	− 13.6
11/8/29	236.53	− 36.98	− 13.5
9/17/32	66.44	− 10.10	− 13.2
10/21/33	83.64	− 11.95	− 12.5
12/12/31	78.93	− 11.21	− 12.4
5/8/15	62.77	− 8.74	− 12.2
6/21/30	215.30	− 28.95	− 11.9

BEST & WORST NASDAQ WEEKS
SINCE 1971 BY POINTS AND PERCENT

BEST TWENTY WEEKS SINCE 1971 BY POINTS

Week Ending	NASDAQ Close	Points Change	% Change
6/2/2000	3813.38	608.27	19.0
2/4/2000	4244.14	357.07	9.2
3/3/2000	4914.79	324.29	7.1
4/20/2000	3643.88	322.59	9.7
12/8/2000	2917.43	272.14	10.3
4/12/2001	1961.43	241.07	14.0
7/14/2000	4246.18	222.98	5.5
1/12/2001	2626.50	218.85	9.1
4/28/2000	3860.66	216.78	5.9
12/23/1999	3969.44	216.38	5.8
4/20/2001	2163.41	201.98	10.3
9/1/2000	4234.33	191.65	4.7
7/2/1999	2741.02	188.37	7.4
1/14/2000	4064.27	181.65	4.7
2/25/2000	4590.50	178.76	4.1
11/3/2000	3451.58	173.22	5.3
1/21/2000	4235.40	171.13	4.2
1/29/1999	2505.89	167.01	7.1
10/20/2000	3483.14	166.37	5.0
3/24/2000	4963.03	164.90	3.4

WORST TWENTY WEEKS SINCE 1971 BY POINTS

Week Ending	NASDAQ Close	Points Change	% Change
4/14/00	3321.29	−1125.16	− 25.3
7/28/00	3663.00	− 431.45	− 10.5
11/10/00	3028.99	− 422.59	− 12.2
3/31/00	4572.83	− 390.20	− 7.9
1/28/00	3887.07	− 348.33	− 8.2
10/6/00	3361.01	− 311.81	− 8.5
5/12/00	3529.06	− 287.76	− 7.5
9/21/01	1423.19	− 272.19	− 16.1
12/15/00	2653.27	− 264.16	− 9.1
12/1/00	2645.29	− 259.09	− 8.9
9/8/00	3978.41	− 255.92	− 6.0
3/17/00	4798.13	− 250.49	− 5.0
10/27/00	3278.36	− 204.78	− 5.9
2/9/01	2470.97	− 189.53	− 7.1
1/7/00	3882.62	− 186.69	− 4.6
6/15/01	2028.43	− 186.67	− 8.4
5/26/00	3205.11	− 185.29	− 5.5
7/23/99	2692.40	− 172.08	− 6.0
2/23/01	2262.51	− 162.87	− 6.7
3/16/01	1890.91	− 161.87	− 7.9

BEST TWENTY WEEKS SINCE 1971 BY %

Week Ending	NASDAQ Close	Points Change	% Change
6/2/2000	3813.38	608.27	19.0
4/12/2001	1961.43	241.07	14.0
4/20/2001	2163.41	201.98	10.3
12/8/2000	2917.43	272.14	10.3
4/20/2000	3643.88	322.59	9.7
10/11/1974	60.42	5.26	9.5
2/4/2000	4244.14	357.07	9.2
1/12/2001	2626.50	218.85	9.1
5/17/2002	1741.39	140.54	8.8
10/16/1998	1620.95	128.46	8.6
12/18/1987	326.91	24.34	8.0
5/2/1997	1305.33	96.04	7.9
1/9/1987	380.65	27.39	7.8
8/3/1984	246.24	16.94	7.4
7/2/1999	2741.02	188.37	7.4
1/29/1999	2505.89	167.01	7.1
10/5/2001	1605.30	106.50	7.1
3/3/2000	4914.79	324.29	7.1
3/8/2002	1929.67	126.93	7.0
1/8/1999	2344.41	151.72	6.9

WORST TWENTY WEEKS SINCE 1971 BY %

Week Ending	NASDAQ Close	Points Change	% Change
4/14/00	3321.29	−1125.16	−25.3
10/23/87	328.45	− 77.88	−19.2
9/21/01	1423.19	− 272.19	−16.1
11/10/00	3028.99	− 422.59	−12.2
7/28/00	3663.00	− 431.45	−10.5
12/15/00	2653.27	− 264.16	− 9.1
12/1/00	2645.29	− 259.09	− 8.9
8/28/98	1639.68	− 157.93	− 8.8
10/20/78	123.82	− 11.76	− 8.7
10/6/00	3361.01	− 311.81	− 8.5
6/15/01	2028.43	− 186.67	− 8.4
9/12/86	346.78	− 31.58	− 8.3
1/28/00	3887.07	− 348.33	− 8.2
3/16/01	1890.91	− 161.87	− 7.9
3/31/00	4572.83	− 390.20	− 7.9
10/12/79	140.71	− 11.58	− 7.6
10/9/98	1492.49	− 122.49	− 7.6
5/12/00	3529.06	− 287.76	− 7.5
12/6/74	58.21	− 4.74	− 7.5
3/7/80	146.19	− 11.84	− 7.5

Based on NASDAQ composite, prior to February 5, 1971, based on National Quotation Bureau indices

BEST & WORST DOW MONTHS
SINCE 1901 BY POINTS AND PERCENT

BEST TWENTY MONTHS SINCE 1901 BY POINTS

Month	DJIA Close	Points Change	% Change
Apr-1999	10789.04	1002.88	10.2
Apr-2001	10734.97	856.19	8.7
Oct-2002	8397.03	805.10	10.6
Mar-2000	10921.92	793.61	7.8
Nov-2001	9851.56	776.42	8.6
Oct-1998	8592.10	749.48	9.6
Aug-2000	11215.10	693.12	6.6
Dec-2003	10453.92	671.46	6.9
Feb-1998	8545.72	639.22	8.1
Dec-1999	11497.12	619.31	5.7
Jul-1997	8222.61	549.82	7.2
Oct-2003	9801.12	526.06	5.7
Nov-1998	9116.55	524.45	6.1
Nov-2002	8896.09	499.06	5.9
Nov-1996	6521.70	492.32	8.2
Apr-2003	8480.09	487.96	6.1
Mar-1999	9786.16	479.58	5.2
Apr-1997	7008.99	425.51	6.5
Jun-1999	10970.80	411.06	3.9
Nov-2004	10428.02	400.55	4.0

WORST TWENTY MONTHS SINCE 1901 BY POINTS

Month	DJIA Close	Points Change	% Change
Aug-1998	7539.07	−1344.22	− 15.1
Sep-2001	8847.56	−1102.19	− 11.1
Sep-2002	7591.93	−1071.57	− 12.4
Feb-2000	10128.31	− 812.22	− 7.4
Jun-2002	9243.26	− 681.99	− 6.9
Mar-2001	9878.78	− 616.50	− 5.9
Oct-1987	1993.53	− 602.75	− 23.2
Aug-1997	7622.42	− 600.19	− 7.3
Aug-2001	9949.75	− 573.06	− 5.4
Sep-2000	10650.92	− 564.18	− 5.0
Nov-2000	10414.49	− 556.65	− 5.1
Jan-2000	10940.53	− 556.59	− 4.8
Dec-2002	8341.63	− 554.46	− 6.2
Jul-2002	8736.59	− 506.67	− 5.5
Oct-1997	7442.08	− 503.18	− 6.3
Sep-1999	10336.95	− 492.33	− 4.5
Apr-2002	9946.22	− 457.72	− 4.4
Jun-2001	10502.40	− 409.54	− 3.8
Feb-2001	10495.28	− 392.08	− 3.6
Jul-1999	10655.15	− 315.65	− 2.9

BEST TWENTY MONTHS SINCE 1950 BY %

Month	DJIA Close	Points Change	% Change
Jan-1976	975.28	122.87	14.4
Jan-1975	703.69	87.45	14.2
Jan-1987	2158.04	262.09	13.8
Aug-1982	901.31	92.71	11.5
Oct-1982	991.72	95.47	10.7
Oct-2002	8397.03	805.10	10.6
Apr-1978	837.32	79.96	10.6
Apr-1999	10789.04	1002.88	10.2
Nov-1962	649.30	59.53	10.1
Nov-1954	386.77	34.63	9.8
Aug-1984	1224.38	109.10	9.8
Oct-1998	8592.10	749.48	9.6
Oct-1974	665.52	57.65	9.5
Dec-1991	3168.83	274.15	9.5
Jul-1989	2660.66	220.60	9.0
Feb-1986	1709.06	138.07	8.8
Apr-2001	10734.97	856.19	8.7
Nov-2001	9851.56	776.42	8.6
Apr-1968	912.22	71.55	8.5
Apr-1983	1226.20	96.17	8.5

WORST TWENTY MONTHS SINCE 1950 BY %

Month	DJIA Close	Points Change	% Change
Oct-1987	1993.53	− 602.75	− 23.2
Aug-1998	7539.07	−1344.22	− 15.1
Nov-1973	822.25	− 134.33	− 14.0
Sep-2002	7591.93	−1071.57	− 12.4
Sep-2001	8847.56	−1102.19	− 11.1
Sep-1974	607.87	− 70.71	− 10.4
Aug-1974	678.58	− 78.85	− 10.4
Aug-1990	2614.36	− 290.84	− 10.0
Mar-1980	785.75	− 77.39	− 9.0
Jun-1962	561.28	− 52.08	− 8.5
Oct-1978	792.45	− 73.37	− 8.5
Jan-1960	622.62	− 56.74	− 8.4
Nov-1987	1833.55	− 159.98	− 8.0
May-1962	613.36	− 51.97	− 7.8
Aug-1981	881.47	− 70.87	− 7.4
Feb-2000	10128.31	− 812.22	− 7.4
May-1956	478.05	− 38.07	− 7.4
Jan-1978	769.92	− 61.25	− 7.4
Sep-1960	580.14	− 45.85	− 7.3
Aug-1997	7622.42	− 600.19	− 7.3

BEST TEN MONTHS 1901-1949 BY %

Month	DJIA Close	Points Change	% Change
Apr-1933	77.66	22.26	40.2
Aug-1932	73.16	18.90	34.8
Jul-1932	54.26	11.42	26.7
Jun-1938	133.88	26.14	24.3
Apr-1915	71.78	10.95	18.0
Jun-1931	150.18	21.72	16.9
Nov-1928	293.38	41.22	16.3
Nov-1904	52.76	6.59	14.3
May-1919	105.50	12.62	13.6
Sep-1939	152.54	18.13	13.5

WORST TEN MONTHS 1901-1949 BY %

Month	DJIA Close	Points Change	% Change
Sep-1931	96.61	− 42.80	− 30.7
Mar-1938	98.95	− 30.69	− 23.7
Apr-1932	56.11	− 17.17	− 23.4
May-1940	116.22	− 32.21	− 21.7
Oct-1929	273.51	− 69.94	− 20.4
May-1932	44.74	− 11.37	− 20.3
Jun-1930	226.34	− 48.73	− 17.7
Dec-1931	77.90	− 15.97	− 17.0
Feb-1933	51.39	− 9.51	− 15.6
May-1931	128.46	− 22.73	− 15.0

BEST & WORST NASDAQ MONTHS
SINCE 1971 BY POINTS AND PERCENT

BEST TWENTY MONTHS SINCE 1971 BY POINTS

Month	NASDAQ Close	Points Change	% Change
Feb-2000	4696.69	756.34	19.2
Dec-1999	4069.31	733.15	22.0
Jun-2000	3966.11	565.20	16.6
Aug-2000	4206.35	439.36	11.7
Nov-1999	3336.16	369.73	12.5
Jan-1999	2505.89	313.20	14.3
Jan-2001	2772.73	302.21	12.2
Apr-2001	2116.24	275.98	15.0
Dec-1998	2192.69	243.15	12.5
Nov-2001	1930.58	240.38	14.2
Oct-1999	2966.43	220.27	8.0
Jun-1999	2686.12	215.60	8.7
Sep-1998	1693.84	194.59	13.0
Oct-2001	1690.20	191.40	12.8
Nov-1998	1949.54	178.15	10.1
Mar-1999	2461.40	173.37	7.6
Oct-2002	1329.75	157.69	13.5
Jul-1997	1593.81	151.74	10.5
Feb-1998	1770.51	151.15	9.3
Nov-2002	1478.78	149.03	11.2

WORST TWENTY MONTHS SINCE 1971 BY POINTS

Month	NASDAQ Close	Points Change	% Change
Nov-2000	2597.93	− 771.70	− 22.9
Apr-2000	3860.66	− 712.17	− 15.6
Feb-2001	2151.83	− 620.90	− 22.4
Sep-2000	3672.82	− 533.53	− 12.7
May-2000	3400.91	− 459.75	− 11.9
Aug-1998	1499.25	− 373.14	− 19.9
Mar-2001	1840.26	− 311.57	− 14.5
Sep-2001	1498.80	− 306.63	− 17.0
Oct-2000	3369.63	− 303.19	− 8.3
Aug-2001	1805.43	− 221.70	− 10.9
Feb-1999	2288.03	− 217.86	− 8.7
Feb-2002	1731.49	− 202.54	− 10.5
Jul-2000	3766.99	− 199.12	− 5.0
Jul-2004	1887.36	− 160.43	− 7.8
Apr-2002	1688.23	− 157.12	− 8.5
Jun-2002	1463.21	− 152.52	− 9.4
Dec-2002	1335.51	− 143.27	− 9.7
Sep-2002	1172.06	− 142.79	− 10.9
Jul-2002	1328.26	− 134.95	− 9.2
Jul-2001	2027.13	− 133.41	− 6.2

BEST TWENTY MONTHS SINCE 1971 BY %

Month	NASDAQ Close	Points Change	% Change
Dec-1999	4069.31	733.15	22.0
Feb-2000	4696.69	756.34	19.2
Oct-1974	65.23	9.56	17.2
Jan-1975	69.78	9.96	16.6
Jun-2000	3966.11	565.20	16.6
Apr-2001	2116.24	275.98	15.0
Jan-1999	2505.89	313.20	14.3
Nov-2001	1930.58	240.38	14.2
Oct-2002	1329.75	157.69	13.5
Oct-1982	212.63	24.98	13.3
Sep-1998	1693.84	194.59	13.0
Oct-2001	1690.20	191.40	12.8
Jan-1985	278.70	31.35	12.7
Dec-1998	2192.69	243.15	12.5
Nov-1999	3336.16	369.73	12.5
Jan-2001	2772.73	302.21	12.2
Jan-1987	392.06	42.73	12.2
Jan-1976	87.05	9.43	12.1
Dec-1991	586.34	62.44	11.9
Aug-2000	4206.35	439.36	11.7

WORST TWENTY MONTHS SINCE 1971 BY %

Month	NASDAQ Close	Points Change	% Change
Oct-1987	323.30	− 120.99	− 27.2
Nov-2000	2597.93	− 771.70	− 22.9
Feb-2001	2151.83	− 620.90	− 22.4
Aug-1998	1499.25	− 373.14	− 19.9
Mar-1980	131.00	− 27.03	− 17.1
Sep-2001	1498.80	− 306.63	− 17.0
Oct-1978	111.12	− 21.77	− 16.4
Apr-2000	3860.66	− 712.17	− 15.6
Nov-1973	93.51	− 16.66	− 15.1
Mar-2001	1840.26	− 311.57	− 14.5
Aug-1990	381.21	− 57.03	− 13.0
Sep-2000	3672.82	− 533.53	− 12.7
May-2000	3400.91	− 459.75	− 11.9
Aug-2001	1805.43	− 221.70	− 10.9
Aug-1974	62.37	− 7.62	− 10.9
Sep-2002	1172.06	− 142.79	− 10.9
Sep-1974	55.67	− 6.70	− 10.7
Feb-2002	1731.49	− 202.54	− 10.5
Dec-2002	1335.51	− 143.27	− 9.7
Oct-1979	135.53	− 14.45	− 9.6

Based on NASDAQ composite, prior to February 5, 1971, based on National Quotation Bureau indices

159

BEST & WORST DOW AND NASDAQ YEARS

DOW SINCE 1901 BY POINTS AND PERCENT

BEST FIFTEEN YEARS SINCE 1901 BY POINTS

Year	DJIA Close	Points Change	% Change
1999	11497.12	2315.69	25.2
2003	10453.92	2112.29	25.3
1997	7908.25	1459.98	22.6
1996	6448.27	1331.15	26.0
1995	5117.12	1282.68	33.5
1998	9181.43	1273.18	16.1
1989	2753.20	584.63	27.0
1991	3168.83	535.17	20.3
1993	3754.09	452.98	13.7
1986	1895.95	349.28	22.6
1985	1546.67	335.10	27.7
2004	10783.01	329.09	3.1
1975	852.41	236.17	38.3
1988	2168.57	229.74	11.8
1983	1258.64	212.10	20.3

WORST FIFTEEN YEARS SINCE 1901 BY POINTS

Year	DJIA Close	Points Change	% Change
2002	8341.63	−1679.87	−16.8
2001	10021.50	−765.35	−7.1
2000	10786.85	−710.27	−6.2
1974	616.24	−234.62	−27.6
1966	785.69	−183.57	−18.9
1977	831.17	−173.48	−17.3
1973	850.86	−169.16	−16.6
1969	800.36	−143.39	−15.2
1990	2633.66	−119.54	−4.3
1981	875.00	−88.99	−9.2
1931	77.90	−86.68	−52.7
1930	164.58	−83.90	−33.8
1962	652.10	−79.04	−10.8
1957	435.69	−63.78	−12.8
1960	615.89	−63.47	−9.3

BEST FIFTEEN YEARS SINCE 1901 BY %

Year	DJIA Close	Points Change	% Change
1915	99.15	44.57	81.7
1933	99.90	39.97	66.7
1928	300.00	97.60	48.2
1908	63.11	20.07	46.6
1954	404.39	123.49	44.0
1904	50.99	15.01	41.7
1935	144.13	40.09	38.5
1975	852.41	236.17	38.3
1905	70.47	19.48	38.2
1958	583.65	147.96	34.0
1995	5117.12	1282.68	33.5
1919	107.23	25.03	30.5
1925	156.66	36.15	30.0
1927	202.40	45.20	28.8
1938	154.76	33.91	28.1

WORST FIFTEEN YEARS SINCE 1901 BY %

Year	DJIA Close	Points Change	% Change
1931	77.90	− 86.68	− 52.7
1907	43.04	− 26.08	− 37.7
1930	164.58	− 83.90	− 33.8
1920	71.95	− 35.28	− 32.9
1937	120.85	− 59.05	− 32.8
1974	616.24	− 234.62	− 27.6
1903	35.98	− 11.12	− 23.6
1932	59.93	− 17.97	− 23.1
1917	74.38	− 20.62	− 21.7
1966	785.69	− 183.57	− 18.9
1910	59.60	− 12.96	− 17.9
1977	831.17	− 173.48	− 17.3
1929	248.48	− 51.52	− 17.2
2002	8341.63	−1679.87	− 16.8
1973	850.86	− 169.16	− 16.6

NASDAQ SINCE 1971 BY POINTS AND PERCENT

BEST TEN YEARS SINCE 1971 BY POINTS

Year	NASDAQ Close	Points Change	% Change
1999	4069.31	1876.62	85.6
2003	2003.37	667.86	50.0
1998	2192.69	622.34	39.6
1995	1052.13	300.17	39.9
1997	1570.35	279.32	21.6
1996	1291.03	238.90	22.7
1991	586.34	212.50	56.8
2004	2175.44	172.07	8.6
1993	776.80	99.85	14.7
1992	676.95	90.61	15.5

WORST TEN YEARS SINCE 1971 BY POINTS

Year	NASDAQ Close	Points Change	% Change
2000	2470.52	−1598.79	− 39.3
2002	1335.51	− 614.89	− 31.5
2001	1950.40	− 520.12	− 21.1
1990	373.84	− 80.98	− 17.8
1973	92.19	− 41.54	− 31.1
1974	59.82	− 32.37	− 35.1
1984	247.35	− 31.25	− 11.2
1994	751.96	− 24.84	− 3.2
1987	330.47	− 18.86	− 5.4
1981	195.84	− 6.50	− 3.2

BEST TEN YEARS SINCE 1971 BY %

Year	NASDAQ Close	Points Change	% Change
1999	4069.31	1876.62	85.6
1991	586.34	212.50	56.8
2003	2003.37	667.86	50.0
1995	1052.13	300.17	39.9
1998	2192.69	622.34	39.6
1980	202.34	51.20	33.9
1985	324.93	77.58	31.4
1975	77.62	17.80	29.8
1979	151.14	33.16	28.1
1971	114.12	24.51	27.4

WORST TEN YEARS SINCE 1971 BY %

Year	NASDAQ Close	Points Change	% Change
2000	2470.52	−1598.79	− 39.3
1974	59.82	− 32.37	− 35.1
2002	1335.51	− 614.89	− 31.5
1973	92.19	− 41.54	− 31.1
2001	1950.40	− 520.12	− 21.1
1990	373.84	− 80.98	− 17.8
1984	247.35	− 31.25	− 11.2
1987	330.47	− 18.86	− 5.4
1981	195.84	− 6.50	− 3.2
1994	751.96	− 24.84	− 3.2

Based on NASDAQ composite, prior to February 5, 1971, based on National Quotation Bureau indices

STRATEGY PLANNING & RECORD SECTION

CONTENTS

PORTFOLIO AT START OF 2006

DATE ACQUIRED	NO. OF SHARES	SECURITY	PRICE	TOTAL COST	PAPER PROFITS	PAPER LOSSES

PORTFOLIO AT START OF 2006

DATE ACQUIRED	NO. OF SHARES	SECURITY	PRICE	TOTAL COST	PAPER PROFITS	PAPER LOSSES

ADDITIONAL PURCHASES

DATE ACQUIRED	NO. OF SHARES	SECURITY	PRICE	TOTAL COST	REASON FOR PURCHASE PRIME OBJECTIVE, ETC.

ADDITIONAL PURCHASES

DATE ACQUIRED	NO. OF SHARES	SECURITY	PRICE	TOTAL COST	REASON FOR PURCHASE PRIME OBJECTIVE, ETC.

ADDITIONAL PURCHASES

DATE ACQUIRED	NO. OF SHARES	SECURITY	PRICE	TOTAL COST	REASON FOR PURCHASE PRIME OBJECTIVE, ETC.

SHORT–TERM TRANSACTIONS

Pages 167–176 can accompany next year's income tax return (Schedule D). Enter transactions as completed to avoid last minute pressures.

NO. OF SHARES	SECURITY	DATE ACQUIRED	DATE SOLD	SALE PRICE	COST	LOSS	GAIN

TOTALS:

Carry over to next page

SHORT–TERM TRANSACTIONS *(continued)*

NO. OF SHARES	SECURITY	DATE ACQUIRED	DATE SOLD	SALE PRICE	COST	LOSS	GAIN

TOTALS:

Carry over to next page

NO. OF SHARES	SECURITY	DATE ACQUIRED	DATE SOLD	SALE PRICE	COST	LOSS	GAIN

TOTALS:
Carry over to next page

SHORT–TERM TRANSACTIONS *(continued)*

NO. OF SHARES	SECURITY	DATE ACQUIRED	DATE SOLD	SALE PRICE	COST	LOSS	GAIN

TOTALS:

Carry over to next page

170

SHORT–TERM TRANSACTIONS *(continued)*

NO. OF SHARES	SECURITY	DATE ACQUIRED	DATE SOLD	SALE PRICE	COST	LOSS	GAIN

TOTALS:

Carry over to next page

SHORT-TERM TRANSACTIONS (continued)

NO. OF SHARES	SECURITY	DATE ACQUIRED	DATE SOLD	SALE PRICE	COST	LOSS	GAIN

TOTALS:

LONG–TERM TRANSACTIONS

Pages 167–176 can accompany next year's income tax return (Schedule D). Enter transactions as completed to avoid last minute pressures.

NO. OF SHARES	SECURITY	DATE ACQUIRED	DATE SOLD	SALE PRICE	COST	LOSS	GAIN

TOTALS:

Carry over to next page

LONG–TERM TRANSACTIONS *(continued)*

NO. OF SHARES	SECURITY	DATE ACQUIRED	DATE SOLD	SALE PRICE	COST	LOSS	GAIN

TOTALS:
Carry over to next page

174

NO. OF SHARES	SECURITY	DATE ACQUIRED	DATE SOLD	SALE PRICE	COST	LOSS	GAIN

TOTALS:

Carry over to next page

NO. OF SHARES	SECURITY	DATE ACQUIRED	DATE SOLD	SALE PRICE	COST	LOSS	GAIN

TOTALS:

INTEREST/DIVIDENDS RECEIVED DURING 2006

SHARES	STOCK/BOND	FIRST QUARTER		SECOND QUARTER		THIRD QUARTER		FOURTH QUARTER	
		$		$		$		$	

BROKERAGE ACCOUNT DATA 2006

	MARGIN INTEREST	TRANSFER TAXES	CAPITAL ADDED	CAPITAL WITHDRAWN
JAN				
FEB				
MAR				
APR				
MAY				
JUN				
JUL				
AUG				
SEP				
OCT				
NOV				
DEC				

PORTFOLIO AT END OF 2006

DATE ACQUIRED	NO. OF SHARES	SECURITY	PRICE	TOTAL COST	PAPER PROFITS	PAPER LOSSES

PORTFOLIO AT END OF 2006

DATE ACQUIRED	NO. OF SHARES	SECURITY	PRICE	TOTAL COST	PAPER PROFITS	PAPER LOSSES

PORTFOLIO PRICE RECORD 2006 (FIRST HALF)

Place purchase price above stock name and weekly closes below

STOCKS Week Ending	1	2	3	4	5	6	7	8	9	10
JANUARY 6										
13										
20										
27										
FEBRUARY 3										
10										
17										
24										
MARCH 3										
10										
17										
24										
31										
APRIL 7										
14										
21										
28										
MAY 5										
12										
19										
26										
JUNE 2										
9										
16										
23										
30										

PORTFOLIO PRICE RECORD 2006 (FIRST HALF)

Place purchase price above stock name and weekly closes below

STOCKS	11	12	13	14	15	16	17	18	Dow Jones Industrial Average	Net Change For Week
JANUARY Week Ending										
6										
13										
20										
27										
FEBRUARY 3										
10										
17										
24										
MARCH 3										
10										
17										
24										
31										
APRIL 7										
14										
21										
28										
MAY 5										
12										
19										
26										
JUNE 2										
9										
16										
23										
30										

PORTFOLIO PRICE RECORD 2006 (SECOND HALF)

Place purchase price above stock name and weekly closes below

STOCKS / Week Ending	1	2	3	4	5	6	7	8	9	10
JULY 7										
14										
21										
28										
AUGUST 4										
11										
18										
25										
SEPTEMBER 1										
8										
15										
22										
29										
OCTOBER 6										
13										
20										
27										
NOVEMBER 3										
10										
17										
24										
DECEMBER 1										
8										
15										
22										
29										

PORTFOLIO PRICE RECORD 2006 (SECOND HALF)

Place purchase price above stock name and weekly closes below

STOCKS Week Ending	11	12	13	14	15	16	17	18	Dow Jones Industrial Average	Net Change For Week
JULY										
7										
14										
21										
28										
AUGUST										
4										
11										
18										
25										
SEPTEMBER										
1										
8										
15										
22										
29										
OCTOBER										
6										
13										
20										
27										
NOVEMBER										
3										
10										
17										
24										
DECEMBER										
1										
8										
15										
22										
29										

WEEKLY INDICATOR DATA 2006 (FIRST HALF)

Week Ending	Dow Jones Industrial Average	Net Change For Week	Net Change On Friday	Net Change Next Monday	S&P Or NASDAQ	NYSE Advances	NYSE Declines	New Highs	New Lows	CBOE Put/Call Ratio	90-Day Treas. Rate	Moody's AAA Rate
JANUARY												
6												
13												
20												
27												
FEBRUARY												
3												
10												
17												
24												
MARCH												
3												
10												
17												
24												
31												
APRIL												
7												
14												
21												
28												
MAY												
5												
12												
19												
26												
JUNE												
2												
9												
16												
23												
30												

WEEKLY INDICATOR DATA 2006 (SECOND HALF)

Week Ending	Dow Jones Industrial Average	Net Change For Week	Net Change On Friday	Net Change Next Monday	S&P Or NASDAQ	NYSE Ad-vances	NYSE De-clines	New Highs	New Lows	CBOE Put/Call Ratio	90-Day Treas. Rate	Moody's AAA Rate
JULY												
7												
14												
21												
28												
AUGUST												
4												
11												
18												
25												
SEPTEMBER												
1												
8												
15												
22												
29												
OCTOBER												
6												
13												
20												
27												
NOVEMBER												
3												
10												
17												
24												
DECEMBER												
1												
8												
15												
22												
29												

MONTHLY INDICATOR DATA 2006

	DJIA% Last 3 + 1st 2 Days	DJIA% 9th - 11th Trading Days	DJIA% Change Rest Of Month	DJIA% Change Whole Month	% Change Your Stocks	Gross Domestic Product	Prime Rate	Trade Deficit $ Billion	CPI % Change	% Unem-ployment Rate
JAN										
FEB										
MAR										
APR										
MAY										
JUN										
JUL										
AUG										
SEP										
OCT										
NOV										
DEC										

INSTRUCTIONS:

Weekly Indicator Data (pages 184-185). Keeping data on several indicators may give you a better feel of the market. In addition to the closing DJIA and its net change for the week, post the net change for Friday's Dow and also the following Monday's. A series of "down Fridays" followed by "down Mondays" often precedes a downswing. Tracking either the S&P or NASDAQ composite, and advances and declines, will help prevent the Dow from misleading you. New highs and lows and put/call ratios (www.cboe.com) are also useful indicators. All these weekly figures appear in weekend papers or *Barron's*. Data for 90-day Treasury Rate and Moody's AAA Bond Rate are quite important to track short- and long-term interest rates. These figures are available from:

> Weekly U.S. Financial Data
> Federal Reserve Bank of St. Louis
> P.O. Box 442
> St. Louis, MO 63166
> **http://research.stlouisfed.org**

Monthly Indicator Data. The purpose of the first three columns is to enable you to track the market's bullish bias near the end, beginning and middle of the month, which has been shifting lately (see pages 88, 136 & 137). Market direction, performance of your stocks, Gross Domestic Product, Prime Rate, Trade Deficit, Consumer Price Index, and Unemployment Rate are worthwhile indicators to follow. Or, readers may wish to gauge other data.

IF YOU DON'T PROFIT FROM YOUR INVESTMENT MISTAKES, SOMEONE ELSE WILL

No matter how much we may deny it, almost every successful person in Wall Street pays a great deal of attention to trading suggestions—especially when they come from "the right sources."

One of the hardest things to learn is to distinguish between good tips and bad ones. Usually the best tips have a logical reason in back of them, which accompanies the tip. Poor tips usually have no reason to support them.

The important thing to remember is that the market discounts. It does not review, it does not reflect. The Street's real interest in "tips," inside information, buying and selling suggestions, and everything else of this kind emanates from a desire to find out just what the market has on hand to discount. The process of finding out involves separating the wheat from the chaff—and there is plenty of chaff.

HOW TO MAKE USE OF STOCK "TIPS"

- The source should be **reliable**. (By listing all "tips" and suggestions on a Performance Record of Recommendations, such as below, and then periodically evaluating the outcomes, you will soon know the "batting average" of your sources.)

- The story should make sense. Would the merger violate anti-trust laws? Are there too many computers on the market already? How many years will it take to become profitable?

- The stock should not have had a recent sharp run-up. Otherwise, the story may already be discounted and confirmation or denial in the press would most likely be accompanied by a sell-off in the stock.

PERFORMANCE RECORD OF RECOMMENDATIONS

STOCK RECOMMENDED	BY WHOM	DATE	PRICE	REASON FOR RECOMMENDATION	SUBSEQUENT ACTION OF STOCK

INDIVIDUAL RETIREMENT ACCOUNTS: MOST AWESOME INVESTMENT INCENTIVE EVER DEVISED

MAX IRA INVESTMENTS OF $4,000 A YEAR COMPOUNDED AT VARIOUS RATES OF RETURN FOR DIFFERENT PERIODS

Annual Rate	5 Yrs	10 Yrs	15 Yrs	20 Yrs	25 Yrs	30 Yrs	35 Yrs	40 Yrs	45 Yrs	50 Yrs
1%	$20,608	$42,267	$65,031	$88,957	$114,103	$140,531	$168,308	$197,501	$228,184	$260,431
2%	21,232	44,675	70,557	99,133	130,684	165,518	203,977	246,440	293,322	345,084
3%	21,874	47,231	76,628	110,706	150,212	196,011	249,104	310,653	382,006	464,723
4%	22,532	49,945	83,298	123,877	173,247	233,313	306,393	395,306	503,482	635,095
5%	23,208	52,827	90,630	138,877	200,454	279,043	379,345	507,359	670,741	879,262
6%	23,901	55,887	98,690	155,971	232,626	335,207	472,483	656,191	902,032	1,231,024
7%	24,613	59,134	107,552	175,461	270,706	404,292	591,654	854,438	1,223,007	1,739,944
8%	25,344	62,582	117,297	197,692	315,818	489,383	744,409	1,119,124	1,669,704	2,478,687
9%	26,093	66,241	128,014	223,058	369,296	594,301	940,499	1,473,167	2,292,744	3,553,764
10%	26,862	70,125	139,799	252,010	432,727	723,774	1,192,507	1,947,407	3,163,181	5,121,198
11%	27,651	74,246	152,760	285,061	507,995	883,653	1,516,658	2,583,308	4,380,675	7,409,344
12%	28,461	78,618	167,013	322,795	597,336	1,081,170	1,933,852	3,436,570	6,084,871	10,752,082
13%	29,291	83,257	182,687	365,880	703,400	1,325,260	2,470,997	4,581,943	8,471,224	15,636,972
14%	30,142	88,178	199,921	415,074	829,331	1,626,948	3,162,692	6,119,634	11,812,975	22,775,017
15%	31,015	93,397	218,870	471,240	978,848	1,999,828	4,053,383	8,183,815	16,491,591	33,201,495
16%	31,910	98,932	239,700	535,362	1,156,353	2,460,646	5,200,108	10,953,914	23,038,871	48,421,410
17%	32,827	104,800	262,595	608,554	1,367,051	3,030,015	6,675,978	14,669,562	32,195,080	70,618,868
18%	33,768	111,021	287,756	692,084	1,617,088	3,733,275	8,574,596	19,650,365	44,989,044	102,957,802
19%	34,732	117,614	315,401	787,390	1,913,722	4,601,550	11,015,657	26,321,986	62,848,299	150,013,001
20%	35,720	124,602	345,769	896,102	2,265,509	5,673,032	14,152,037	35,250,518	87,750,288	218,386,516

TOP 140 EXCHANGE TRADED FUNDS BY MARKET VALUE
(As of July 29, 2005 — See pages 80 and 116 for Sector Seasonalities)

Ticker	Exchange Traded Fund	MV $mil	Ticker	Exchange Traded Fund	MV $mil
HHH	Internet HOLDRs	60,590	PEY	PowerShares High Yield	339
SPY	S&P 500 Spyder	45,541	EWZ	iShares Brazil	313
MTK	streetTRACKS High Tech 35	24,940	IYZ	iShares DJ US Telecom	309
QQQQ	NASDAQ 100	21,490	VNQ	REIT VIPERS	284
IVV	iShares S&P 500	10,848	XLY	SPDR Consumer Discretionary	282
DVY	iShares DJ Select Dividend	6,838	IWW	iShares Russell 3000 Value	279
DIA	Diamonds DJIA 30	6,505	TTH	Telecom HOLDRs	277
EWJ	iShares Japan	5,799	IYF	iShares DJ US Financial	257
MDY	S&P Mid Cap 400 SPDR	3,772	IYJ	iShares DJ US Industrial	250
IWD	iShares Russell 1000 Value	3,689	VXF	Extended Market VIPERS	250
VTI	Vanguard Total Market VIPERS	3,639	EWA	iShares Australia	238
EFA	iShares EAFE	3,464	IYC	iShares DJ US Consumer Cyc	226
IWM	iShares Russell 2000	3,272	EWS	iShares Singapore	214
LQD	iShares Corporate Bond	2,547	IGM	iShares Technology	205
IVE	iShares S&P 500/BARRA Value	2,520	RKH	Regional Bank HOLDRs	197
IWF	iShares Russell 1000 Growth	2,429	BBH	Biotech HOLDRs	192
TIP	iShares Lehman TIPS Bond	2,244	IOO	iShares S&P Global 100	183
XLE	SPDR Energy	1,990	IGE	iShares Natural Resources	182
IVW	iShares S&P 500 BARRA Growth	1,905	EWW	iShares Mexico	168
IWO	iShares Russell 2000 Growth	1,904	IXJ	iShares S&P Global Healthcare	162
IWV	iShares Russell 3000	1,833	IGN	iShares Multimedia Networking	152
SHY	iShares Lehman 1-3 Yr Bonds	1,793	IGW	iShares Semiconductor	144
IWB	iShares Russell 1000	1,698	ONEQ	Fidelity NASDAQ Composite	138
AGG	iShares Lehman Aggregate Bond	1,693	IGV	iShares Software	137
XLU	SPDR Utilities	1,633	VDE	Energy VIPERS	137
SMH	Semiconductor HOLDRs	1,280	OIH	Oil Service HOLDRs	136
GLD	streetTRACKS Gold	1,199	EWG	iShares Germany	125
IBB	iShares NASDAQ Biotech	1,170	VTV	Vanguard Value VIPERS	125
IJH	iShares S&P Mid Cap 400	1,149	ILF	iShares S&P Latin America 40	123
XLF	SPDR Financial	1,045	IWZ	iShares Russell 3000 Growth	123
XLK	SPDR Tech	1,032	EZA	iShares S Africa Index	122
FXI	iShares FTSE/Xinhua China 25	988	IYG	iShares DJ US Financial Serv	120
IJR	iShares S&P Small Cap 600	981	TMW	streetTRACKS Fortune 500	116
IWR	iShares Russell Mid Cap	950	UTH	Utilities HOLDRs	114
IEV	iShares S&P Europe 350	935	PWC	PowerShares Dynamic Market	109
EEM	iShares Emerging Market Income	933	RTH	Retail HOLDRs	103
XLV	SPDR Healthcare	892	BDH	Broadband HOLDRs	102
IJT	iShares S&P Sm Cp 600 BARRA Gr	882	WMH	Wireless HOLDRS	102
IWN	iShares Russell 2000 Value	866	VUG	Vanguard Growth VIPERS	100
EPP	iShares Pacific Ex-Japan	836	IAH	Internet Architecture HOLDRs	97
IJJ	iShares S&P Md Cp 400/BARRA Va	798	ITF	iShares S&P/TOPIX 150	79
RSP	Rydex S&P Equal Weight	786	EWO	iShares Austria	79
IYH	iShares DJ US Healthcare	770	FEZ	streetTRACKS DJ Euro STOXX 50	79
IWS	iShares Russell Mid Cap Value	748	EWQ	iShares France	76
IJS	iShares S&P Sm Cp 600/BARRA Va	708	VGK	European VIPERS	75
IWP	iShares Russell Mid Cap Growth	707	PWO	PowerShares OTC	74
XLB	SPDR Materials	686	VB	Small Cap VIPERS	72
XLP	SPDR Consumer Staples	669	EWM	iShares Malaysia	72
ICF	iShares Cohen & Steers Realty	628	PBE	PowerShares Dynamic Bio&Genom	70
XLI	SPDR Industrial	624	VWO	Emerging Markets VIPERS	67
IEF	iShares Lehman 7-10 Year	602	DSV	streetTRACKS DJ Small Cap Val	66
IDU	iShares DJ US Utilities	592	ISI	iShares S&P 1500	66
IYE	iShares Energy	585	EKH	Europe 2001 HOLDRs	65
EWH	iShares Hong Kong	544	RWR	StreetTRACKS Wilshire REIT	64
IJK	iShares S&P Md Cp 400/BARRA Gr	509	JKF	iShares Morningstar Lg Cap Val	61
PPH	Pharmaceutical HOLDRs	496	XLG	Rydex Russell Top 50	61
EWU	iShares United Kingdom	478	EWP	iShares Spain	59
OEF	iShares S&P 100	461	JKD	iShares Morningstar Large Cap	56
EWT	iShares Taiwan	454	MKH	ML Market 2000+ HOLDRs	55
TLT	iShares Lehman 20+yr Bond	447	JKE	iShares Morningstar Lg Cp Gr	55
EWC	iShares Canada	436	VPU	Utilities VIPERS	54
IYY	iShares DJ US Total Market	434	PGJ	PowerShares Gold Dragon Health	53
EWY	iShares South Korea	434	VBK	Small Cap Growth VIPERS	52
EZU	iShares EMU	409	VPL	Pacific VIPERS	50
IXC	iShares S&P Global Energy	392	EWL	iShares Switzerland	50
IYR	iShares DJ US Real Estate	390	KLD	iShares KLD Select Social	50
IAU	iShares Comex Gold	380	IYT	iShares DJ Transports	44
IYK	iShares DJ US Consumer Goods	372	PSI	PowerShares Dynamic Semis	43
IYW	iShares DJ US Tech	363	JKJ	iShares Morningstar Small Cap	43
IYM	iShares DJ US Basic Materials	341	SWH	Software HOLDRs	42

G.M. LOEB'S "BATTLE PLAN" FOR INVESTMENT SURVIVAL

LIFE IS CHANGE: Nothing can ever be the same a minute from now as it was a minute ago. Everything you own is changing in price and value. You can find that last price of an active security on the stock ticker, but you cannot find the next price anywhere. The value of your money is changing. Even the value of your home is changing, though no one walks in front of it with a sandwich board consistently posting the changes.

RECOGNIZE CHANGE: Your basic objective should be to profit from change. The art of investing is being able to recognize change and to adjust investment goals accordingly.

WRITE THINGS DOWN: You will score more investment success and avoid more investment failures if you write things down. Very few investors have the drive and inclination to do this.

KEEP A CHECKLIST: If you aim to improve your investment results, get into the habit of keeping a checklist on every issue you consider buying. Before making a commitment, it will pay you to write down the answers to at least some of the basic questions—How much am I investing in this company? How much do I think I can make? How much do I have to risk? How long do I expect to take to reach my goal?

HAVE A SINGLE RULING REASON: Above all, writing things down is the best way to find "the ruling reason." When all is said and done, there is invariably a single reason that stands out above all others why a particular security transaction can be expected to show a profit. All too often many relatively unimportant statistics are allowed to obscure this single important point.

Any one of a dozen factors may be the point of a particular purchase or sale. It could be a technical reason—an increase in earnings or dividend not yet discounted in the market price—a change of management—a promising new product—an expected improvement in the market's valuation of earnings—or many others. But, in any given case, one of these factors will almost certainly be more important than all the rest put together.

CLOSING OUT A COMMITMENT: If you have a loss, the solution is automatic, provided you decide what to do at the time you buy. Otherwise, the question divides itself into two parts. Are we in a bull or bear market? Few of us really know until it is too late. For the sake of the record, if you think it is a bear market, just put that consideration first and sell as much as your conviction suggests and your nature allows.

If you think it is a bull market, or at least a market where some stocks move up, some mark time and only a few decline, do not sell unless:

✓ You see a bear market ahead.

✓ You see trouble for a particular company in which you own shares.

✓ Time and circumstances have turned up a new and seemingly far better buy than the issue you like least in your list.

✓ Your shares stop going up and start going down.

A subsidiary question is, which stock to sell first? Two further observations may help:

✓ Do not sell solely because you think a stock is "overvalued."

✓ If you want to sell some of your stocks and not all, in most cases it is better to go against your emotional inclinations and sell first the issues with losses, small profits or none at all, the weakest, the most disappointing, etc.

Mr. Loeb is the author of *The Battle for Investment Survival*, John Wiley & Sons.

G.M. LOEB'S INVESTMENT SURVIVAL CHECKLIST

OBJECTIVES AND RISKS

Security		Price	Shares	Date

"Ruling reason" for commitment	Amount of commitment $ _____
	% of my investment capital _____%

Price objective	Est. time to achieve it	I will risk _____ points	Which would be $ _____

TECHNICAL POSITION

Price action of stock:

☐ hitting new highs   ☐ in a trading range

☐ pausing in an uptrend   ☐ moving up from low ground

☐ acting stronger than market   ☐ _____

Dow Jones Industrial Average

Trend of Market

SELECTED YARDSTICKS

	Price Range		Earnings Per Share Actual or Projected	Price/Earnings Ratio Actual or Projected
	High	Low		
Current Year				
Previous Year				

Merger Possibilities	Years for earnings to double in past
Comment on Future	Years for market price to double in past

PERIODIC RE-CHECKS

Date	Stock Price	D.J.I.A.	Comment	Action taken, if any

COMPLETED TRANSACTIONS

Date Closed	Period of time held	Profit or loss

Reason for profit or loss

191

IMPORTANT CONTACTS

NAME	TELEPHONE	E-MAIL